On This Day

Volume 2

More Irish Histories from *Drivetime* on RTÉ Radio 1

Myles Dungan

Illustrations by Annie West

NEW ISLAND

ON THIS DAY – VOLUME 2
First published in 2017 by
New Island Books
16 Priory Hall Office Park
Stillorgan
County Dublin
Republic of Ireland

www.newisland.ie

Print ISBN: 978-1-84840-636-0
Epub ISBN: 978-1-84840-637-7
Mobi ISBN: 978-1-84840-638-4

Typeset by JVR Creative India
Cover design by Mariel Deegan

New Island Books is a member of Publishing Ireland.

Cover images: The White House South Lawn © Mark Skrobola; John Lawrence Sullivan © Joe Maria Mora; Éamon de Valera in Indian headdress, 18 October 1919 (Reproduced by kind permission of UCD-OFM Partnership); Nora Joyce, courtesy of Alamy; RMS Titanic © FGO Stuart.

Printed and bound in Great Britain by
TJ International Ltd, Padstow, Cornwall

To Dr Eileen Butler,
Dr Deirdre Lynch and Mr Barry McGuire,
without whom ... !

Acknowledgements

My profound thanks are due to the estimable and indispensable Tom Donnelly, producer of the RTÉ Radio One *Drivetime* programme, for keeping faith with this relentlessly non-topical Friday column. Thanks also to my affable and accomplished RTÉ *History Show* producer Alan Torney for his indulgence in allowing me to record much of the material for broadcast on his dollar. John Davis, now retired, again played a huge part in improving the items and making them something more than a mere four-minute spoken dirge.

I am, as before, grateful to Edwin Higel and Dan Bolger of New Island Books for taking this project on in the first place and, despite the wisdom of hindsight, for agreeing to follow up with two more years of anniversary etchings. Thanks to them also for persuading the redoubtable Annie West to shelve whatever useful project she was working on at the time and get involved in illustrating twelve of the stories in this and the previous volume. To Shauna Daly, thank you for saving me from myself. And to all those who had the good sense and generosity to be born, die or do something noteworthy on a Friday, I am eternally in your debt.

And finally, to the ever accommodating and supportive Nerys Williams and to the ever sceptical Amber, Rory, Lara, Ross and Gwyneth, thank you all for the grounding – and here we go yet again.

Foreword

And so, once more with feeling. Or *encore une fois*, as the French would say. Or should that be '*encore un fois*'? I could never hack that masculine/feminine thing in French.

'On This Day' has now survived for an entire American presidential term. Especially if William Henry Harrison is the president in question. The poor man died after only one month in office, helped to the pearly gates by giving a two-hour inauguration address, hatless and coatless, on a cold and wet March day in Washington, D.C. It is sobering to think that his inauguration speech was the equivalent of about six months of 'On This Day'. But enough about William Henry Harrison.

As I mentioned in the distinguished preceding volume, the idea for 'On This Day' was stolen from the 1980s. It was already a tried and tested broadcasting format, allowed to pass on, before being triumphantly resurrected. It will inevitably lapse as a successful column in a few years, only to be picked up by some other concept thief in 2035. And so on. One wonders whether, a century from now, when tour operators are running sun holidays to Antarctica, it will re-emerge triumphantly. What will the slick, plausible 'On This Day' presenter of 2116 make of the events of 2016?

Will listeners to *Drivetime* on 23 June 2116 shudder to hear that an obscure monarchy called the United Kingdom (now four distinct political entities), voted for political and economic self-immolation, one hundred years ago, on this day. And what about 8 November 2116? How will it be fondly remembered? The event that ultimately led to the secession of over half the states of the Union – the election of Donald Trump as forty-fifth and final President of the United States of America – took place one hundred years ago, on this day.

Not to worry, though. Columns like this will most likely be redundant in a world where only tropical aquatic creatures still survive. Is this unseemly pessimism? I'm sure it is. And if not, I warrant the sharks and ghost shrimp won't carp.

So, what's new this time around?

In *On This Day – Volume 2*, you can thrill to the horrors of the 'Night of the Big Wind' and the Invincibles, gasp at the genius of novelists Laurence Sterne and Arthur Conan Doyle, hiss at the iniquity of the informer Francis Magan, the Norman warlord Strongbow, and 'Half-hanged' McNaughton, and sob at the fate of the hapless *RMS Titanic*, the fearless Rollo Gillespie, and the luckless Kevin Barry. And you can, once again, enjoy Annie West's idiosyncratic take on some of the narratives included in this volume.

In fact, if you have had the good sense to purchase this collection in November, you will be in a position to savour, in advance of broadcast, more than half a dozen columns. This will enable you, should you engineer a communal audience for *Drivetime* in December, to astonish all your friends with your intimate knowledge of Irish history. You will also be able to correct some of the more egregious errors *before* they are broadcast. This is the literary equivalent of the practice in horse racing of 'past-posting'. However, be wary of how you use this dizzying power, as you may find yourself in the vicinity of an even greater pedant, with his or her own copy of *On This Day – Volume 2* in hand.

Apologies for the prosaic nature of the title, by the way. Some of the more colourful suggestions were rejected, such as *On This Day – The Golden Years, On This Day – Go Set a Watchman*, and *On This Day – Dead Man's Chest.*

As always, any errors are attributable to the mistakes, exaggerations and downright lies of the biographers and historians from whom the information contained in these columns has been culled. The author, himself an innocent victim of such fraud, #fakenews, special pleading or laxity, is entirely blameless.

Two years ago, in the foreword to the preceding volume, I asserted confidently that 'I certainly have made nothing up'. Unfortunately, I must confess that is not the case here. One column is entirely fictional. The fact that 1 April 2016 fell on a Friday was just too tempting to resist.

Someday I am sure I will run out of interesting stories. But we're not there yet.

Myles Dungan
April 2017

January

Another average day at Ennis Train station

29 January 1768

Oliver Goldsmith's first play, *The Good-Natured Man*, opens in London

Oliver Goldsmith must have been the despair of his mother – his father didn't live long enough to see him fail at almost everything to which he turned his hand. Eventually he would write one of the finest plays, one of the best novels, and one of the most ambitious long poems of the eighteenth century, but not before he had managed to destroy almost every opportunity that came his way.

Goldsmith was born the son of a Church of Ireland curate, either in Longford or Roscommon, in November 1728. In 1730 the family moved to Westmeath when his father was appointed rector to a parish in that county. In 1744 Goldsmith was admitted to Trinity College. There he learned to drink, gamble and play the flute. Although neither he nor the college greatly profited from his brief tenure, his subsequent fame has earned him one of the two most prominent statues in that venerable institution, overlooking College Green.

His father died around the time he graduated, and Goldsmith moved back into the family home so that he could be a burden on his poor mother, rather than on himself. He obtained a position as a tutor, and quickly lost it after a quarrel. After this, he decided to emigrate to America, but managed to miss his boat. He then took fifty pounds with him to Dublin, to help establish himself as a student of law, but he lost it all at gambling. He pretended to study medicine in Edinburgh, but rather than knuckle down he took off on a grand tour of Europe, keeping body and soul together by busking with his flute.

Eventually he settled in London and began to churn out hack writing to keep him gambling in the manner to which he had become accustomed. Due to the fact that he, in spite of himself, also occasionally published something of merit, he came to the attention of the famous wit and lexicographer, Samuel Johnson. He became a founder member of the club of writers and intellectuals unimaginatively entitled 'The Club', which included Johnson, his biographer James Boswell, the actor-manager David Garrick, the statesman and philosopher Edmund Burke, and the painter Joshua Reynolds. Heady company for a young ne'er do well from Ballymahon.

In 1760 he wrote the epic poem, *The Deserted Village*, elements of which schoolchildren of a certain age were forced to learn by heart. The poem tells the story of the fictional village of Auburn, laid to waste in order to make way for the ornamental gardens of a local landowner.

> … the man of wealth and pride
> Takes up a space that many poor supplied;
> Space for his lake, his park's extended bounds,
> Space for his horses, equipage, and hounds:
> The robe that wraps his limbs in silken sloth
> Has robbed the neighbouring fields of half their
> growth.

He followed this poem with his charming novel, *The Vicar of Wakefield*, in 1766, and one of the greatest comic plays in the

English language, *She Stoops to Conquer* in 1773. Prior to the play, he had a modicum of success with *The Good-Natured Man*, which bombed on the London stage but managed to sell a large number of copies when the text was published.

Success enabled Goldsmith to carry on with a lifestyle that virtually guaranteed an early exit. And so it proved. He continued to gamble and drink on a spectacular scale, and ended up in debt and in bad health. He died in 1774 at the age of forty-five.

Despite all his achievements as a novelist, playwright and poet, he is probably best remembered today for his *Elegy on the Death of a Mad Dog*, an inspired piece of doggerel (no pun intended). The title gives away the ending, but the short verse is a satire on hypocrisy and corruption in which a man of acknowledged standing, guilty of these vices, is bitten by a dog and left for dead by the commentariat. Then comes the sting in the tail (and yes, the pun is intended this time).

> But soon a wonder came to light,
> That showed the rogues they lied:
> The man recovered of the bite,
> The dog it was that died.

Oliver Goldsmith's play, *The Good-Natured Man*, opened in London to less-than-ecstatic reviews, two hundred and forty-eight years ago, on this day.

Broadcast 29 January 2016

15 January 1825

The suicide of banker Thomas Newcomen

If you thought Irish banking failures and inquiries were peculiar only to the twenty-first century, then think again. As Woody Guthrie pithily put it:

> Some men rob you with a gun
> And some with a fountain pen.

The Irish banker has been ruining himself and his customers, as well as cleverly masking his losses, since the early 1800s.

Let us look at some of the most spectacular Irish banking collapses of the nineteenth century. Most of them involve politicians as well as bankers. Strange that.

To begin, there was the scandal of the Tipperary Joint Stock Bank. It was run by the Irish Liberal MP for Carlow, John Sadlier, and his brother James, MP for Tipperary. When the bank ran out of money in 1856, John Sadlier committed suicide on Hampstead Heath, leaving James to face the music. This he did for a while, before he absconded. He ended his days in Switzerland, the natural home of the dodgy banker. Investigations revealed that the collapse of the bank was due to John Sadlier's embezzlement of funds on an outrageous scale. Before he shuffled off his mortal coil, he'd stolen nearly £300,000 from the vaults. The whole episode is said to have provided Charles Dickens with the inspiration to create the dubious financier, Mr Merdle, in *Little Dorritt*, published in 1857.

Fast forward to 1869, and to an egregious example of Ireland's capacity to forgive a scoundrel, another MP, Joseph Neale McKenna, Chairman and Managing Director of the National Bank of Ireland in the 1850s and 60s. He somehow managed to combine in one person the roles later held by Sean Fitzpatrick and David Drumm of Anglo Irish Bank. Either Seanie and David were total slackers or McKenna was an absolute hive of fiduciary energy.

McKenna successfully ran the bank into the ground due to a number of unwise investments in pursuit of growth and greater market share. Aren't we fortunate that our bankers shrugged off that bad habit a century and a half later? By the time he was forced out in 1869, accused of cronyism and being far too generous with his own paycheque – other habits utterly alien to the modern equivalent – the National Bank of Ireland had debts of almost £400,000. The bank did manage to survive, however, and McKenna, MP for Youghal, lost his seat, but later re-invented himself as a Parnellite and was re-elected in South Monaghan. This proves the theory that if Charles Stewart Parnell had nominated a pile of pigeon droppings for a nationalist constituency, they would have won the seat with a thumping majority.

Another flawed banker, however, was not so lucky where the Uncrowned King of Ireland was concerned. William Shaw briefly held the leadership of the Home Rule Party after Isaac Butt died in 1879 until, in 1880, he got the bum's rush when Parnell stood against him. Interestingly, Shaw was supported in the leadership contest by one James McNeale McKenna. These banker/politicians do seem to stick together. Shaw was also founder and Chairman of the Munster Bank. In 1885 he resigned, having received loans to the value of £80,000 – twice the amount of the rest of the directors combined. Again, we are fortunate that this practice was completely stamped out before the twenty-first century. The Munster Bank did not outlive his chairmanship for long. It went bust the following year.

Finally, we go quickly to the 1820s, and Thomas Newcomen, a Viscount and, surprise surprise, a politician. He inherited the Newcomen Bank, voted for the Act of Union in 1800, spent much of his time in the bank's fine new headquarters – now the Rates Office beside Dublin Castle – and proceeded to drive the family business into the ground, taking many depositors with him. Newcomen was described as a reclusive, Scrooge-like figure who enjoyed gloating over the precious metals left in his safe keeping.

Thomas Newcomen, driven to distraction by the collapse of his family bank, took his own life, one hundred and ninety-one years ago, on this day.

Broadcast 15 January 2016

6 January 1839

The night of 'The Big Wind'

Snow fell over much of the country on 5 January 1839, but then, as often happens in Ireland, the weather changed completely. Temperatures rose, and the snow rapidly melted. For a few hours, the country basked in unseasonable warmth. No one had the slightest idea what lay in store.

Gradually, during the day of the 6 January, the winds rose. The first area affected was Co. Mayo, where a strong breeze and heavy rains swept in from the Atlantic at around midday. Nollaig na mBan, the religious feast of the Epiphany, wasn't going to be that pleasant a day after all.

There was a belief among the impressionable that the world would come to an end, that the Apocalypse would descend on 6 January and that one Nollaig na mBan would finally prove to be the day of Final Judgement. And that was *before* the Apocalypse of the Night of the Big Wind.

The squalls that first appeared on the west coast quickly moved eastwards, and worse weather followed in its wake. The storm began to gather strength, and soon it was powerful enough to blow down the steeple of the Anglican church in Castlebar. As it moved across the midlands, the wind gusted at over one hundred knots – roughly one hundred and eighty-five kilometres an hour. According to the scale devised in 1805 by the Navan-born hydrographer and naval officer Sir Francis Beaufort, that was a force twelve, or hurricane force.

It was the most destructive wind to hit Europe in more than a century – another damaging, continent-wide hurricane in 1703 had largely bypassed Ireland. But our geographical position on the western periphery of the continent meant that this time early Victorian Ireland bore the brunt of nature's awe-inspiring strength. By the time the wind had blown itself out, upwards of three hundred people were dead; many had died at sea. Forty-two ships had sunk. Most of the shipping damage was on the badly hit west coast. So strong were the surging winds that some inland flooding was caused by seawater.

The Big Wind spared no one. Well-built aristocratic homes and military barracks were destroyed or badly damaged, as were the bothies and cottages of the rural poor. Exposed livestock were vulnerable, not only to the Big Wind itself, but to the aftermath, as crops and stores of fodder were obliterated.

Ironically, given the prevailing conditions, much of the damage was caused by fire. The winds fanned the embers of turf fires abandoned overnight in hearths. The sparks set fire to thatched roofs. These conflagrations were then spread to adjacent roofs, especially in small towns like Naas, Kilbeggan, Slane and Kells. Seventy-one houses were burned in Loughrea, and over one hundred in Athlone.

County Meath was right in the path of the wind. The *Dublin Evening Post* reported that:

> The damage done in this county is very great. Not a single demesne escaped, and tens of thousands of trees have been snapped in twain or torn up by the roots, and farming produce to an immense amount destroyed.

The city of Dublin did not escape either. The tremendous gusts devoured a quarter of the buildings in the capital as the wind raced across the Irish Sea to Britain and continental Europe before finally dissipating. The River Liffey rose and flooded the quays in the centre of the city. A noon service at the Bethesda Chapel in Dorset Street had given thanks, on 6 January, for deliverance from a potentially destructive fire – that night the wind whipped up the embers of the fire and consumed the church.

One of the unexpected consequences of the Night of the Big Wind came almost seventy years later, when the British Government introduced an old-age pension for the over-seventies. As the formal registration of births in Ireland had only begun in 1863, many septuagenarians were entitled to a pension, but had no birth certificates to prove their age. One of the methods used to ascertain their age was devised by civil servants, who would ask the question 'Do you remember the Night of the Big Wind?' If they did remember it, they got their pension, as they were deemed old enough to qualify.

Hurricane-force winds destroyed property and killed hundreds of people and animals when 'The Night of the Big Wind' struck Ireland, one hundred and seventy-eight years ago, on this day.

Broadcast 6 January 2017

8 January 1871

The birth of Sir James Craig

The most familiar photograph of James Craig is of a rather startled but steely-eyed elderly man with rapidly receding hair and a prominently thick, grey moustache. He looks like someone you wouldn't want to trifle with. In this instance, looks were not deceptive.

Craig was born in Belfast in 1871, the son of a distiller. He was a millionaire by the age of forty, with much of his money coming from his adventures in stockbroking. This meant that he had plenty of resources to devote to his favourite pastime, keeping Ulster in the Union. This he was very good at indeed.

As did many a younger son of a well-established family, he first distinguished himself in the army. Everybody had enjoyed the first Boer War so much that they decided to do it all over again. So, from 1899, Craig served as an officer in the Third Royal Irish Rifles. He was, at one point, imprisoned by the Boers, and was finally forced home due to dysentery in 1901.

His name is, of course, as indelibly associated with that of Edward Carson as is Butch Cassidy's with that of the Sundance Kid. Craig came into his own in 1912 in the organisation of unionist opposition to the prospect of Irish Home Rule. He was central to the creation of the Ulster Volunteer Force (UVF) and the promulgation of the Ulster Solemn League and Covenant, in which Ulster said 'no' with an emphatic flourish. While Carson made the speeches and was the most public opponent of Irish devolution, Craig was seen as the organisational genius who developed the muscular element to back up Carson's rhetoric. Craig was, for example, one of the men behind the Larne gun running of 1914, which brought 20,000 rifles to the UVF.

Unlike Carson, Craig was perfectly content with the exclusion of the six counties from the ambit of Home Rule. The Government of Ireland Act of 1920 gave Ulster, somewhat ironically, a Home Rule parliament of its own. In February 1921, Craig succeeded Carson as leader of the Ulster Unionist party. Later that year he fought the 1921 election, while asking unionist supporters to 'Rally round me that I may shatter our enemies and their hopes of a republic flag. The Union Jack must sweep the polls. Vote early, work late.' If you were expecting 'vote often' there … well, that wasn't Craig's style. In June 1921 he became the first Prime Minister of Northern Ireland.

His most famous speech was made in the Northern Ireland Parliament in 1934 and, we are told, is often misquoted. He did not actually refer to that assembly as a 'Protestant parliament for a Protestant people'. What he did say was, 'my whole object [is] in carrying on a Protestant Government for a Protestant people.' You might well be forgiven for wondering what the difference is.

He also reflected, on one occasion in the Northern Ireland House of Commons, that:

It would be rather interesting for historians of the future to compare a Catholic State launched in the South, with a Protestant State launched in the North, and to see which gets on the better, and prospers the more. It is most interesting for me at the moment to watch how they are progressing. I am doing my best always to top the bill, and to be ahead of the South.

Arguably, he achieved that ambition during his tenure as Prime Minister, though large-scale fiscal transfers from London, as well as the Anglo-Irish Economic War of the 1930s, undoubtedly helped the Northern Irish economy to keep its nose ahead of the under-performing Irish Free State.

Craig was almost obsessive in his desire to have Northern Ireland treated as an integral part of the United Kingdom, to such an extent that he occasionally acted contrary to the apparent interests of its population. This can be seen clearly in his insistence, in 1940, that conscription be introduced in Northern Ireland when World War II broke out. Winston Churchill wisely passed on that particular poisoned chalice, fearing the inevitable backlash from the sizeable nationalist population and the reaction in the Irish Free State.

Towards the end of his days, Craig began to take on an uncanny physical resemblance to the man who, in later life, would become the Rev. Ian Paisley. When Craig died in November 1940, aged sixty-nine, he was still Northern Ireland Prime Minister.

Captain James Craig, later First Viscount Craigavon, was born one hundred and forty-five years ago, on this day.

Broadcast 8 January 2016

22 January 1879

James Shields is elected Senator for Missouri

James Shields from Co. Tyrone was an extraordinary Irishman, though his name is virtually unknown in his native country. He had an uncle of the same name who emigrated to the US and became a senator for Ohio. Not to be outdone, James Shields Jr left Ireland at the age of twenty, and went on to represent not one but *three* states in the US Senate. A unique achievement, unlikely ever to be repeated.

In 1849 he served one term as a US senator for the state of Illinois... His election was helped by what came to be known as the 'lucky Mexican bullet'. This had struck him while he was a brigadier general in the Mexican-American war in 1846, and he used it for all it was worth in his campaign. His opponent for the Illinois seat was the incumbent Sydney Breese, a fellow Democrat. A political rival wrote of Shields's injury:

> What a wonderful shot that was! The bullet went clean through Shields without hurting him, or even leaving a scar, and killed Breese a thousand miles away.

Shields is also unusual in that he replaced himself in the Senate. When he was first elected in 1849 it emerged that he had not been a citizen of the US for the required nine years. He had only been naturalized in October 1840, leaving him a few weeks short, so his election was declared null and void. However, he would be entitled to take his seat after a special election was immediately called to replace him as he had by then been naturalized for the required period. He stood again, and won the seat for a second time.

When he failed in his bid to be re-elected six years later, in 1855, he moved to what was then the Minnesota 'territory', from where he was returned in 1858 as one of the new State's first two senators, after Minnesota achieved statehood. Later, during the Civil War, he distinguished himself as a union general and then settled in Missouri.

He had obviously taken a liking to the Senate chamber, because in 1879 he contrived to get re-elected to that house, from Missouri, at the age of seventy-three. He died shortly after taking office.

But Shields is possibly even more important for something he didn't do.

In 1842 he was already well known in his adopted home of Illinois. He was a lawyer, and was serving in the State Legislature as a Democrat. After one of those periodic economic recessions hit the nation in the 1840s, Shields, as State auditor, issued instructions that paper money should no longer be taken as payment for State taxes. Only gold or silver would be acceptable. A prominent member of the Whig party, one Abraham Lincoln, took exception to the rule, and wrote an anonymous satirical letter to a local Springfield, Illinois newspaper, in which he called Shields a fool, a liar and a dunce. This was then followed up by Lincoln's wife-to-be, Mary Todd, with an equally scathing letter of her own. When Shields contacted the editor of the newspaper to find out who had written the second letter, Lincoln himself took full responsibility. A belligerent Shields, accordingly, challenged the future US president to a duel. The venue was to be the infamous Bloody Island in the middle of the Mississippi river, dueling being illegal in Illinois.

Lincoln, having been challenged, was allowed to choose the weapons and set the rules. He did this to his own considerable advantage, opting for broadswords as opposed to pistols. While Shields was a crack shot, he was only five feet nine inches in height, as opposed to Lincoln's towering six feet four inches. When the rivals finally met on 22 September 1842, Lincoln quickly demonstrated his huge reach advantage by ostentatiously lopping off a branch above the Irishman's head with his weapon of choice.

When the seconds ticked by and other interested parties intervened, peace was negotiated between the two men, though it took some time to placate the pugnacious Shields and persuade him to shake hands with Lincoln.

The man who might have abruptly ended the life and career of Abraham Lincoln, and subsequently change the course of American history, James Shields from Co. Tyrone, was elected as Senator for Missouri, one hundred and thirty-seven years ago, on this day.

Broadcast 22 January 2016

13 January 1880

The Irish film director, Herbert Brenon, is born

They weren't presented with anywhere near the same sort of pizzazz or pomp first time around as they are now, but the 1927 and 1928 Academy Awards – the first of their kind, at a time before they became known as 'the Oscars' – were still hugely important to the burgeoning Hollywood community of film-makers.

At the private dinner for the nominees at the Hollywood Roosevelt Hotel in Los Angeles, there was a significant Irish presence. The dinner was hosted by the president of the relatively newly formed Academy of Motion Picture Arts and Sciences, Douglas Fairbanks, on 16 May 1929. It cost five dollars to get in, there were almost three hundred invited guests, a dozen categories, with two to four nominees in each category. The entire ceremony lasted fifteen minutes – about the length of Billy Crystal's opening monologue these days. It remains the only Academy Award ceremony not to have been broadcast on radio or TV.

But who was the Irish-born nominee that night? It wasn't the celebrated Dubliner Rex Ingram, whose brilliant career was coming to an end. Neither was it the Dublin-born art director Cedric Gibbons, though he did design the winner's statuettes, which, at the time, were yet to be iconic. The Irish nominee, in the Best Director category, was another

24

Dubliner, Herbert Brenon, director of over three hundred movies, in a career that dated back to the migration of the film industry to the west coast, and to its new home in the Hollywood Hills in Los Angeles.

Brenon was born in Dublin in 1880, son of an English father – who was a drama critic – and an Irish mother, Frances, who was a writer. He had emigrated to the USA at the age of sixteen and began performing on the vaudeville stage almost immediately. In the early 1900s, with vaudeville beginning to provide slim pickings, he joined Carl Laemmle's Independent Motion Picture Company as a screen writer, working with glamorous stars like Florence Lawrence and Mary Pickford.

He directed his first film in 1912, and was quickly ranked alongside some of the Hollywood greats of the silent era, like Cecil B. de Mille, D.W. Griffiths, and his own compatriot, Rex Ingram. While some of his output was frivolous, much of what he created dealt with difficult and challenging subjects, like the fall of the Romanov dynasty, and life in a Jewish ghetto. His only obvious genuflection to his country of origin was *Kathleen Mavourneen*, made in 1913.

He worked with some of the biggest names of the silent era: Theda Bara, Ronald Colman, Lon Chaney, Clara Bow and Pola Negri. He also had an adventurous career. While making the film *Neptune's Daughter* (1949), he was badly injured when a tank exploded. Later, while making a film on location in Italy, he was kidnapped by bandits.

In 1926 Brenon became the first director to try his hand at adapting F. Scott Fitzgerald's *The Great Gatsby* (1925) for the screen. Not an easy thing to do convincingly, with no dialogue available during the silent movie era. Brenon's version was produced by the legendary Adolph Zukor and Jesse Lasky, and released by Paramount.

Two years before, the same team had produced and directed the first full-length film adaptation of J. M. Barrie's classic children's story *Peter Pan* (1911). Brenon was also first to direct the film version of *Beau Geste* (1924), the French Foreign Legion novel by P. C. Wren.

On the night of 16 May 1929, he waited – not for too long given the length of the ceremony – to find out whether he had won the first Best Director Academy Award for a film called *Sorrell and Son* (1927). He hadn't. The gold-plated gong went instead to Frank Borzage for *Seventh Heaven* (1927).

Like a lot of his contemporaries, Brenon wrote off the 'talkies' as a passing fad. His illustrious career did not prosper when Hollywood adopted sound, and his career ended with a number of undistinguished movies made in England. He made his last film in 1940 and died in Los Angeles in 1958.

Alexander Herbert Reginald St. John Brenon, to give him his full name, was born in Dublin, one hundred and thirty-seven years ago, on this day.

Broadcast 13 January 2017

27 January 1885

Charles Stewart Parnell turns the first sod for the West Clare Railway

In extenuation for his many crimes, it was once suggested that at least Benito Mussolini, the Italian Fascist leader, 'made the trains run on time'. It is hardly enough, however, to erase the invasion of Abyssinia, his alliance with Nazi Germany, nor the liquidation of a number of inconvenient political opponents from our minds.

But you can't offer that excuse in the case of one of the great villains of Irish history, Captain William Henry O'Shea. The reason O'Shea didn't make the trains run on time was because he was one of the great parliamentary champions of the notoriously dilatory West Clare Railway. This narrow-gauge iron road ran, if that particular word doesn't suggest too much urgency, between Ennis and Moyasta, and thence west to Kilrush, or east to Kilkee, whichever was your preference. It travelled the route via Ennistymon, Lahinch and Milltown Malbay. It was the last operating narrow-gauge passenger railway in the country. The problem was that it just wasn't very reliable.

Only twenty-seven miles long when it opened in 1887, it was actually two railways, the West Clare and the South Clare, that met at Milltown Malbay. Hardly comparable to the iconic junction of America's Union Pacific and Central Pacific railroads at Promontory Point in Utah, but very exciting nonetheless for the good citizens of Clare, who now found it much easier to travel around and connect with the country's main rail network at Ennis. The line was later extended to forty-eight miles in overall length.

Although work had already started the previous November, the sod was not officially turned on the original construction site until January 1885. O'Shea, the semi-detached Nationalist MP for Clare, wanted his pound of flesh after months of lobbying Parliament to ensure that funds were made available for the project, so the party leader himself, Charles Stewart Parnell, was recruited to pop over from his unwedded bliss with O'Shea's wife Katharine in London, and do the needful with a shovel. Also in attendance was the man chosen to build the railway, one William Martin Murphy, who would have his own days in the sun during the infamous Dublin Lockout of 1913.

Of course, the railway was immortalized by its hilarious brush with the songwriter and performer Percy French. He successfully sued the line for loss of earnings after arriving four and a half hours late for an engagement in Kilkee on 10 August 1896, thanks, he alleged, to the rather relaxed attitude of the railroad employees towards the joys of timetabling. He won £10 and costs at the Ennis Quarter Sessions in January 1897.

Now, most sensible corporations, when in a hole, stop digging. But not the West Clare Railway. They appealed the decision at the next Clare Spring Assizes, held before the formidable jurist, Chief Baron Palles. French might have forfeited the case, as he arrived an hour late for the hearing. But his explanation that he 'took the West Clare Railway here, Your Honour', probably sealed the case in his favour.

In the course of his contribution, French offered a couplet that suggested he had a certain composition in mind already. He informed the Chief Baron that, 'If you want to get to Kilkee/ You must go there by the sea'. The lines didn't actually make it into his final revenge on the hapless railway line: 'Are Ye Right There Michael', which begins:

> You may talk of Columbus's sailing
> Across the Atlantical Sea
> But he never tried to go railing
> From Ennis, as far as Kilkee

Incidentally, on the same day as Percy French's court appearance, one Mary Anne Butler from Limerick was also suing the railway, alleging that she had been attacked by a malevolent donkey on the platform in Ennis.

The line eventually closed down in 1961, but thanks to a group of local enthusiasts, the West Clare Railway lives once more. Part of the line, between Moyasta and Kilkee, has been restored, and one of the original engines, the exquisite Slieve Callan, is back in use.

The national press reported that the first sod of the West Clare Railway was turned by Charles Stewart Parnell, one hundred and thirty-two years ago, on this day.

Broadcast 29 January 2017

20 January 1902

Kevin Barry, medical student and nationalist revolutionary, is born in Dublin

He was from a working-class background. His father died when he was six years old. But that didn't stop the young Dubliner, Kevin Barry, from getting a scholarship to University College Dublin to study medicine, at the age of seventeen. Two years before, while a rugby-playing student and an enthusiastic hurler at Belvedere College, he joined the Irish Volunteers. By 1920 the Volunteers had become the Irish Republican Army, and he was carrying a Mauser pistol on military raids in Dublin and Wicklow.

On 20 September 1920, his unit, 'C' Company of the Dublin 1st Battalion, was given orders to capture the much-needed weapons of a British Army unit in Church Street. Things went smoothly at first, and it looked like the operation would be a complete success with no loss of life, but then firing broke out.

Accompanying Barry on that arms raid was seventeen-year-old T. P. McKenna from Mullagh in Co. Cavan, a good friend and a fellow medical student who had just begun his studies in Trinity College. McKenna and most of the other members of the raiding party managed to escape, but Kevin Barry was captured. Three young British soldiers were killed in the fire-fight, and Barry became the first member of the Irish Volunteers to be taken prisoner since 1916.

His treatment in custody, in the North Dublin Union, was anything but exemplary. The authorities were looking for information – they wanted the names of the other members of Barry's unit – and used intimidation and violence in their attempt to acquire them. Barry resisted physical and psychological torture, and refused to give up the names of the other members of his Volunteer unit.

Barry was then court-martialled under a new piece of legislation, the Restoration of Order in Ireland Act. It was an extension of the war-time Defence of the Realm Act, and had been introduced by the British Government so that it could deal with IRA insurrection without introducing martial law. Barry achieved another unenviable first, becoming a test case for the effectiveness of the new legislation. He was charged with the murder of one of the three soldiers, twenty-year-old Private Marshall Whitehead. He was tried by military court, consisting of nine British officers. This he refused to recognise.

Although there was no proof that Barry had personally shot Whitehead, who had been killed by a bullet from a Colt pistol, not a Mauser, the Crown only had to prove that he had participated in the exchange of fire. They established the facts to the court's satisfaction and the young medical student was sentenced to death for the murder of Private Whitehead.

He hoped to be executed by firing squad; instead, he was to die by hanging. Despite a national and international campaign for a reprieve – which included interventions from the US and the Vatican – the sentence was carried out in Mountjoy Prison on Monday 1 November 1920, less than a week after the death of the hunger-striking Lord Mayor of Cork, Terence McSwiney, and barely three weeks before the Bloody Sunday atrocities in Dublin. Barry was buried in an unmarked grave near the Mountjoy Women's Prison. In

October 2001 his remains, along with those of nine other Republicans, were exhumed and re-interred in Glasnevin Cemetery, after a State funeral.

Shortly after his death, a song written in Kevin Barry's honour began to circulate. The tune was taken from the melancholy sea shanty 'Rolling Home'. It has since been recorded by artists as diverse as The Dubliners, Lonnie Donegan, Paul Robeson and Leonard Cohen.

Kevin Gerard Barry, medical student and executed teenage IRA Volunteer, was born one hundred and fifteen years ago, on this day.

Broadcast 20 January 2017

February

"Take your time, Mr. Pigott"

26 February 1797

Bank of Ireland suspends gold payments

The expression 'It's money in the bank' was once widely used but, in the wake of the fiscal, financial and credit crises of 2008, phraseology like this is fairly redundant. That axiom has gone the way of 'It's as safe as houses' or 'I am a markets' trader, trust me'. Today, we think more in terms of 'It's money under the mattress' or 'It's as safe ... as this large amount of cash I'm carrying around in my pocket because the interest rate is higher on my backside than in an investment account'.

Where did it all go wrong? Well, maybe it started, in this country at least, in 1797, when Bank of Ireland took an unprecedented step. In those days, cash was king, and cash was gold, or silver. No gold, no goods. Unless you were a member of the ten thousand or so landed Irish aristocratic families who were allowed to run up debts. But you still had to settle your account with gold at some point ... didn't you?

Anyway. It's the end of the eighteenth century and, as usual, Britain is at war. Which is really to say that England is at war, and everybody else is expected to chip in and help pay for it. In this case the opposition was provided, as usual – or *comme d'habitude* – by France. Where would England have been without France? Clearly, at war with somebody else.

What the British Government required above all, to conduct its war with Napoleon, was gold. There wasn't enough to go around. There certainly wasn't enough in the vaults of the Bank of England to be sending any of it over to the Irish. So, in 1797, the Bank of Ireland was obliged to stop issuing gold it didn't have, and rely on banknotes – already well established at that time – to keep money in circulation.

A few weeks later, the stance taken by the bank was approved by Irish legislators in the Irish Parliament. Anyone starting to get a feeling of *déjà vu* here?

One of the noticeable phenomena prior to the withdrawal of gold, and the increased issuing of notes in its stead, was the establishment in Ireland of a number of private banks who were allowed to issue their own notes. In 1799 there were eleven. In 1803, the year Robert Emmet was hung, drawn and quartered for the sake of the economy, this number had increased to forty-one. That's not forty-one branches, mind you, that's forty-one banks! Many of these went bust and subsequently destroyed the lives of their customers. In those days the partners who ran the financial institutions were identified on the banknotes they issued. This meant that when the banks went into liquidation, their clients could see the names, but unfortunately not the addresses, of the men who had screwed them.

Perhaps we should thank the Bank of Ireland for the fact that we are no longer weighed down with gold whenever we go to the supermarket or the pub. Their action in withdrawing the precious metal from circulation was certainly to the benefit of our clothing. Pockets are no longer subjected to excessive strain. Jackets are not weighed down by heavy metal, except in the case of angry people who wander around carrying Motorhead CDs. But, as we don't have much to thank our banks for these days, let's not bother.

The Bank of Ireland relieved itself of the necessity to issue payment in gold, two hundred and nineteen years ago, on this day.

Broadcast 26 February 2016

24 February 1841

Birth of John Philip Holland

The next time a Royal Navy submarine engages in one of the force's favourite pastimes, namely 'snagging an Irish trawler', its crew might pause to reflect on the fact that the man who invented their vessel was brought up speaking Irish, and was once a Christian Brother.

John Philip Holland didn't learn English until he went to national school in Liscannor, Co. Clare, just as the Famine was beginning to take hold in the west of Ireland.

His father, an employee of the British Coastguard Service, would probably not have approved of the first intended use of his new invention – it was built at the behest of the Fenians to blow up British shipping.

Holland was born in 1841 and left Ireland in 1873 after a stint as a schoolteacher in a variety of locations, including the North Monastery in Cork. It seems that he had already been working on his invention before he left Ireland. He settled down in Paterson, New Jersey, and developed a patent, which he first offered to the US Navy in 1875. They rejected it as 'a fantastic scheme of a civilian landsman'.

Holland's brother, who lived in Boston, happened to be a member of the Fenian Brotherhood, and it was through his sibling that Holland met John Devoy and Jeremiah O'Donovan Rossa. Devoy, leader of the extreme republican Clan na Gael organisation, was impressed by

Holland's nationalism and by the potential for havoc with his invention. Money was appropriated from O'Donovan Rossa's infamous 'Skirmishing Fund' – collected from Irish-American nationalists for use in freeing the 'old sod' –and Holland was engaged to build a prototype.

Holland gave up his teaching job and worked on the project full time. He used Rossa's fund to develop his first model in 1878, the *Holland 1,* a one-man, fourteen-foot craft with a two-cylinder engine.

By 1881 he had refined his original design and produced a three-man vessel, thirty-one feet long, which became known as *The Fenian Ram*, which, unfortunately, could not sustain extended periods of use underwater.

While he was working for the Irish republican, Holland could never seem to get it absolutely right. If he designed a submarine that could remain underwater for long periods, it would develop engine trouble. He also got into difficulties with port authorities in New York and New Haven, who considered him, quite literally, a danger to shipping. After an investment of sixty thousand dollars, with little or nothing to show for it other than three interesting models, the Clan and Holland parted company. Fortunately, Clan na Gael had no comptroller or auditor general among their ranks to issue a negative report about the waste of good Skirmishing Fund money, funds that might have been better used in the dynamite campaign then going on in London.

Holland continued to experiment. He developed a fourth prototype, which didn't seem to excite anybody too much either, until he attracted the attention of a wealthy lawyer, J. B. Frost, who staked him until he got it right. He hit gold with 'Model No. 6'. It was fifty-three feet long, had a six-man crew, could dive to sixty feet, and could stay under for nearly two days. It was also armed with torpedoes. In 1900 the US Navy gave him one hundred and fifty thousand dollars for it, named it the *USS Holland*, and asked for six more, please. Oh, yes – and then they really annoyed the inventor by selling the plans to the British Navy.

Holland died in 1914, barely a week after the beginning of the global war that was to see his invention kill thousands of people, including women and children on board commercial vessels like the *Lusitania*, which sank in 1915.

John Philip Holland, Clare man, ex-Christian Brother, native Irish speaker, and inventor of one of the most lethal weapons in military history, was born, one hundred and seventy-six years ago, on this day.

Broadcast 24 February 2017

12 February 1848

John Mitchel publishes the first *United Irishman* newspaper

He was one of the great propagandists of his day, although the causes he espoused often placed him on the wrong side of the angels. He was loved and loathed in equal measure, and was one of the few Irishmen to have incurred the wrath of the British Government and the Federal administration of the USA.

John Mitchel was born near Dungiven in Co. Derry in the year of the Battle of Waterloo, 1815. He probably would have been on Napoleon's side, if only because the opposing army was largely British. Son of a Presbyterian clergyman, Mitchel created his own pulpit in a series of journalistic enterprises in Dublin, Tennessee, Virginia and New York.

Mostly raised in Newry, Co. Down, Mitchel's first political association was with the Young Ireland movement of the 1840s, and the famous *Nation* newspaper, founded by Charles Gavan Duffy, Thomas Davis and John Blake Dillon in 1842. But long before the abortive Young Ireland rebellion of 1848, Mitchel had moved on, finding the editorial policies of the *Nation* rather too bland for his tastes. He founded his own rival nationalist weekly newspaper, the *United Irishman*, which, in its inaugural edition, claimed that, 'the world was weary of Old Ireland and also of Young Ireland', thus attacking both Daniel

O'Connell and his younger antagonists with the same broadsword. Mitchel aimed to be an equal-opportunities offender, and succeeded admirably.

The *United Irishman*, however, was not responsible for the destruction of many trees, as it was closed down by the British authorities after a mere sixteen issues. Mitchel was later tried before an elegantly and efficiently packed jury, found guilty of treason-felony, and deported to Tasmania, then known as Van Diemen's Land. The result was one of the greatest works of Irish political history, *The Jail Journal* (1854), in which Mitchel wrote about his own experience of deportation and advocated a far more militaristic approach to Ireland's 'English problem' than would have been popular heretofore.

He followed this up, in 1861, with a white-hot diatribe, *The Last Conquest of Ireland (Perhaps)*, in which he accused the British Government of operating genocidal policies in its Irish colony during the Great Famine. The latter work was written in the safety of the USA, as his escape from Tasmania had been engineered in 1853.

So far so good, at least if you are an Irish nationalist, especially one of a more militant stripe. But it is from here on in that Mitchell's career becomes problematic. Settling in New York, he established the radical newspaper, *The Citizen*. He used this publication as a platform for continued attacks on British policy in Ireland, but also employed its columns for full-blooded assaults on advocates for the end of slavery. An abolitionist he was not.

When the American Civil War began, he moved lock, stock and barrel to the South, settling first in Knoxville, Tennessee, where he published the *Southern Citizen* newspaper. In its pages, he attacked the Union, once describing Abraham Lincoln as 'an ignoramus and a boor'.

He also had a go at Irish-American political and military leaders, like his erstwhile Young Ireland ally, Thomas Francis Meagher, who fought on the Union side. He compared the South to Ireland, and suggested that black slaves experienced better economic and social conditions than Irish tenant farmers. He didn't expend all his vitriol on attacking the North either. Confederate President Jefferson Davis, who was far too much of an old softy for Mitchell, was also a frequent target. One of the ironies in all of this was that his advocacy of the Confederacy put him on the same side in the conflict as the British Government, which was officially non-aligned, but neutral for the South.

After the war, however, Mitchel shared the fate of Jefferson Davis, spending a short time in jail for his anti-Union spleen. His imprisonment would have given him plenty of time to reflect on the deaths of two of his sons in the war. A third son lost an arm. The latter years of his life were spent in the service of the Fenian movement, for whom he worked in Paris. He also stood, successfully, albeit *in absentia*, for election in Tipperary in 1875. His success at the polls was nullified by the authorities on the grounds that he was a convicted felon. In those days, you could commit all the felonies you liked AFTER you were elected, but not before. Mitchel died suddenly in 1875 at the age of fifty-nine. His grandson, John Purroy Mitchel, later became Mayor of New York.

John Mitchel published his political manifesto, in the shape of the first issue of the *United Irishman* newspaper, one hundred and sixty-eight years ago, on this day.

Broadcast 12 February 2016

17 February 1857

Birth of Samuel McClure

Campaigning investigative journalism, or 'muckraking' in American parlance, came into its own in the USA during what is known as the Gilded Age, towards the end of the nineteenth century. As with all halcyon eras, it was 'gilded' only for the privileged few. Such fabulously wealthy individuals often had few compunctions about how they acquired their gold.

Newspapers and magazines uncovered and exposed the excesses of corrupt politicians, and the illegal and unethical activities of the so-called 'robber barons' of the period – staggeringly rich men, as well as major corporations, who wished to become even wealthier. The 'muckrakers' – the term was coined by President Theodore Roosevelt, who meant it as a compliment – held corporate and political America up to close scrutiny, and generally found it wanting.

At the centre of this tsunami of investigative journalism was a monthly magazine called *McClure's*, which employed some of the greatest campaigning writers of the nineteenth and early twentieth centuries. It was owned and edited by an Irishman, Samuel McClure. McClure was from Ballymoney, Co. Antrim. He was the son of a carpenter, whose mother was forced to take him and his siblings to the USA after her husband died in an industrial accident when young Sam was nine years old. McClure had a tough childhood, but his mother was determined that he would get a good education. This eventually brought him to one of the best liberal arts academies in the USA, Knox College in Illinois, and after that into a career in New York journalism.

He was already well-established when he started *McClure's* in 1893. It sold for ten cents a copy, or a dollar a year. Among his achievements was the nurturing of new literary voices such as Jack London and Willa Cather. He also introduced the teaching methods of Maria Montessori to the American public. But McClure's enduring significance lies in the fact that he championed an entirely new form of writing: the well-researched exposé. McClure was almost unique among editors in not demanding instant and regular copy from his employees. Instead, he was prepared to finance painstaking but thoroughly researched reporting that would reveal the corruption and injustice of nineteenth century American society. He did this with the help of the so-called 'Big Four', the talented, tenacious and courageous quartet of Lincoln Steffens, William Allen White, Ida Tarbell, and Ray Stannard Baker.

Steffens once said of his editor that:

He was a flower that did not sit and wait for the bees to come and take his honey and leave their seeds. He flew forth to find and rob the bees.

The bees McClure robbed were amongst the wealthiest, most ruthless, and most powerful individuals in late nineteenth (and early twentieth) century America. Men like John D. Rockefeller, whose Standard Oil company was a particular target for Ida Tarbell in a series of articles between 1902 and 1904. Rockefeller dismissed her as 'Ida Tarbarrel', a sure sign that she was getting under his skin.

Or Andrew Carnegie, whose activities within the US Steel Corporation were laid bare by Ray Stannard Baker in 1901. Steffens, who became editor of *McClure's* in 1902, tended to focus his attention on crooked politicians and corrupt civic administrations, many of whom were in the pockets of the 'robber barons'.

The muckrakers challenged the power of an apparently invulnerable class of super-rich industrialists and their allies in urban machine politics. The turn of the nineteenth century in the USA was a period, on the one hand, of unregulated capitalism, and on the other, of a burgeoning progressive reform movement. *McClure's* magazine was in the vanguard of reform, providing progressive politicians with the ammunition they needed to curtail the power of a monopolistic oligarchy.

None of which made the mercurial Sam McClure easy to work with. He was often idiosyncratic and inconsistent, though highly supportive of his invaluable contributors. Finally, in 1906, Tarbell, Baker, White and Steffens, having had enough of his eccentricities, departed from what they called McClure's 'house of bondage', and founded the equally radical *American Magazine.* To the astonishment of all, McClure, who parted with his stars on generous terms, simply dusted himself off and started over again as a dangerous pest to the elites he had already been stinging for years.

At its height, *McClure's* was selling four hundred thousand copies a month. Gradually, however, its influence declined, as did McClure's personal interest in his pet project. By 1914 he had moved on to other things. These included three philosophical musings on the workings of democracy, two of which were published in the 1930s. McClure lived to the age of ninety-two, and died in 1949.

Samuel Sidney McClure, scourge of the American entitled, was born in Co. Antrim, one hundred and sixty years ago, on this day.

Broadcast 17 February 2017

10 February 1889

Richard Pigott is exposed
as a forger

Charles Russell, born in Newry, Co. Down, was the man who would become Baron Killowen, and who would later torment the infamous forger Richard Pigott in the witness box in his defence of Charles Stewart Parnell. He was one of five siblings, and was the only sibling in the Russell family who did not enter the religious life. His three sisters all became nuns, his brother a Jesuit priest.

He was a highly successful Queen's Counsel in London, a moderate nationalist MP, and rose to become Lord Chief Justice of England, the first Catholic to hold the office for centuries. However, it is for his forensic grilling of the dubious journalist, turncoat, and pornographer, Richard Pigott at the *Times* Commission hearings in 1889 that he is justly celebrated.

Pigott had fallen on hard times by the 1880s – he had, at one point, been a relatively prosperous newspaper proprietor who, in 1868, went to jail on a point of principle after defending the Manchester Martyrs in one of his newspapers. He had been affiliated with the Fenians, but accusations of his embezzlement of IRB funds put paid to that association. In 1881 he sold his newspapers to Parnell, but went through the four thousand pounds he received from the Land League in short order.

Pigott had conned the *Times* … at least twice over. He had passed on, for payment, a letter that suggested Parnell supported those who carried out the brutal Phoenix Park murders of the Chief Secretary of Ireland, Lord Frederick Cavendish, and the Under Secretary, Thomas H. Burke, in May 1882. Parnell vehemently denied the veracity of the letter. A commission was established which, in essence, pitched the *Times* newspaper against Parnell, and most of the senior members of his party.

The letter in question, published in facsimile by the *Times* in April 1887, was one of a number that had been forged, quite cleverly, by Pigott himself. He had, however, left a couple of hostages to fortune in the material he had supplied to the *Times*. Pigott was not quite as literate as one might expect a former newspaper editor to be. He was a dreadful speller. Observers who closely examined the cache of correspondence he had provided to the *Times* noted a couple of howlers. In one case, he had spelt the word 'hesitancy' as h-e-s-i-t-e-n-c-y.

When Russell began his cross-examination of this crucial *Times* witness, he puzzled the onlookers by handing Pigott a sheet of paper and asking him to write a number of words on it. One of those was 'hesitancy'. He then casually took back the paper, glanced at it, and ignored it for most of the next two days.

Russell then proceeded to reduce Pigott to a gibbering wreck, catching him out in his elaborate system of deception. Before the future Lord Chief Justice was finished, most of the observers, and even the three presiding judges had been reduced to tears of laughter at Pigott's many contradictions and obvious lies.

Then, as a *coup de grâce*, Russell returned to the mysterious page. After a few more barbed questions, he pointed out that in one of the letters retained by the *Times*, and handed over to the defence under 'discovery', the word 'hesitancy' had been misspelt. The erroneous spelling, he demonstrated, was precisely that chosen by Pigott the previous day when asked to write the word on the piece of paper. Pigott went a couple of stages beyond a gibbering wreck, and no one in the court had the slightest doubt but that he had forged all the letters upon which the *Times* depended to make its case.

Pigott fled shortly after the commission of inquiry adjourned, admitted his guilt in a letter to the tribunal, and in order to avoid arrest, shot himself dead in Madrid a few days later. Parnell subsequently sued the *Times* for defamation in a London libel court, and won £5,000. In subsequent years, at public meetings, when a heckler wished to suggest that a platform speaker had 'sold out' or betrayed his cause, the aggrieved party would yell 'Spell hesitancy!' at the top of his voice.

Charles Russell, inquisitor *extraordinaire*, destroyed the credibility of the hapless forger Richard Pigott, one hundred and twenty-eight years ago, on this day.

Broadcast 10 February 2017

3 February 1911

The death of Robert Tressell

He was something of a contradiction – he had a number of different names for a start, was an avowed socialist who sent his only child to private schools while he could afford it, and, despite writing one of the definitive working-class novels of the early twentieth century, once had a black manservant.

We know him as Robert Tressel, author of one of the most influential left-wing novels of the last one hundred years, *The Ragged-Trousered Philanthropists* (1914), but his original name was Robert Croker. He was the product of an extra-marital relationship between his mother, Mary Noonan, and a Royal Irish Constabulary inspector, Samuel Croker, who died five years after his birth.

He was born in Wexford Street in Dublin in 1870 and, largely thanks to his mother, whose name he later adopted, he was well-educated up to the time he left Ireland at the age of sixteen. By 1890 he was in South Africa working as a sign-writer and writing articles for Cape Town newspapers. He had one child, Kathleen, from an unhappy and short-lived marriage there. In 1897 he moved with Kathleen to Johannesburg, where he became involved with the centenary commemoration of the 1798 rebellion. He also became acquainted with Irish nationalists John MacBride and Arthur Griffth in the Transvaal province, and later helped to establish the Irish Brigade, which fought against the British Army in the Boer War. Whether or not he actually participated in the conflict himself is one of the many imponderables of his short life.

He returned to England in the early 1900s, settling down on the south coast, and worked again as a sign-writer and house painter. Here he joined the Social Democratic Federation, a forerunner of the Independent Labour Party. It was during this period that he began work on what was to be a hugely significant novel.

The Ragged-Trousered Philanthropists – it may originally have been called *The Ragged-Arsed Philanthropists* – was finished in 1910, and amounted to a virtually unpublishable 400,000 words. It was rejected by the first three publishing houses Noonan approached. Thoroughly depressed, and also suffering from tuberculosis, he is said to have attempted to burn the manuscript. His daughter Kathleen, who played a huge part in the novel's eventual success, apparently rescued it from destruction.

The Ragged-Trousered Philanthropists is set in the fictional southern coastal town of Mugsborough – Hastings in disguise. The names of many of the characters are as subtle as the naming of the location. They include Botchit, Grinder, Leavitt, Starvem, Crass and Slyme. The philanthropists in question are house painters – the *nom de plume* chosen by Noonan – Robert Tressel – is a pun on one of their essential pieces of equipment, the trestle table. Their philanthropy, according to the central character, the socialist Frank Owen, lies in the offering of their services to their employers for such low wages – 'benefactors in ragged trousers who willingly hand over the results of their labour … to the rich'.

Having failed to secure a publisher for his work, Noonan decided to emigrate to Canada in 1911, but only made it as far as Liverpool. He died of pulmonary tuberculosis en route. He was only forty years old.

And that might have been the end of the road for *The Ragged-Trousered Philanthropists*, were it not for Noonan's devoted daughter. Kathleen managed to persuade the writer and journalist Jessie Pope, infamous for some dreadful patriotic WWI poetry, to look at the manuscript in 1913. She recommended it to her publisher, and undertook to edit the volume herself. In the process, she redacted much of the socialist content and produced a highly bowdlerized version of the material. A second edition, published in 1918, was also abridged, but was closer to the original source.

A 1940 Penguin edition of the work was widely read by the British soldiers of World War II, and is said to have influenced the outcome of the 1945 general election, which saw Labour return to power. Though that's quite a claim for a mere book. *The Ragged-Trousered Philanthropists* did not appear in its original form until 1955. Since then it has been adapted multiple times for radio and TV.

Noonan, or Tressel if you'd prefer, was buried in an unmarked grave in Liverpool, and his final resting place was not identified until 1968. It now bears a memorial, as does the house of his birth in Dublin.

The author of *The Ragged-Trousered Philanthropists* died, one hundred and six years ago, on this day.

Broadcast 3 February 2017

19 February 1921

Percy Crozier quits the Auxiliaries in disgust

He is the author of one of the most tastelessly titled autobiographies ever published, *The Men I Killed* (1937). He was a career soldier, a martinet, bounced a few big cheques in his day, and then, in one of the great 'Road to Damascus' stories of the early twentieth century, ended his life as a pacifist. Frank Percy Crozier was nothing if not a mass of contradictions.

His main contribution to Irish history came in 1921, when he confirmed something that everybody in this country had known for at least twelve months: namely, that the fine body of men he commanded, the Royal Irish Constabulary Auxiliary Division, harboured some of the lowest scum to represent the interests of the Crown in Ireland. When he resigned from the force in disgust, he substantiated the axiom that the only creature lower than an 'Auxie' was a 'Black and Tan'. He returned to tend to his garden, write some books and give a few lectures.

So just who was this delicate flower whose stomach was turned by the extra-curricular activities of his own men? Well, it has to be said that in the past he had not displayed a notable sensitivity or delicacy of feeling.

Crozier, born in Bermuda of British stock on New Year's Day 1879, had served in the Boer War before taking charge of one of the battalions of the 36th Ulster Division in the Great

War. He became commanding officer of the 9th Royal Irish Rifles, loyalists from Protestant West Belfast. While colonel of the battalion, he took a particular interest in excessive drinking in the ranks – he was a reformed alcoholic – and the sexual antics of his charges. In the latter instance, his concern was not merely puritanical; a soldier with venereal disease was a soldier out of the trenches and not fulfilling his duty, the duty of dying horribly for King and Country.

A small pudgy figure with a thin wispy moustache, he was, in many respects, the epitome of the stereotypical British officer class. Crozier had the honour, if that is the word I'm after, of leading his men – he called them 'my Shankhill boys' – into battle at the village of Thiepval, on that infamous date, 1 July 1916, the first day of the greatest cock-up in British military history, the Battle of the Somme. Of course, he should not have been in no man's land, as commanding officers were given strict instructions not to go 'over the top'. Crozier was one of two colonels in the 36th Division to ignore the order. In the heat of battle he recorded that he was obliged, on more than one occasion, to threaten the lives of sensible combatants whose response to the murderous German fusillade was to turn tail and run back to their own trenches. Crozier, waving a revolver in the air, turned these potential deserters around and sent them back to almost certain death or injury.

Crozier survived the opening day of the Somme campaign and was recommended for a Victoria Cross. The men who had sought the safety of the trenches during the battle didn't have any say in the matter. He was told through various channels that it was uncertain as to whether he would receive a Victoria Cross or a court martial for insubordination. A compromise was reached, and he received neither! A highly successful recruiting officer for the 36th, he once promised the family of one young soldier, with whom he happened to share a surname, that he would look after their son in the war. He discharged this obligation by subsequently officiating at the execution of said son, young James Crozier, for cowardice.

After the war, where he rose to the rank of Brigadier General, he assumed control of the Auxiliaries, a force of British ex-servicemen sent to reinforce the Royal Irish Constabulary in the fight against the IRA. The RIC Auxiliary rapidly became just as unpopular as the better-known, but no better loved, RIC Special Reserve, or the infamous 'Black and Tans'. He quickly became disillusioned with the levels of indiscipline and the predilection for drunken retaliation among the members of the force. In February 1921 he dismissed twenty-one temporary cadets, as they were officially known, for their depredations during raids on Trim and Drumcondra. When he was overruled by his own commanding officer, Chief of Police Henry Hugh Tudor, he submitted his resignation. Probably not the first time a Percy was slapped around by a Tudor.

This principled gesture cost him dearly. England expected, and Crozier had not lived up to those expectations. He resorted to writing and lecturing in order to earn a living. He also became a pacifist and a supporter of the anti-war Peace Pledge Union, established in Britain in 1934. Crozier died in 1937 at the age of fifty-eight.

Francis Percy Crozier, commanding officer of the RIC Auxiliary Division, resigned from his post in disgust at the behaviour of his own men, ninety-five years ago, on this day.

Broadcast 19 February 2016

5 February 1960

The first commercial screening
of *Mise Éire*

As a young boy, in a rather grim Irish boarding school in the 1960s, one of the few attempts by the prison authorities to break the monotony was the occasional screening of a film in the school library. These would often be of an 'improving' nature, designed to elevate and inform rather than to entertain. So, *The Song of Bernadette* (1943) was more likely to turn up than the latest James Bond adventure.

One screening which greatly appealed to this particular teenage nerd, though it might not have been quite as well-received by some of the less historically oriented students, was a stirring, archive-based account of the build-up to the 1916 Rising and its aftermath. *Mise Éire* (1959) was like nothing we had ever seen before. It combined the talents of two of the country's greatest ever artists, filmmaker George Morrison and composer Seán Ó'Riada.

Mise Éire was commissioned in the late 1950s and premiered at the 1959 Cork Film Festival. The feature-length documentary, entirely in Irish, with suitably portentous narration by Padraig O'Raghallaigh, had been directed or, more accurately, assembled, by Morrison, then in his thirties. Morrison, who had been a Trinity College medical student before he was eaten alive by the dreaded film bug, visited archives all over Europe and collected 300,000 feet of silent black and white film, which he then painstakingly edited into a full-length documentary. For this he was apparently paid a measly £375. Unfortunately, he didn't haggle for residuals, and made nothing further from his efforts. Some compensation for this came with his election to Aosdána in 2005 and a Lifetime Contribution Award at the Irish Film and Television Awards in 2009, when he was eighty-seven years old.

The events represented visually in *Mise Éire* – the first theatrically released film/documentary to be recorded in the Irish language – had already become the stuff of legend long before it was released. It contained footage of the funeral of O'Donovan Rossa in 1915, with shots of the old Fenian's open coffin and the graveside oration by Pearse. It is probably the only existing documentary film coverage of either man.

There is also unique footage of James Larkin leading a protest march after the 1914 Bachelor's Walk killings, and of the main motive force behind the Rising, the arch plotter himself, Thomas Clarke. Members of the Irish Citizen's Army are depicted in training. Members of the Irish Volunteers are shown on their way to take up their positions on Easter Monday 1916 in Dublin. And then, of course, there is the representation of the Rising itself. We see the impact of the conflict on the fabric of Dublin city centre, and the Volunteers, post surrender, being marched off to Frongoch prison in North Wales. Later material from the War of Independence includes rare shots of Michael Collins – speaking at the funeral of hunger striker Thomas Ashe – and of Éamon de Valera campaigning in the decisive 1918 general election.

But, of course, there is a huge irony at the heart of *Mise Éire*. Despite the gargantuan achievement of Morrison in collecting and collating all this invaluable material, what sticks in the mind is not so much the images as the music in the background. The score for the film was written by the great Seán Ó'Riada. Making ingenious use of well known traditional pieces, like 'Róisin Dubh' and 'Boolavogue', Ó'Riada created a soundtrack that underlined the significance of the images on screen, but it also stood on its own as abiding symphonic music. The soundtrack was recorded in the Phoenix Hall on 19 May 1959, with Ó'Riada conducting the Radio Éireann Symphony Orchestra.

Some trivia associated with the film: it includes one of the earliest photographs ever taken in Ireland, a still dating from the Famine period, when photography was in its infancy. George Morrison later wanted to add an English-language version of the film's voice-over; Anglo-Irish film star Peter O'Toole was recruited for the task, but, in the face of opposition from the producers, Gael Linn, this version was never recorded. Today the DVD of the film includes English-language subtitles.

Mise Éire, blessed by the images collected and assembled by George Morrison, and exalted by the music of Seán Ó' Riada, had its commercial release, fifty-six years ago, on this day.

Broadcast 5 February 2016

March

"If I miss, sir, I will hit you hard with a double negative"

3 March 1766

How did Dollar Bay in Co. Wexford get its name?

Dollar Bay in Co. Wexford gets its name from an act of piracy in 1765 on the part of four men, George Gidley, Richard St. Quintin, Andreas Zeckerman and Peter McKinley – the latter being the only Irishman amongst this motley, homi-cidal and felonious crew. The four were ordinary seaman on a vessel named *The Earl of Sandwich*, which was travelling from the Canaries to London in November of that year, car-rying silk, gold dust, jewellery and Spanish doubloons. The transport of this wealthly cargo was the responsibility of two partners, a Captain Cochrane, and a Scottish sailor, Captain George Glass. Glass was the son of a fire-breathing Scottish preacher, the Reverend John Glass, whose followers were known, predictably enough I suppose, as Glassites.

Glass Junior, a seafaring type, did not possess much of that quality which carries many of us through life, namely, good luck. He had just been released from a Canary Island dungeon when he took ship for London with Cochrane and a cargo that the aforementioned felons were anxious to acquire for themselves.

Some way into the voyage the four would-be pirates took over the ship, beat Cochrane to death with an iron bar, stabbed Glass, and threw both bodies overboard. They were soon followed into the sea by their unfortunate wives.

The four conspirators then changed course and set sail for Ireland. The ship was scuttled off the south-east coast, with the loss of the rest of the crew, and the pirates landed near Duncannon Fort in a longboat on 3 December 1765. They buried their treasure on a beach known ever since as, you've guessed it, Dollar Bay – a slight underestimation of the value of the booty – and headed for New Ross with as much gold as they could carry.

In New Ross they got so drunk that they managed to lose twelve hundred dollars to a second-phase robbery – the gold thieves becoming the only real beneficiaries of the entire affair. The following day they sold a further twelve hundred dollars worth of gold – a move which excited considerable comment. When the wreck of *The Earl of Sandwich* came ashore, the authorities began to ask questions about the four jolly sailors, and the hapless pirates decided it might be a good idea to make a hasty escape to Dublin. There they took rooms in the Black Bull tavern on Thomas Street and settled in for some more hard drinking.

It wasn't long before they were arrested. They confessed to their crimes and informed the authorities where the loot was buried – apologies if you thought it might be worth checking over Dollar Bay with a metal detector.

The four were quickly tried, convicted and hanged together in St. Stephen's Green. Their remains were then gibbetted on the South Wall in Ringsend – convicted pirates' bodies were often displayed at the entrances to harbours in order to discourage the practice of mutiny, robbery and murder on the high seas. However, after the gulls and decomposition had taken their toll, locals who liked to walk near the South Wall began to complain about the eyesore and the stench.

Two of the bodies – no one is exactly sure which two, but one was probably that of McKinley – were transferred to the Muglins, an outcrop of rocks near Dalkey Island, where they continued to fester in chains until they were eventually disposed of by the birds, the wind and the sea.

The lamentably unsuccessful, but undoubtedly murderous pirates, George Gidley, Richard St. Quintin, Andreas Zeckerman and Peter McKinley, were hanged, two hundred and fifty-one years ago, on this day.

Broadcast 3 March 2017

31 March 1790

The Curran-Hobart duel

By the early nineteenth century, Ireland had acquired a reputation as 'the land of the duel'. Some reputations are palpably unfair and unearned. This one wasn't. Ireland *was* the land of the duel, and had become so during the eighteenth century. Is it any wonder that the Dublin-born playwright Richard Brinsley Sheridan named the Irish aristocratic buffoon in his great comedy *The Rivals* (1775), Sir Lucius O'Trigger? Sheridan himself had fought a couple of duels with the man on whom O'Trigger was based. William Makepeace Thackeray based his truculent character 'The O'Mulligan' (*The Irish Sketchbook*, 1842) on the Irish nineteenth-century duellist The O'Gorman Mahon.

So popular was duelling in Ireland that in 1777 a new *code duello* was adopted at the summer assizes in Clonmel – and yes, the assizes were courts of law. The new code was devised 'by the gentlemen of County Tipperary, County Galway, County Mayo, County Sligo and County Roscommon, and prescribed for general adoption throughout Ireland'. The Irish code soon gained wide acceptance in Britain and North America. Under the Irish code the practice of firing into the air or the ground to avoid wounding an opponent was discouraged. So it will be no surprise to learn that while the fatality rate in British duels was one in fourteen, in Ireland it was one in four. A total of nineteen establishments in Dublin made or sold duelling pistols for their crust.

One of the country's most enthusiastic duellists was the distinguished barrister John Philpot Curran. He fought in at least four duels, the first against an Irish MP named David Walsh – Lance Armstrong would undoubtedly have approved – in which neither man was injured.

The most interesting was probably in 1785 against the future Lord Chancellor, John Fitzgibbon, later the Earl of Clare. Fitzgibbon, a formidable personality, had observed in the Irish House of Commons that the Irish nation, while easily angered, was just as easily appeased. In response to this rather innocuous assertion, Curran speculated that Fitzgibbon had arrived at his opinion of the nation from studying his own character. Fitzgibbon retaliated with a personal insult against his opponent, alleging that 'Curran was no lawyer and the monstrous nonsense that came from him was fit only for [the] Sadler's Wells [opera]'. A challenge was issued, shots were exchanged, but neither man was injured.

Five years later, Curran picked a quarrel with the Chief Secretary, Major Robert Hobart, who was MP for Portarlington. Curran had been affronted by some public criticism from the parliamentary reporter and all-round hack, John Giffard, a Dublin Castle stooge. Rather than challenge a lowly journalist on the field of honour, Curran picked a fight with his boss. When Hobart refused to fire Giffard, Curran challenged him. It was all a bit tenuous, but Hobart had no option but to take up the gauntlet – I use the term metaphorically as the actual wearing of gauntlets, a medieval practice, was not conducive to firing duelling pistols with hair triggers.

'Occasioned by some words spoken in Parliament', according to a contemporary newspaper account, the duel was fought in Luttrelstown in Co. Dublin, on the estate of Lord Carhampton, who was Hobart's second. Curran was attended by a gentleman by the name of Egan. The report of the encounter went as follows:

> Being put to their ground, and having agreed to fire as they chose, Mr Curran fired first, without effect; whereupon Major Hobart said he hoped Mr Curran was satisfied. Mr Egan then called out to Major Hobart that he had not fired, as did Mr Curran. The Major, advancing a step or two towards Mr Curran, repeated what he had said before. Mr Curran replied: 'I am sorry, Sir, you have taken this advantage; but you have made it impossible for me not to be satisfied.'

Of course, it might just have been bluster on the part of the barrister, but from his response it appears that Curran had come to get his man, and felt cheated of his prize. Hobart went on to have the capital city of Tasmania named after him. By then Curran was dead, or he might have issued another challenge, based on the fact that nothing much was named after him other than a street in Cork city.

Major Robert Hobart and John Philpot Curran fought a duel, two hundred and twenty-seven years ago, on this day.

Broadcast 31 March 2017

24 March 1829

Birth of George Francis Train

He was an exceptionally wealthy eccentric who stood for the American presidency. When making speeches he spoke mostly about himself and his exploits, was prone to repetition and frequently wandered off the subject. He was also a racist who, when he failed to become president, decided a better option was to become the nation's dictator.

If that all sounds familiar, then perhaps you've already heard of George Francis Train, one of the most appropriately named mavericks in nineteenth-century America – Train made his fortune from building a railway line. He was one of the founding men behind the Union Pacific, which built the east/west section of the American transcontinental railroad in the 1860s, and royally ripped off America in the process.

But Train is even more interesting for a number of reasons: he campaigned to allow more Irish migrants to enter the USA in the 1840s (not a very popular position to adopt); he became involved in the building of a horse-tramway in Cork (which didn't succeed); he became an advocate for Fenianism; wrote a book in 1865 called *Irish Independency*; and he landed himself in a Dublin prison for ten months in 1868 for carrying pro-Fenian literature on board a ship which landed in Ireland.

George Francis Train was either a con man supreme, a fraudster *par excellence*, a deluded maniac, a feminist, a vegetarian, a communist, a capitalist leech, a pacifist, or the 'Great American Humbug' – he was called all of the above, and a lot more besides. Oh yes, and lest we forget, he was also the model for the character of Phileas Fogg in Jules Verne's *Around the World in Eighty Days* (1873).

He made his first fortune in shipping in the USA and Australia before returning to America in the 1860s. In the US, he threw in his lot with one of the most crooked business cabals in a long and undistinguished history of crooked American business cabals: the Union Pacific Railroad Corporation. Train and his associates realised that there were huge sums of money to be made from building their half of the transcontinental railroad, but only if they helped themselves to as much of the available funds as they could lay their grubby hands on. This is where Train's neat idea of the Credit Mobilier paid off handsomely. It may sound like a French bank but, in fact, it was a company set up to actually build the eastern half (from Nebraska to Idaho) of the transcontinental railroad for the Union Pacific.

Naturally the construction costs were inflated, and the Union Pacific insiders, including Train, pocketed the difference between the actual cost of building the railroad and the prices charged by Credit Mobilier for its construction. By the time the scam was exposed by the *New York Sun* newspaper in 1873, Train had long since taken his profit and moved on. He had become an acolyte of Fenianism, a supporter of equal rights for women and a vegetarian.

His progressive credentials, however, did not extend as far as advocating equal rights for freed slaves, which became apparent when he sought the Democratic party nomination for the presidency in 1864, 1868 and 1872.

As mentioned, Train's exploits in shipping had influenced Verne in the creation of the character of Phileas Fogg in

Around the World in Eighty Days. In 1890, when the *New York World* newspaper despatched its ace reporter Nellie Bly to circumnavigate the globe – she did it in seventy-two days – the real George Train rose to the challenge on behalf of the fictional Fogg, and completed the same journey in sixty-seven days. Two years later he did it all over again, this time in sixty days.

Towards the end of his life, Train used the columns of his newspaper, *The Revolution,* to defend a campaigner for free love who had been arrested for obscenity. In the process, Train was charged with the same offence himself. His lawyers got him off by pleading insanity. Train was not best pleased. But he *was* probably the victim of some form of mental debilitation that went well beyond so-called 'eccentricity', a euphemism for mental illness if you were wealthy.

He died in 1904 of smallpox. Sadly, fear of the infectious nature of the disease led to many of his personal papers being destroyed after his death.

The extraordinary George Francis Train, American robber baron, suffragist and Irish nationalist, was born, one hundred and eighty-eight years ago, on this day.

Broadcast 24 March 2017

25 March 1840

Birth of Captain Myles Keogh

The Little Bighorn, which sounds like a bit of a contradiction in terms, is a river in the American state of Montana and Wyoming. As a river, it is unremarkable; it is not famous for the qualities of its drainage. It is infamous for what happened there in June 1876, when a flamboyant, egotistical cavalry officer, George Armstrong Custer, led his Seventh Cavalry to the worst and last significant military defeat ever inflicted on the US Army by the Lakota, Blackfeet and Cheyenne Indian tribes. This took place at what they called 'The Battle of the Greasy Grass'. No prizes for guessing what it was that greased the grass of the river's banks.

Five of the twelve companies of the Seventh Cavalry were wiped out on 25 June, including 'I' Company, led by Carlow-born Captain Myles Keogh, the most senior of thirty-two Irish-born fatalities in the battle.

Keogh, from Leighlinbridge, had found his way to his date with destiny by a circuitous route. He had, in 1860, as a twenty-year-old man from a relatively prosperous Catholic family, volunteered for service in the army of the Pope. He wasn't dressed in a striped uniform guarding the Vatican City however; he was fighting, unsuccessfully, to save the Pope's last remaining territorial possessions in Italy. When the American Civil War broke out, the Roman Catholic Archbishop of New York, John Hughes, recruited Keogh and a number of his colleagues to join the Union Army. He served with distinction through most of the Civil War as a cavalry officer, fighting at Fredericksburg and Gettysburg, and rose to the rank of Lieutenant Colonel.

After the war the American Army was greatly reduced in size, but Keogh stayed on. Like most other officers he lost his exalted war-time rank, but was not demobilized. He was sent west to join Custer's Seventh Cavalry, charged with keeping the peace on the great American Plains, and ensuring that tribes like the Lakota – better known as the Sioux – the Cheyenne, and the Blackfeet behaved themselves and remained on the relatively useless patches of land that had been set aside for them as 'reservations'.

Keogh was undoubtedly handsome, dynamic, vigorous and physically courageous. However, he was also described by some colleagues as intemperate, drunken and violent. Although he respected the Native Americans of the American Plains as military opponents, he had no time for their culture or way of life. He viewed them, quite simply, as savages who needed to be kept permanently in check.

He was part of an army that had a huge Irish element. Ten thousand soldiers were stationed in the American West, a quarter of whom were born in Ireland. The Irish influence can clearly be seen in Custer's Seventh. The muster roll in 1876 included one hundred and twenty-six Irish-born soldiers out of eight hundred and twenty-two members of the regiment. Keogh was the only officer. The regiment's two marching tunes were the Irish airs 'Garryowen' and 'The Girl I Left Behind Me'.

The story of Custer's massive miscalculation in sending his six hundred-strong force against an Indian village that contained up to five thousand fighting men has become the stuff of legend. He made matters even worse by dividing his command, sending more than half the regiment, under the command of Major Marcus Reno and Captain Frederick Benteen, to attack from the southern end of the camp. Everyone who fought with Custer, died with Custer. The only survivor was Keogh's horse, Comanche. Keogh himself was killed a few hundred yards away from Last Stand Hill, where his colonel died. Although Keogh is buried in New York state, a gravestone bearing his name marks the spot where he perished, surrounded by the other members of Company 'I'. Keogh's body was one of the few not to have been mutilated by the victorious Sioux and Cheyenne. He wore a Papal medal, awarded in 1860 by a grateful Pope, and this token may have been what saved his corpse from evisceration. The Lakota and Cheyenne, who wore pendants of all kinds to ward off evil spirits, may have been wary of the Pontiff's decoration.

Captain Myles Walter Keogh, commanding officer of Company 'I' of the Seventh Cavalry, was one of two hundred and sixty-eight US cavalrymen to die at the Battle of the Greasy Grass, or the Little Bighorn. He was born, one hundred and seventy-six years ago, on this day.

Broadcast 25 March 2016

18 March 1847

The Choctaw collect money for Irish Famine relief

Although there was a respite from the potato blight in 1847, the year is still remembered in Irish history as 'Black '47'. So few potatoes had been planted that the absence of blight made little difference to a starving, diseased and demoralized people. Thousands more died of hunger and disease, or chose the emigrant ship as the only possibility of escape. However, the plight of eight million Irish people was not being ignored, except, perhaps, by the Liberal Government of Lord John Russell in London. Money poured in from Europe, the USA, and as far away as Australia.

In March of 1847, an unexpected donation arrived from the USA. While America had been the source of much of the famine-relief funds that found their way to Ireland, this particular charitable gift was different. It didn't come from Irish-American migrants on the east coast of the USA. It didn't even come from smaller pockets of Irish migrants in the midwest or the west. It came from the state of Oklahoma, a region that was not generally favoured for settlement by the Irish diaspora.

The donation amounted to one hundred and seventy dollars, and it was collected by members of the Choctaw Native American nation. Some sources give the sum involved as seven hundred and ten dollars, but the amount actually donated is immaterial. Either way, it was a huge sum of money for a nation of impoverished Native Americans, consigned more than a decade before to life on the comfortably-sounding but demonically devised reservation. The Choctaw probably empathized with the starving Irish because their own history also had much of the tragic about it.

In the war of 1812, fought by the new American nation against their former British colonial overlords, the Choctaws had aided the victorious forces, led by future US president General Andrew Jackson. Abject defeat could well have led to the end of the great American democratic experiment. Not that democracy proved to be of much use to the Choctaw. Their reward, in 1831, was expulsion from their homes in the south-east during Jackson's presidency, and banishment to the badlands of Oklahoma. This forced transportation, known as the 'Trail of Tears', had caused the deaths of almost a quarter of the 20,000 or so Choctaw obliged to decamp to the mid-west. Their fate was shared by the Cherokee, Chickasaw, Creek and Seminole nations, all forced into exile, starvation and cultural suppression. The white man wanted their land, and what the white man wanted, he got. The punitive Treaty of Dancing Rabbit Creek, signed in 1830, attended to the detail of the wholesale dispossession of the Choctaw. Similar barbed treaties achieved the same result with the other four so-called 'Five Civilised Tribes'.

1831 was one of the coldest winters on record, and the Federal Government was not about to waste valuable tax-payers money on providing adequate food, clothing and transportation to mere Indians to protect them from the elements, during such an arduous trip westwards into the even colder interior.

It is not difficult to see why the Choctaw, having heard of the Great Famine, empathised with the Irish people.

What must have been more difficult was raising such a significant sum. Only in recent years has their generosity been recognized in Ireland, and today, former president Mary Robinson is an honorary chieftain of the Choctaw nation. A plaque commemorating their charity has been erected outside Dublin's Mansion House. Other monuments around the country – including the spectacular sculpture recently unveiled in Midleton, Co. Cork — recognize their immensely charitable gesture.

The Choctaw, originally from the modern state of Mississippi, more than earned their designation as one of the 'Five Civilised' tribes when they collected a charitable donation worth at least one hundred thousand dollars in today's money to the relief of famine victims in Ireland, one hundred and sixty-nine years ago, on this day.

Broadcast 18 March 2016

11 March 1858

The birth of Thomas Clarke

When it comes to the issue of the organization of the 1916 insurrection, we have to look well beyond the esoteric, if palpably sincere, philosophizing of Pearse, and even the military *nous* and pragmatism of Connolly, and look to the quiet man in the midst of the fury.

Thomas Clarke, the self-effacing tobacconist, was the spine, the heart and the genius of the Easter Rising. While he was surrounded by capable and resourceful allies, it was Clarke who drove the rebellion.

The first oddity associated with the life of Tom Clarke is his place of birth. He was actually born in England, in the Isle of Wight. The second was his association with the British Army: his father was a serving soldier.

At the age of twenty, Clarke made the decision that was to inform the rest of his life. He joined the Irish Republican Brotherhood in Dungannon, Co. Tyrone. Two years later he was forced to flee to the US to avoid arrest.

Clarke was sent from America to London in 1883 to lead the bombing campaign masterminded by O'Donovan Rossa. He did so under the alias Henry Wilson, and it was under this name that he served fifteen years in British prisons after his arrest and conviction. While in jail he met the fellow Fenian John Daly. After his release in 1898 Clarke married Daly's niece Kathleen. Her family did not approve, despite their own staunch republicanism. She was twenty-one years younger than her husband, and marriage to a felon, albeit a republican felon, was not exactly what they had in mind for their daughter. In addition, Clarke, after a tough decade and a half in prison, looked far older than his years.

After spending almost a decade in the USA, the Clarkes returned to Ireland in 1907 and Tom opened a humble tobacconist's shop in Dublin. While outwardly settled and law-abiding, Clarke continued his work with the Irish Republican Brotherhood, most notably as a member of its Military Council. He became a sort of mentor to the likes of Denis McCullough, Bulmer Hobson and, in particular, Sean McDermott. Because of his background as a convicted felon, however, Clarke steered clear of overt political involvement. He left it to others to infiltrate, at the highest level, organisations like the GAA, the Gaelic League and, from 1913 on, the Irish Volunteers.

Because of his age, in 1916 Clarke became a link to the nineteenth-century Fenians, who had risen in 1867, although he himself was only a child at that time. Acting on the republican axiom that 'England's difficulty is Ireland's opportunity', he was determined to take advantage of the outbreak of the Great War in 1914. He worked assiduously to make plans for a rising around the country, with the IRB at its core, and using the Volunteers as their battering ram. A reluctant Hobson and McCullough were jettisoned along the way; the likes of Pearse, Connolly, Plunkett and McDonagh were recruited.

The seven members of the Military Council – Eamon Ceannt being the one often ignored –became signatories of the 1916 Proclamation. As the most senior IRB man, Clarke should have become president of the Provisional Government, but preferred to leave that honour to the more flamboyant and better-known Pearse. Clarke himself was an anonymous figure, familiar only to fellow revolutionaries and 'G' Division of the Dublin Metropolitan Police.

Clarke was stationed in the GPO during the Rising and was the second leader, after Pearse, to be executed. His last message to Kathleen ended with the words 'we die happy'. Familiar photographs of Clarke depict a thin, bespectacled, elderly man. Despite appearancs, he was only fifty-nine years of age at the time of his death.

Thomas Clarke, conspirator, Republican, tobacconist and victim of the 1916 firing squad, was born, one hundred and fifty-eight years ago, on this day.

Broadcast 11 March 2016

10 March 1888

Birth of actor Barry Fitzgerald

He has played some of the worst-named characters in cinematic history, is unique in the annals of the Academy Awards, had an Irish stamp devoted to him on the centenary of his birth in 1988, and, for more than twenty years, was a mainstay of the Abbey Theatre Company. His real name was William Joseph Shields, but we know him better as Barry Fitzgerald.

Fitzgerald was born on Walworth Road in Portobello, Dublin, eight years before his brother Arthur, another celebrated Abbey actor, and a 1916 Volunteer. As William Shields, he worked as a civil servant in the unemployment insurance division. He could have joined the British Army and been killed or maimed in WWI, but chose the safer alternative of staying at home. He gave up his pension in 1929 to become a professional actor; no doubt he wondered whether he would end up availing of the services of his former colleagues in the unemployment insurance division of the Civil Service.

He was a good friend and roommate of Sean O'Casey, and appeared in a number of O'Casey's productions, including *The Silver Tassie* (1929), controversially rejected for the Abbey by W. B. Yeats. Fitzgerald played Fluther Good in the original production of *The Plough and the Stars* in 1925, and took on an outraged punter who stormed the stage during opening week, having paid good money for the right to be offended. Accounts vary as to whether Fitzgerald or the protestor won the fight. O'Casey himself gave it to Fitzgerald on points.

In 1936 Hollywood beckoned in the shape of the great American film director, John Ford, who cast Fitzgerald in his film version of *The Plough and the Stars*.

After the *Plough and the Stars*, he would appear in four other movies directed by John Ford: *Four Men and a Prayer* (1938), *The Long Voyage Home* (1940), *How Green Was My Valley* (1941) – in which he played a Welshman – and, most famously, *The Quiet Man* (1952), as the wily matchmaker who tried his best to get John Wayne and Maureen O'Hara to stop taking lumps out of each other and settle down.

His most famous role was undoubtedly that of the irascible old priest with the heart of gold, Father Fitzgibbon, in Leo McCarey's 1944 film, *Going My Way*. He starred opposite Bing Crosby, who played the young Father O'Malley, and in the course of the film was forced to endure his co-star singing 'Too-Ra-Loo-Ra-Loo-Ral' to put him to sleep. He survived the experience, and is unique in the history of the Academy Awards in that he was *then* – and still *is*, because the rules were subsequently changed – the only actor ever nominated in two categories for the same part. He won Best Supporting Actor award in 1944, but had also been nominated, alongside Crosby, for Best Actor, which Crosby duly won. The Best Song award also went to *Going My Way*, but sadly it wasn't carried off by the unforgettable 'Too-Ra-Loo-Ra-Loo-Ral', and went instead to the Jimmy van Heusen number 'Swinging on a Star'.

Although the fictional Fr Fitzgibbon in *Going My Way* takes a dim view of Father O'Malley's habit of skiving off and playing golf, Barry Fitzgerald himself was a great lover of the sport. So much so that an errant practice swing beheaded his Oscar statuette. Wartime Oscars were, apparently, made of plaster. There is no record of which club he used to achieve this sporting feat, but we can assume it wasn't a putter. The Academy agreed to replace the decapitated statuette.

After *Going My Way*, Fitzgerald found himself typecast as a stage Irishman. The names of the characters he played tell a story of their own; they included Britches, Zipper, Cocky, Icky, Cooky, O'Doul, Stooky O'Meara, Murphy, Terence O'Feenaghty, Dan Muldoon, Denno Noonan, and Micheleen óg Flynn in *The Quiet Man*. Fitzgerald returned to Dublin in 1959, and died on 4 January 1961.

William Joseph Shields, aka Barry Fitzgerald, was born, one hundred and twenty-nine years ago, on this day.

Broadcast 10 March 2017

4 March 1978

The death of Emmet Dalton

James Emmet Dalton, known to his friends as Emmet, might have ended up being better-known for the distinguished company he kept rather than for anything he did himself, but he managed to avoid such a fate. Nonetheless, the story of his life is dominated by two events: the deaths of two of this country's most significant twentieth-century figures.

Dalton was born in America in 1898 to an Irish-American father and an Irish mother, and the family moved back to Dublin when the young Emmet was two years old. His remarkable military career began in 1913 when he joined the Irish Volunteers. Note the date. He was fifteen at the time. He was still underage when he joined the British Army in 1915 as a second lieutenant in the Royal Dublin Fusiliers. He saw action at the Somme in September 1916, and it was here that he crossed paths with the first of those two great Irishmen: the poet, economist and politician, Thomas Kettle. Kettle, a fellow officer, was a good friend of Dalton's father. In an RTÉ radio interview given in the 1960s, Dalton recalled how Kettle had read to him his most famous poem, the poignant sonnet, 'To My Daughter Betty a Gift from God', a couple of days before the Battle of Ginchy. Kettle's death in the battle was witnessed by Dalton, who himself won a Military Cross and was promoted to Major.

In an RTÉ television interview with Cathal O'Shannon, which took place in the year of his death, Dalton admitted to having been taken completely by surprise by the 1916 Rising, and believed that 'we thought it was madness'. He was, however, to become closely associated with one of the minor figures being swept up by the British Army and transported to Frongoch prison in North Wales. This was a previously obscure London-based IRB man by the name of Michael Collins.

Despite his opposition to the Rising, when Dalton was demobilised in 1919 he quickly threw in his lot with the IRA. Putting his war experience to good use, he became their director of training. He also gained considerable kudos by talking his way into Mountjoy prison in a failed attempt to effect the escape of the IRA leader Seán MacEoin.

His association with Collins brought him to London for the Anglo-Irish Treaty negotiations in late 1921 and, unsurprisingly, given his huge admiration for Collins, he took the pro-Treaty side in the Civil War. It was Dalton who commanded the artillery bombardment of Rory O'Connor's rebel garrison in the Four Courts, the event that precipitated the bitter fraternal conflict.

It was against Dalton's advice that Collins made his final fateful journey to Cork in 1922. The killing of his mentor at Béal na Bláth on 22 August traumatised the young man, who, despite his seniority in military terms – he was a Major General – was still only twenty-four years old.

What do you do when you have been through eight years at the sharp end of continuous warfare? In the case of Dalton, you get into the film industry, and you eventually set up Ardmore Studios. This he did at the age of sixty, a time when most men would be thinking of slowing down. In this capacity, he brought films like *The Spy Who Came in from the Cold* (1965), *The Blue Max* (1966), and *The Lion in Winter* (1968) to the Co. Wicklow studio facility.

As an interesting footnote, the Slievenamon, the ill-fated armoured car against which a desperate Dalton propped Collins as he tried to save his life at Béal na Bláth, later featured in an Ardmore-based Hollywood movie, *Shake Hands with the Devil* (1959), which starred James Cagney.

Emmet Dalton died on his eightieth birthday, but he was born, one hundred and eighteen years ago, on this day.

Broadcast 4 March 2016

April

"I'm James Joyce's Daughter, you know"
"Oh really. Well I shot Mussolini"

8 April 1861

The mass evictions of
John George Adair on his Donegal estate

If he is fondly remembered anywhere, a remote possibility, then it is in the USA rather than the country of his birth. John George Adair did little for his fellow countrymen, or for his own reputation. Born in the 1820s, the son of a gentleman farmer from Co. Laois, he once stood as a Tenant Right candidate in a parliamentary election in the 1850s, and was described by the Young Ireland newspaper, *The Nation*, as 'a cultured young squire', which is rather ironic, as by the 1860s he had journeyed about as far from the Tenant Right cause as it was possible to travel while still remaining on Planet Earth. He also once trained as a diplomat, which is another irony in itself. Had he pursued a career in this area, he would have been to diplomacy what Donald Trump is to self-deprecation.

One account of his life includes references to his purchasing bankrupt estates after the Famine, from which he then evicted tenants wholesale. He was certainly responsible for one of the most notorious mass evictions in Irish history. In 1857 he had begun to acquire land (around thirty thousand acres) in the Glenveagh/Derryveagh area of Donegal. Later, in 1867, he would build the magnificent Glenveagh House on the land he had purchased. Exactly what prompted him to clear the estate is disputed. It may have been the murder of his steward,

James Murray, in 1861, or it may have been when he was surrounded and intimidated by tenants while he exercised the hunting rights he claimed over their land. Whatever the cause, the outcome was a bitter and vindictive campaign in the course of which two hundred and forty-four men, women, and children, from forty-seven families, were thrown out of their holdings and left to fend for themselves. Such was the outcry at the time that the Donegal Relief Committee was formed, which paid for the passage of most of the evictees to Australia, where they were given plots of land to work.

Tiring somewhat of his status as a member of the Irish landed gentry, and, perhaps, slightly chastened by the notoriety he had acquired, even among his own rapacious class, Adair established himself in New York in the mid 1860s. He married well – to Cornelia Wadsworth Ritchie of blue-blooded Connecticut stock – and began making a fortune that enabled him to divide his time between the USA and his Donegal estate.

Adair gained fame in America because of his business association with one of the most significant figures of the American West, Charles Goodnight. In the 1860s, Goodnight, along with his partner Oliver Loving, had brought his herd from the agriculturally depressed Texas in search of a decent market price for his cattle. In doing so, Goodnight and Loving achieved fame for creating what became known as the Goodnight–Loving Trail. As a rancher, Goodnight had frequent need of capital. Adair had plenty of that, and in the early 1880s Adair became a business partner of Goodnight in the JA Ranch in Palo Duro Canyon in Texas. Although Adair didn't know the horns of a steer from the more unpleasant end of his anatomy, the spread – which extended for more than five thousand square kilometres – was still named after the Irish money-man.

Although Adair was largely a sleeping partner, he had clearly made this particular investment as something of an indulgence, an attempt to identify himself with the romance and adventure of the West. He and his wife insisted on accompanying Goodnight on the inaugural trip from Colorado to Texas with the cattle that would form the basis of their herd of over one hundred thousand steers. In the course of the journey the Adairs reported to their host that they had spotted a party of Indians through their field glass. Upon examination, an exasperated Goodnight discovered that what they had in fact seen was a rather less threatening US cavalry troop.

Adair became the butt of some practical cowboy jokes when the party reached Palo Duro. On one occasion, when he ordered that a mount be saddled for him by a group of cowboys who were breaking in some wild horses, the hands picked out the meanest and most untameable beast for Adair. As luck would have it, when he mounted him, the horse shrugged off the habits of a lifetime and behaved like a sweet-natured Shetland pony.

The two men fell out over the terms of their partnership and their arrangement ended some time before Adair's death in 1885. The night before his burial a dead dog was thrown into Adair's grave in his native Co. Laois, an indication of the feelings of tenant farmers towards this ruthless landlord.

John George Adair began the process of clearing the tenants off his Co. Donegal estate one hundred and fifty-five years ago, on this day.

Broadcast 8 April 2016

1 April 1872

The birth of Irish-American bootlegger Katherine Daly

She was born Katherine Rose Daly in Oakland, California in 1872. Her father, Bill Daly, was from Roscrea, Co. Tipperary. Katherine was a wild child, one of twelve young Dalys who was allowed to roam the heights of Oakland in her untutored youth. The knowledge she gained of the hills proved very useful to the family business. Her father manufactured what *he* called 'poteen' and his customers called 'moonshine'. Katherine's intimate knowledge of her local environment helped the Dalys to escape the clutches of the authorities, who never seemed able to locate the family's illicit stills.

When the attentions of the forces of law and order became too intrusive, the entire Oakland operation was moved, in the 1880s, to the boom town of Tombstone. However, the law eventually caught up with Bill Daly when he was killed in a shoot-out with Wyatt Earp not long after the infamous gunfight at the OK Corral in October 1881. Daly, a supporter of the Clantons and the McLaurys, the losers in that shoot-out, simply chose the wrong side. Katherine, however, kept the family business going.

If some of this seems rather familiar to you, it might be because of a certain well known folk song that tells the story of Katherine Daly's life:

Come down from the mountain, Katie Daly
Come down from the mountain, Katie do
Oh, can't you hear us calling, Katie Daly
We want to drink your Irish mountain dew.

With her old man, Katie came from Tipperary
In the pioneering year of forty-two
Her old man he was shot in Tombstone city
For making of the Irish mountain dew.

Soon after her father's death, Katherine Daly, better known as Katie, escaped the Earps and took herself to Chicago. There she continued to manufacture moonshine for the next three decades. Prohibition in the 1920s should have been good to her. Her famous 'mountain dew' was streets ahead of the bathtub gin of Al Capone, but the notorious Italian-American hoodlum had more military hardware at his disposal than the ageing Katie.

After the St Valentine's Day massacre, in which Capone's goons slaughtered seven members of the rival Moran gang, Katie headed back home to the west coast and began operating in San Francisco. There she made a fatal error. Had she confined her activities to the Bay Area, who knows what she might have achieved. But she got just a bit too greedy and began shifting bootleg whisky across the state border into Nevada. This brought down on her head the ire of the burgeoning criminal element in the Silver State and enabled the very non-Irish FBI to take an interest in her activities as well. She was probably fortunate that the Feds got to her first. Hence the verse of the song that goes:

Wake up and pay attention, Katie Daly,
I am the judge that's goin' to sentence you,

And all the boys in court have drunk your whiskey,
And to tell the truth, dear Kate, I drank some too.

Katie went down for a fifteen-year stretch. If you know the song well enough, you will be aware that she did not survive her incarceration as the only female inmate of the notorious Alcatraz prison in San Francisco Harbour.

So off to jail, they took poor Katie Daly,
But very soon, the gates they opened wide,
An angel came, for poor old Katie Daly,
And took her, far across the Great Divide.

She may have derived some small satisfaction before her demise from the fact that she survived another famous inmate of Alcatraz, Alphonse 'Scarface' Capone, who joined her on 'The Rock' after he was found guilty of evading Federal taxes.

Katherine Daly, bootlegger, distiller of Irish poteen, based on an old family recipe, was born, one hundred and forty-four years ago, on this day.

Broadcast 1 April 2016

21 April 1874

Birth of tank designer Walter Gordon Wilson

A century ago, the Great War was still raging, still deadlocked. Two inventions would play a huge role in the resolution of the conflict, and both were originally designed by Irishmen. As already mentioned, John Philip Holland, a Fenian sympathiser from Co. Clare, had invented the submarine in the late nineteenth century as a way of attacking British shipping. Walter Gordon Wilson, on the other hand, developed the tank with a view to assisting the cause of the United Kingdom against Germany in the Great War.

Wilson was born in Blackrock, Co. Dublin in 1874. The son of a barrister, he trained as a British naval cadet before completing his education at King's College, Cambridge, where he got a first in mechanical science.

His story includes one of the great 'what ifs' of aviation history. In 1897 he formed a partnership with Percy Pilcher, a gliding enthusiast. Their aim was simple: to be the first to achieve controlled, powered, heavier-than-air flight by developing an aero-engine. They nearly made it, and might have done so had Pilcher not been killed in a glider accident in 1899. Shocked at the death of his charismatic partner, Wilson abandoned the project, although he had already designed a prototype engine. Four years later Orville and

Wilbur Wright made aeronautical history with their flying machine at Kitty Hawk, North Carolina.

Wilson next moved into the burgeoning automobile industry, adapting his aeronautic engine for the new 'horseless carriage'. Although Percy Pilcher was dead, Wilson paid homage to his partner in naming the Wilson-Pilcher motor car in 1900. He continued to develop the design – which included a revolutionary gearbox – until the outbreak of war in 1914.

Wilson re-joined the British Navy in 1914. He was sent to Belgium and France to protect British aircraft using armoured vehicles. He was then taken on by the highly secretive Landships Committee to develop what would become the tank. The committee wanted nothing more or less than an armoured vehicle capable of withstanding German machine guns and small arms sailing through barbed wire and over trenches. So no pressure.

But Wilson and his new partner, fellow engineer William Tritton, were up to the task. Their first effort was nicknamed – no sniggering at the back, please – 'Little Willie'. It was called after Wilson or the Kaiser – depending on who you believe – and was chronically unstable. So probably the Kaiser then. A high mid-section meant it had a tendency to keel over when sent into experimental action. Wilson went back to the drawing board and developed an armoured vehicle with a lower centre of gravity and tracks running around the whole body. Its official name was 'The Wilson'. Then it was renamed 'The Centipede'. But it was better known by its nickname, 'Big Willie'. I kid you not. It went into production in February 1916, and the first models were ready for action during the second phase of the Somme offensive.

Well, sort of. They just weren't very good in 1916. They were unbelievably hot and noisy, and tended to break down long before they got near the enemy trenches. Wilson and Tritton kept at it and continued to improve the design until the tank, by 1918, was a vital and integral part of the Allied victory over Germany. Its most successful appearance was probably at the Battle of Cambrai in 1917. One of Wilson's great contributions was epicyclic steering, which allowed the tank to turn, a rather useful characteristic in a war.

Wilson transferred from the Navy to the Army in 1916, was promoted to Major, mentioned in dispatches twice, and, in 1917, was appointed Companion of the Order of St Michael and St George, or a CMG to you and me.

After the war he continued his career as an innovative engineer, developing and exploiting the Wilson self-changing gearbox and setting up his own company in Coventry to manufacture it.

Walter Gordon Wilson, the man who designed one of the most lethal and decisive weapons of the Great War, the tank, was born in Blackrock, Co. Dublin, one hundred and forty-three years ago, on this day.

Broadcast 21 April 2017

22 April 1905

Captain William O'Shea dies

We don't use the word 'cuckold' much these days. Neither do we use the expression 'criminal conversation' very often. As it happens, the two are related. A cuckold is the *victim* of criminal conversation. He – and it's always a 'he' – is a wronged husband. The fact that the term for the female equivalent, 'cuckquean', is utterly obscure, says a lot. There tend to be more 'cuckqueans' than 'cuckolds' in the world of marital infidelity.

The most famous Irish cuckold – in truth 'notorious' is probably a better word – was undoubtedly William Henry O'Shea. His estranged wife, Katharine, entered into a relationship with Charles Stewart Parnell in 1880 that ended with his death in 1891. In the interim, O'Shea, who of course played the part of the injured husband in the sensational divorce trial of 1890, turned a blind eye to what was, in effect, a second marriage for Katharine.

O'Shea, son of a Dublin lawyer who purchased many bankrupt estates after the Famine – making him a sort of nineteenth-century client of NAMA – was educated in England, and then at the Catholic University (later University College, Dublin). There he was such a troublemaker that he was the despair of the rector, the celebrated cleric John Henry Newman, who later escaped to become a cardinal.

The young O'Shea joined the Hussars, and was encouraged by his father to spend a lot of money on 'entertainment'. I'll repeat that in case you think you misread. He was encouraged by his father to spend a lot of money on entertainment. What is a young man to do when a parent is foolish enough to say 'go waste my fortune on wine, women and song, and make as many influential friends as possible'? Of course it ended in tears when the young O'Shea nearly sent his old man to the same bankruptcy courts that had helped him acquire the basis of his fortune in the first place.

O'Shea never really succeeded at anything much, other than being an accomplished cuckold and a pompous, self-serving politician. In his twenties he tried banking and breeding horses. He failed at both. Then he went into politics, standing as a candidate in Co. Clare in the 1880 general election. After he won a seat in the House of Commons he insisted his wife, from whom he was long separated by then, should invite influential MPs to a series of *soirées* over which she would officiate.

In 1881 the gallant Hussar found out about his wife's newly established relationship with Parnell and challenged the Irish Party leader – his political boss – to a duel. When Parnell accepted with a tad too much enthusiasm, O'Shea suddenly changed his mind about pistols at dawn. From then on he extracted as much advantage as he could out of the relationship while waiting for Katharine's rich aunt to die and leave her a fortune, from which he assumed he would benefit.

Between 1881 and 1889, he managed to overlook the fact that his wife and Parnell had three children together, and that the Irish leader even moved his horses and beloved scientific equipment into the establishment he kept with Katharine.

It was only when the aged aunt died and left her money to her niece in such a way that O'Shea – he pronounced the name 'O'Shee' by the way – couldn't touch a penny, that he 'discovered' – to his utter shock and horror – that Katharine had been carrying on behind his back. Who knew? Well, actually, half of London knew, but we'll let that go. He sued for divorce on Christmas Eve 1889.

As we know, Parnell's career was destroyed by the divorce case, though he was able to marry Katharine a few weeks before he died unexpectedly in October 1891.

O'Shea lingered on for another fourteen years. His funeral in 1905 was attended by two people, one of whom was his son. He died, one hundred and eleven years ago, on this day.

Broadcast 22 April 2016

15 April 1912

The *Titanic* sinks on her maiden voyage

Nowadays we celebrate human disaster almost as much as success, but we call it 'commemoration'. That's the rationale behind the magnificent Titanic Experience in Belfast. Remembrance = tragedy + time. You'd have thought the citizens of Belfast would not be so keen to remind the world that the R.M.S. *Titanic*, which sank in 1912 in the North Atlantic with the loss of over one thousand lives, was built in the Harland and Wolff shipyard in East Belfast. But somebody has to cater for our fascination with this doomed vessel, so why not the descendants of the people who built it?

The facts of this marine catastrophe are well known. The White Star liner R.M.S. *Titanic* was the largest ship afloat when it collided with an iceberg on its maiden voyage at 11:40 p.m. on 14 April 1912 and, to the shock of all concerned, sank at 2:20 a.m. the following morning, bringing the majority of its passengers with it. Just as Belfast is the port associated with its birth, Cork is the harbour closest to its demise.

The *Titanic* arrived in Cork Harbour on its maiden voyage from Southampton on Thursday 11 April. It was too big to land in Cobh (then known as Queenstown), so tenders were used to bring passengers on board. One of the travellers who had made the trip from England was the Jesuit priest Father Francis Browne, one of the most enthusiastic amateur photographers of the early twentieth century. He was only booked for the first leg of the journey, and spent most of the trip taking the last pictures ever seen of the ship, and many of its passengers. An American couple offered to pay his way to New York and back. Browne telegraphed the provincial of the Jesuit order to seek permission. The response was rapid, terse and probably saved Browne's life – the telegram read, 'Get off that ship'. Think of the amazing pictures we would have lost had Browne's boss been the fuzzy indulgent type.

Even more fortunate was *Titanic* stoker John Coffey, a native of Cobh. Stricken by homesickness, he sneaked off the ship by hiding among the mailbags being taken by one of the tenders to the Cobh dock.

Among the more prominent citizens who went down with the ship were its designer, Thomas Andrews; its captain, Edward Smith; the multi-millionaires John Jacob Astor and Benjamin Guggenheim; and the campaigning journalist W.T. Stead. The gazillionaire J. P. Morgan was also supposed to make the trip but cancelled at the last minute.

One prominent citizen who did not go down with the ship was J. Bruce Ismay, managing director of the White Star Line. That meant he was around to field all the awkward questions about how the apparently unsinkable ship could have succumbed to an iceberg. There were also a number of awkward questions about how he managed to survive the sinking to field the other awkward questions.

Most of the Irish passengers were travelling in third class – or steerage – having paid just over seven pounds (around six hundred pounds today) for the privilege. Contemporary reports suggest that they were enjoying the trip until interrupted by the iceberg. One account has Irish steerage passengers chasing a rat around the lower decks – presumably it was exercising that unerring instinct of rodents and was already on its way to deserting the sinking ship.

In case this all seems like a remote historic event removed from us by over a century, it should be pointed out that the last surviving passenger of the ill-fated vessel, Elizabeth Dean, died in 2009, aged ninety-seven. She had been a babe in arms when rescued.

And sorry to disappoint, but Jack Dawson and Rose Calvert never sailed on the *Titanic* – they are both merely lucrative figments of the imagination of filmmaker James Cameron.

The R.M.S. *Titanic*, pride of the White Star Line, sank to the bottom of the Atlantic Ocean, one hundred and four years ago, on this day.

Broadcast 15 April 2016

29 April 1916

Patrick Pearse agrees to an
unconditional surrender

It was never going to be much more than a futile gesture
to begin with, but few of those who gathered in Dublin
on Monday 24 April 1916 for Irish Volunteer manoeuvres
would have expected the rebellion they had planned to last
as long as a week. The failure of the German steamer the *Aud*
to land twenty-five thousand rifles and a million rounds of
ammunition on Good Friday, the arrest of Roger Casement
in Kerry, and the decision of Volunteer commander Eoin
MacNeill to countermand the order for units to assemble
on Easter Sunday had lengthened the odds against the Easter
Rising being anything other than a brief skirmish.

That it lasted almost a week was down to British
incompetence as much as it was to Irish luck, or pluck. There
were inefficiencies on both sides. While the rebels famously
failed to take the wide-open Dublin Castle, the well-
positioned Trinity College and the strategically important
Crow Street Telephone Exchange, the flower of the British
administration in Ireland was enjoying its recreational
downtime at Fairyhouse Racecourse while they were being
made fools of in Dublin.

Two myths, among many. Number one: Patrick Pearse
did not read the Proclamation of the Irish Republic from the
steps of the General Post Office. He read it from the front

of the building. The GPO, then, and now, doesn't have any steps. Number two: the document he was reading bore the signatures of the members of the Military Council of the Irish Republican Brotherhood, and James Connolly representing the Irish Citizen's Army. But it was not their death warrant. The document Pearse was reading was of no use to a prosecutor even in the improvised courts-martial that followed the rebellion. The reason for this was simple – the names of the leaders were printed. The authorities would have had to produce a signed original for it to be of any practical assistance in convicting the signatories.

As the British sought to take back the city of Dublin, most of the fatalities incurred were civilians, more than two hundred and fifty of them. Forty of those were under the age of sixteen. One of the civilian fatalities was the pacifist Francis Sheehy Skeffington, brutally murdered by an improvised firing squad on the orders of a British officer, Captain J. C. Bowen Colthurst—later adjudged insane—as he went about the city trying to prevent looting. Sixty-four members of the Volunteers, or the Irish Citizens Army, lost their lives, as did one hundred and sixteen British soldiers. Most of the soldiers were from the Sherwood Foresters, picked off on Mount Street Bridge by a small unit sent from Boland's Mills by Third Battalion Commandant Eamon De Valera. When the Foresters disembarked in Kingstown – now Dun Laoghaire – they were surprised to hear people speaking English. They assumed they'd landed in wartime France.

James Connolly may or may not have claimed that capitalists would never destroy property, even to end a rebellion – he is unlikely to have been sufficiently naïve to have ever said any such thing – but destroy it they did. Much of the centre of Dublin was laid waste by the shells of the gunboat, *Helga*, and British artillery stationed in Phibsborough and Trinity College.

The Volunteers' headquarters in the General Post Office was never actually taken by the British forces – it was abandoned by the Volunteers before its total destruction by shelling. Shortly after the evacuation of the GPO, the rebel leadership bowed to the inevitable, six days after the Rising started. That began a busy day for Nurse Elizabeth O'Farrell, who was given the dangerous job of informing the other garrisons, most of which remained untaken, that the Rising was at an end.

Patrick Pearse, President of the Provisional Irish Republic, agreed to an unconditional surrender of the Irish Volunteers and Irish Citizen's Army, one hundred years ago, on this day.

Broadcast 29 April 2016

14 April 1919

The Limerick Soviet

Many have discovered, to their cost, not least the All Blacks, that you don't mess with Limerick. In 1919 the city put itself on a par with Moscow and St Petersburg by establishing its very own soviet, or council. It only lasted two weeks, but it sent a shiver up the spine of the British establishment, and probably up the spines of quite a few Irish 'conservative revolutionaries' as well. It also garnered huge international publicity.

The incident that sparked the establishment of the soviet occurred on 9 April 1919, when, three months into the War of Independence, the IRA attempted to engineer the escape of a sympathiser, Robert Byrne, from the Limerick workhouse where he was on hunger strike. The botched operation led to the deaths of Byrne and of one of his captors.

The response of the Crown forces in Ireland was to deploy troops and armoured cars to the city and declare it a Special Military Area under the Defence of the Realm Act. This meant that anyone wanting to leave the city had to get a permit from the Royal Irish Constabulary.

Limerick people love their city, but they do like to leave from time to time, and in 1919 they didn't see why they should have to ask the RIC for permission. They weren't going to oblige.

On 13 April a general strike was called by the Limerick United Trades and Labour Council for the following day.

The organising committee, rather colourfully, described itself as a 'soviet', despite the absence of any obvious Russian connections. Coincidentally, a transatlantic air race had been scheduled to leave from Bawnmore in Limerick that day, so there were dozens of foreign journalists in the area. They immediately sought out the leaders of the 'soviet', John Cronin and James Casey. Their interviews, however, were interrupted at noon when the leaders of the strike, in a rather un-Lenin-like move, excused themselves briefly so that they could recite the Angelus.

Lenin would have been much more excited by the printing of Limerick soviet currency. Banknotes, if one is allowed to use the term 'bank' in this context, bore the legend: 'The workers of Limerick promise to pay the bearer one shilling', and were signed by Cronin and Casey on behalf of the Limerick Trades Council. By and large, the currency was honoured in local shops.

The response to the strike call was encouraging. Even the pubs closed. Some cinemas were allowed by the Strike Committee to remain open under a special dispensation, and bakers were asked to go back to work. There was support for the soviet outside of the city as well. Any goods dispatched from Limerick to Dublin were not handled by members of the Irish Transport and General Workers' Union. One problem, however, was the refusal of many of the city's trade unions, headquartered in Britain, to support the strike, as it was seen as a political (i.e. nationalist) action rather than legitimate trade union activity. This opposition also ensured that the Limerick strike would not expand to outside the city.

Food prices were strictly controlled by the soviet, and food was distributed to the forty thousand people of the city. Farmers from Co. Clare sent supplies that were sold below prevailing market prices. British troops and the RIC, however, were left to fend for themselves. But not everyone co-operated. Local coal merchants, for example, refused to supply coal. Many larger businesses complained that they were forced to close down by the strike and refused to continue paying workers.

The Roman Catholic Church authorities in Limerick, initially supportive, turned against the strike, and the soviet came to an end on 27 April after a proclamation by the Catholic bishop Denis Hallinan.

The historian of the soviet, former RTÉ journalist Liam Cahill, described the protest as being based 'on essentially nationalist and humanitarian grounds, rather than … on socialist or even trade union aims'.

The people of Limerick briefly rose up and lost their chains, in the only soviet of the War of Independence, ninety-eight years ago, on this day.

Broadcast 14 April 2017

28 April 1920

The tribulations and triumphs of Georgina Frost

Georgina Frost was both an unremarkable and quite a remarkable woman. She was the daughter of Thomas Frost, a Petty Sessions clerk from Co. Clare. She assisted her father in administering two of the courts presided over by the Resident Magistrates of the county before the advent of independence in 1922.

Born in 1879, and motherless from the age of eight, Georgina Frost was no Countess Markievicz, nor a Hannah Sheehy-Skeffington. She was to be royally shafted by the 'conservative revolutionaries' of the Free State Government. But, in 1920, she struck her own small blow for Irish women when her tenacity and perseverance, as well as the justice of her cause, extracted a minor but highly significant concession from the male-dominated establishment.

She was known to one and all as 'Georgie', and when her father retired in 1915 as Petty Sessions clerk for Sixmilebridge and Newmarket on Fergus, the Co. Clare Resident Magistrates sensibly decided that, as she had already been doing the job for a number of years, Georgie was the right person to take over from her father. The position is the equivalent of a District Court clerk today.

But when their decision was conveyed to the Lord Lieutenant, Lord Wimborne, he objected on the grounds that 'Georgie' was actually Georgina, a female. It wasn't that she couldn't do the job, clearly she was very good at it. But according to Wimborne, there were issues of decorum at stake, with what was described in a court case as 'the unfitness of certain painful and exacting duties in relation to the finer qualities of women'.

Undoubtedly Georgie Frost had many fine qualities, but she was keen to retain those qualities, as well as the job for which she was eminently suited and experienced. So, she sued, and lost. The case was entitled *Frost v. The King*, which has a certain meteorological flavor to it. It was heard in 1919, and the judge agreed with the Lord Lieutenant that court work was not appropriate for such a delicate flower as a woman. At which point Georgie should have taken her 'finer qualities' and gone back to the family kitchen.

But she was made of sterner stuff. Obviously one of her 'finer qualities' was a refusal to defer to the authorities, all of whose members happened to be men. She appealed. And lost again. Surely now she would get the message and not attempt to inflict those 'painful and exacting duties' on her feeble feminine frame?

No such luck. Georgie wasn't having any of it, and appealed to the House of Lords. At this point the British Government threw up its hands and cried 'mercy'. In December 1919, the King signed a new piece of legislation, the Sex Disqualification (Removal) Act, into law. The first section of the new legislation read as follows:

A person shall not be disqualified by sex or marriage from the exercise of any public function, or from being appointed to or holding any civil or judicial office or post, or from entering or assuming or carrying on any civil profession or vocation, or for admission to any incorporated society.

What that meant in simple English was that Georgina Frost had won. Of course the law had not been introduced because the Government feared that Georgie might impress the Lords and win her second appeal. Perish the thought!

The Lord Lieutenant relented, and the appointment of Miss Georgina Frost as Sixmilebridge Petty Sessions clerk was confirmed and made retrospective. Her tenure was brief but exciting, and included an IRA raid where she was held at gunpoint.

In 1923 the new Free State Government abolished Petty Session courts and Resident Magistrates. Out with the RMs went the clerks. Georgina lost the job which she had fought so hard to secure. Although the District Courts replaced the Petty Sessions, she didn't get her job back. Of course, this had nothing whatever to do with the fact that she was a woman. She was a mere 'tool' of the British establishment, which she had taken on and beaten. She did get a pension of four pounds a week, which she enjoyed up to her death in 1939 at the age of fifty-nine.

The unassuming, but obviously steely Georgina Frost, became, retrospectively, the first woman to hold paid public office in the United Kingdom, ninety-seven years ago, on this day.

Broadcast 28 April 2017

7 April 1926

Violet Gibson attempts to assassinate Mussolini

He had his ardent fans, but the modest Irishwoman, the Honorable Violet Albina Gibson, was certainly not one of them. In 1926 she linked nineteenth-century Irish land purchase with twentieth-century Italian fascism when, around the time he assumed absolute power in Italy, Violet Gibson attempted to assassinate Benito Mussolini.

At the time, Il Duce was saluting his public in the Piazza del Campodoglio in Rome. He had just addressed the International Congress of Surgeons, so he was probably in the right place for some urgent medical attention, had Violet Gibson only been a better shot. As he sat in his Duce-mobile, waiting to be whisked away, the car was approached by a petite, bespectacled, and somewhat shabby fifty-year-old woman. Instead of smiling and waving at the Italian prime minister, she took out a gun and shot him at almost point-blank range.

Gibson was not a particularly good shot, and pistols are notoriously inaccurate in the hands of a novice. She hit Mussolini in the nose, twice, causing a spectacular nosebleed, but leaving him otherwise unscathed. At least one bullet went right through both nostrils. A third attempt to fire led to the gun jamming. Had Mussolini not turned his head at the wrong moment – or the right moment if you're a lover of

Fascist dictators – Violet Gibson might not have failed in her one and only attempt at killing someone other than herself. Mussolini's recorded reaction was one of surprise – that his assailant was a woman.

Gibson was immediately set upon by enthusiastic Fascist spectators eager to demonstrate their devotion to Il Duce, and was almost lynched. The police intervened, and she was quickly overpowered and arrested. She can probably consider herself fortunate. A few months later a teenager tried to kill Mussolini in Bologna; he was captured by a vengeful mob, strangled, knifed, and then shot.

The middle-aged Irish aristocrat was from a celebrated Anglican and Unionist family, but had converted to nationalism and Christian Science before eventually becoming a Catholic in 1902. Her Catholicism, however, did not prevent her from once threatening to shoot the Pope, whom she accused of betraying her beloved Italy. The year before her attempt to prematurely end the illustrious career of Il Duce, she had tried to kill *herself* with a gunshot to the chest. She missed on that occasion too, her inaccuracy probably explaining her inability to kill the Fascist leader from the much greater range of a couple of feet.

After her attempt to take her own life, she spent her days living quietly in a convent in Rome, mostly doing jigsaws. She gave no indication of what she had in mind when she stepped out on 7 April 1926. She did not tell any of the nuns that she was armed.

In the military court that tried her, she claimed to have been ordered to kill Mussolini by God himself, but the prosecution held that 'the deed was not attempted in an unconscious frenzy of delirium, terror or hallucination'. When she was released on Il Duce's orders and deported to Britain, she was committed to the same asylum where James

Joyce's daughter Lucia spent the last thirty years of her life. She died in 1956 at the age of seventy-nine, and is buried in Northampton in England.

Violet's action would not have been welcome in official circles in Britain in 1926, as the King of England had just awarded Mussolini the Order of the Bath. But Mussolini's own lynching in 1945 prompted calls for her to be released. By then, however, her mental state had deteriorated, and she suffered from the delusion that her moods were responsible for the weather. With most of us it's the other way around. On her return to England from Italy she had written many letters to Winston Churchill, and much later, to the future Queen Elizabeth. None were ever posted.

Incidentally, the obscure reference in the first paragraph to Irish land purchase was based on the fact that Violet Gibson was the daughter of Edward Gibson, Baron Ashbourne, the Tory Lord Chancellor whose 1885 legislation sped up the acquisition of the land of Ireland by its tenant farmers, in what became known as the Ashbourne Land Act.

The Honourable Violet Gibson came within inches of changing European history, ninety-one years ago, on this day.

Broadcast 7 April 2017

May

Another dull day at School

27 May 1224

Death of Cathal O'Connor, King of Connacht

We hear a lot about the Red Hand of Ulster these days, but the province of Connacht had a Red Hand of its own. He was Cathal 'Crobhdearg' (Red Claw) O'Connor, who ruled the region for almost thirty-five years at a time when a wet weekend of political domination was the lot of most Irish kings.

Cathal O'Connor was a born survivor who avoided the sudden and painful death he inflicted on many others by always knowing in which direction the wind was blowing. He succeeded his brother Rory, the last High King of Ireland, as ruler of Connacht in 1189. He and Rory were two of the twenty-five sons of Turlough O'Connor, a previous king of Connacht, who survived five of his six wives. We have to assume that Turlough probably had a few daughters as well, but only one has been chalked up to his credit in the annals.

Cathal came to power in the west, at a time when the country was being overrun by Norman invaders, introduced into Ireland by Pope Adrian IV, the only English Pontiff, and his agent, King Henry II. By the time Cathal assumed the throne of Connacht, the Normans were well ensconced in neighbouring Leinster, and were making inroads into his bailiwick too. He could have chosen the military route, but adopted a conciliatory line instead. His first reign lasted ten years before he was usurped by the head of a rival O'Connor family, Cathal Carrach, his own nephew – I hope you're still following this. Irish medieval dynasties are full of scheming warlords with exactly the same names. 'Carrach', by the way, translates as 'scabby', so we can assume that this Cathal – the usurper, not our boy – was not much to look at. Given his disposition it is also unlikely that anyone called him 'Carrach' to his pockmarked face.

Our Cathal O'Connor got the throne back from the other Cathal O'Connor in 1202, when he defeated and killed his blotchy relative in a battle near Boyle, Co. Roscommon. He kept the throne until his death in 1224, no mean achievement with the Normans eyeing the land west of the Shannon and sizing it up for castle building. Cathal wasn't too picky about who he made alliances with, as long as the alliances kept him in power. Sometimes he was in league with Thomond, sometimes with Tyrone. Now and again he even hitched up with the Normans, and on at least one occasion appealed to Dublin to restore his sovereignty.

His constant switches of allegiance resulted, eventually, in his recognition by the King of England as Lord of Ireland. He wrote a letter to Henry III, in which he pointed out that he had offered 'faithful and devoted service' to his father, King John 'of happy memory'. It is an egregious example of brown-nosing the monarch, as nobody in their right minds would ever describe the callous and useless King John as being 'of happy memory' – you would have needed a bad case of amnesia for that.

The Annals of Connacht are equally obsequious when it comes to outlining the merits of Cathal Crobhdearg. The annalists write of him as:

> The king who carried out most plunderings and burn-
> ings against Galls and Gaels who opposed him; the

king who was the fiercest and harshest towards his enemies that ever lived; the king who most blinded, killed and mutilated rebellious and disaffected subjects;

But all the bloodshed was forgiveable because he was also: 'The king who was most chaste of all the kings of Ireland'.

James Clarence Mangan both immortalized and romanticized Cathal Crobhdearg in his poem 'A Vision of Connacht in the Thirteenth Century', where he writes of 'Cathal Mór of the wine-red hand'. The poem is about the gradual Anglo-Norman domination of the old Gaelic world, with Cathal O'Connor as the main transitional figure.

Cathal Crobhdearg O'Connor, monarch and political meteorologist, died seven hundred and ninety-two years ago, on this day.

Broadcast 27 May 2016

20 May 1762

The birth of Sir Eyre Coote

The expression 'as bald as a coot' is well known in this part of the world. In the United States, however, the unfortunate bird is familiar as the basis of an entirely different simile. In America, you can be 'as crazy as a coot'. The assumption has always been that the 'coot' in question is the common 'mud hen', often mistaken for a duck.

But what if the insane 'coot' to which the phrase refers is not the inoffensive animal, but an eccentric Irish-military character with the letter 'e' distinguishing him from the water-loving bird? And the word 'eccentric' is not used lightly. Because Sir Eyre Coote, born in Ireland in 1762, was adjudged to be merely 'eccentric' rather than completely ga-ga by a military board in 1816. But more about that later.

He had the misfortune to be the nephew of, and share a name with, one of the greatest generals in the British Army, who ensured that England rather than France became a tea-drinking nation when he pushed the French out of India in the eighteenth century. His nephew, also called Eyre Coote, joined the army at the age of fourteen and quickly rose through the ranks, helped, no doubt, by his name. Eyre Coote Junior first distinguished himself in the American War of Independence, which began with a dispute over tea and ended with the United States abandoning that beverage for coffee. More significantly, perhaps, it also ended in the defeat of the British Army and the capture of Coote at the pivotal Battle of Yorktown in 1781, when he was only nineteen years of age.

Moving rapidly from opposing the American colonists to the more traditional antagonism with the French, Coote became involved in a military operation designed to flood the part of the Netherlands that was occupied by France in 1798. Flooding northern Holland proved to be relatively simple; getting away afterwards was a bit more difficult. A contrary wind meant that the ships intended to evacuate his force could not land, and after losing more than a hundred of his men, Coote was forced to surrender, again.

Shortly after that, he inherited Uncle Eyre's property and took a seat in the Irish House of Commons. That seat was pulled from under him by the Act of Union in 1800, and he went on to become Governor of Jamaica. Although he left that post in 1808, claiming the climate didn't agree with him and that it affected his brain, he must have had some fun while he was resident in the West Indies, because the former US Secretary of State, General Colin Powell, claims direct descent from him.

But it is for his unorthodox activities in the year of the Battle of Waterloo, 1815, that Coote is most commonly remembered. He had already displayed a talent for what might diplomatically be called 'erratic decision-making', but he surpassed himself when, in November 1815, he wandered into the Mathematical School of Christ's Hospital for Boys in London and offered some of the young inmates money – if he was allowed to flog them. A few volunteered. They were far more receptive when he suggested they might want to flog *him*. Three of the boys duly obliged and were paid three shillings each. Discovered by a school nurse, Coote was charged with indecent behaviour. He escaped jail by donating £1,000 to the hospital, a somewhat disproportionate version of the use of the Trocáire box for traffic offences in modern times. But despite avoiding a criminal charge, he later found himself facing a military tribunal of three generals.

He was ruled not to be insane but merely 'eccentric'. However, his conduct was adjudged to have been unworthy of an officer, and he was dismissed from the army. He was also stripped of his membership of the Order of the Bath. Clearly the affiliates of that august order had no time for flagellation.

Eyre Coote, soldier, politician, ancestor of General Colin Powell and keen masochist, was born, two hundred and fifty-four years ago, on this day.

Broadcast 20 May 2016

19 May 1798

Francis Magan betrays
Lord Edward Fitzgerald

Today, neither a birth nor a death, but an act of supreme betrayal.

Everyone knows that a variety of Irish revolutionary organizations were, over the years, bedevilled by informers. Contrary to Brendan Behan's famous axiom, it would appear that the first item on the agenda of such groups was not 'the split', but the decision on who would be the most effective government spy.

One of the most enthusiastic of those was Francis Magan. His most distinguished victim was the charismatic and highly romanticized Society of United Irishmen leader, Lord Edward Fitzgerald, son of the Duke of Leinster. Fitzgerald was the almost anonymous Magan's polar opposite: aristocratic, idealistic and captivating. He had fought in the British Army in the American War of Independence, journeyed down the Mississippi river with an escaped African-American slave, Tony Small, who had saved his life on the battlefield, was elected to the Irish Parliament as a supporter of the 'Patriot' leader Henry Grattan, and joined the United Irishmen in 1796. Fitzgerald, despite his elevated social status, was pledged to the establishment of an Irish Republic, along French lines. In the planned rebellion of 1798, Fitzgerald was to lead the Dublin-based rebels.

Magan, born in 1774, was a lawyer who came into a decent inheritance and became, therefore, a man of independent means for most of his working life, though not fabulously wealthy like Fitzgerald. However, Magan didn't exactly want for money, so his betrayal of the United Irishmen's cause cannot be explained simply by the pursuit of thirty pieces of silver. He joined the United Irishmen in 1792 and became a prominent member of the organisation's Dublin committee.

Magan's conduit to the government was the infamous Francis Higgins. Known as 'The Sham Squire', Higgins was the proprietor of Dublin Castle's favourite newspaper, *The Freeman's Journal*, and a long-standing government agent. Higgins informed the Under Secretary and Britain's spymaster in Dublin, Edward Cooke, about Magan's availability as well as his unrivalled access to the revolutionary plans of the United Irishmen. Cooke recognized that the lawyer could prove an invaluable asset. He wasn't far wrong. After negotiating a nice little earner for himself – £1,000 for information leading to the arrest of Fitzgerald – Magan went to work.

In order to help him locate Fitzgerald, Magan organized a meeting of the Dublin United Irishmen in his own house on the night of 17 May 1798. Lord Edward may even have spent the night in Magan's home, at No. 20 Usher's Island on the south quays. The authorities failed to apprehend Fitzgerald on that occasion, however. Time was running out for the Castle.

On 19 May Fitzgerald was due to lead more than a thousand rebels in an attempt to seize the capital city. Enter Magan one more time. He kept the Castle informed of Lord Edward's whereabouts – he wasn't too far away from them, on Thomas Street – and this time they got their man. Fitzgerald was wounded in the attempt to arrest him, clung to life for a few days, and eventually died in Newgate Prison on 4 June. As a consequence, the rebellion of the United Irishmen failed utterly in Dublin.

The spies, however, fell out amongst themselves. In 1802 Higgins died without having handed over the £1,000 that had been promised to his protégé. The Castle was under the illusion that Magan had been paid off, and were dismayed when he sued the Higgins estate. They did not particularly want their machinations being discussed in open court, so the erstwhile informer was bought off with an award of £500.

Magan got away with his secret identity during his own lifetime. He died in 1843 and prior to that had been an active member of Daniel O'Connell's Catholic Association. There is no evidence that his career as a 'spook' extended into the nineteenth century, though he did offer to expose a few more rebels in 1801. He was not outed as an informer until 1859, by the historian William J. Fitzpatrick, who also exposed Francis Higgins as a gifted but corrupt 'supergrass'. Fitzpatrick, unaware that Magan was a relatively wealthy man, assumed that his actions had been prompted solely by greed.

Francis Magan successfully betrayed Lord Edward Fitzgerald to the British authorities, two hundred and nineteen years ago, on this day.

Broadcast 19 May 2017

13 May 1842

Arthur Sullivan is born

There are times when you should listen to your parents, and times when it is best to ignore them. On one important issue, that of his future career, Arthur Sullivan chose to disregard the advice of his Irish father and his Irish-Italian mother.

Thomas Sullivan had carved out a living in a certain field, but didn't want his son to follow in his footsteps. The field in question was music – *père* Sullivan was a military bandmaster – and because Arthur ignored the wishes of his old man, the world was able to enjoy the melodies to perennial favourites like *The Pirates of Penzance* (1879) and *The Gondoliers* (1889). Yes! That's the Sullivan in question – the other half of Gilbert and ...

Not that Arthur Sullivan should merely be celebrated as the man who wrote the 'dum-de dum-de-dum' accompaniment to the comic lyrics of his long-time partner, W. S. Gilbert. He was also a serious classical composer. His 1866 'Symphony in E' – the '" Irish" Symphony' – was written when he was only twenty-four years old. While his collaboration with Gilbert brought him international fame and a considerable fortune, he tended to regard the writing of the music for songs like 'I Am the Very Model of a Modern Major General' and 'Three Little Maids from School Are We', as a distraction from his more important musical work.

However, whether he would have liked it or not, he is still best remembered today for his light operatic compositions.

How many people can claim to have seen or heard his only opera *Ivanhoe* (1891)? More of us can probably hum 'A Wandering Minstrel', than the *andante* from The Irish Symphony.

His meeting with Gilbert in 1870 was as important to English music as the coming together of Michael Marks and Thomas Spencer was to retail. Their partnership didn't really get off the ground until the mid 1870s when the impresario Richard d'Oyly Carte commissioned the one-act comic opera *Trial by Jury* (1875). Their first full-length collaboration, *The Sorcerer* (1877), was a modest success, but it was eclipsed by the triumph of their 1879 opera *H.M.S. Pinafore*, which ran for an almost unprecedented five hundred and seventy-one performances at the Opera Comique in London. So popular was *Pinafore* that it spawned one hundred and fifty unlicensed productions in the USA; this would not have pleased Sullivan as he didn't make a penny from them in royalties. Their follow-up, *The Pirates of Penzance*, despite the obvious temptation, had nothing whatsoever to do with copyright theft.

Sometime after he was knighted in 1883, Sullivan began to tire of Gilbert's sense of humour and the 'topsy-turvy' plots – his description – that his collaborator seemed to favour. These tended to rely on mistaken identity, supernatural devices and the taking of occasional magic potions, all of which was a bit *infra dig* for a Knight of the Realm who wanted to write symphonies. He remained in the partnership largely because of a 'handcuff' contract with Richard d'Oyly Carte, and the fact that, in 1885, when their partnership was on its last legs, Gilbert came up with the libretto for *The Mikado*, their most successful work together. Set in a Japan that no Japanese person would have recognized, and packed with superb and memorable melodies, *The Mikado* ran for a Gilbert & Sullivan record of six hundred and seventy-two performances and, of course, spawned a popular variety of biscuit.

Five years later, the partnership came to an acrimonious end when Sullivan sided with d'Oyly Carte in a row with Gilbert over money. Sullivan was finally free of the threat of magic potions and could write that great symphony. Within a couple of years, however, he was back with Gilbert in a relationship that continued to anticipate the marriages of Richard Burton and Elizabeth Taylor. It finally ended in 1896 when Sullivan had less than four years to live.

In the years before his death, one of his more interesting final projects was an homage to the birthplace of his father, the comic opera *The Emerald Isle* or *The Caves of Carrig-Cleena* (1901). Sullivan died at the early age of fifty-eight – his health had never been good. Kidney disease in middle age meant he had to conduct most of his most celebrated works while seated. Gilbert, six years older, survived him by more than a decade.

Arthur Sullivan, son of an Irish bandmaster, and composer of some of the most abiding melodies in popular music was born, one hundred and seventy-four years ago, on this day.

Broadcast 13 May 2016

26 May 1868

Michael Barrett is hanged

Public hangings used to be a form of public entertainment, part of the regime of 'bread and circuses' laid out for the delectation of the *sans culottes*. It didn't offer them trousers, but it kept them amused and in check. After 1868, however, public hangings did not form part of the cultural landscape of modern Britain. In the 1850s, trains had been laid on so that people could attend the hangings. They were often scheduled for noon to facilitate the curiosity of the onlooker. In some cases, to ratchet up the level of morbid fascination, judges would order executions to take place at the scene of the crime. When a 'toff' was being stretched, as opposed to just another unfortunate like themselves, the *hoi polloi* would show up in droves. This was especially so in the case of the banker Henry Fauntleroy in 1824. He had been found guilty of defrauding the Bank of England of five thousand pounds. His execution was witnessed by more than one hundred thousand people. The public hanging of rogue bankers is, fortunately, frowned upon today.

The last public hangings in England took place in 1868. The final public execution of a woman, Frances Kidder, who had murdered her twelve-year-old stepdaughter, was witnessed by a mere two thousand people, many of them women. It took place outside Maidstone Prison on 2 April. Five weeks later, the last man was hanged in public. The execution of Michael Barrett was particularly well-attended

– he was found guilty of involvement in the bombing of Clerkenwell Prison in London, one of the great Fenian atrocities of the nineteenth century,

The unintentionally catastrophic explosion had taken place on 13 December 1867, a few months after the abortive Fenian rebellion. It was the last act in a sequence of events that had begun with the arrest in Manchester of Fenian leaders Timothy Deasy and Thomas Kelly. The arrest resulted in the engineering of their escape from a prison in Manchester and the consequential death of a police sergeant. The man who had masterminded the escape attempt, Richard O'Sullivan Burke, had himself been arrested and was being held in Clerkenwell Prison on remand.

On the night of 13 December, a group of Fenians placed barrels of gunpowder outside the walls of the prison in an attempt to secure Burke's escape. But the charge was well in excess of anything required to breach the walls of the prison, and the resultant massive explosion destroyed a number of nearby homes. It killed twelve civilians, injured dozens more, and terrified the already nervous population of Britain. It was a classic Fenian 'own goal'. Even Karl Marx commented that:

> The London masses, who have shown great sympathy towards Ireland, will be made wild and driven into the arms of a reactionary government. One cannot expect the London proletarians to allow themselves to be blown up in honour of Fenian emissaries.

Retribution quickly followed. Whether justice was done is a moot point.

Michael Barrett, a Fermanagh-born Fenian, was arrested in Glasgow, charged with complicity in the Clerkenwell explosion, and brought to London for trial. The main evidence against him, as was common at the time, came from what was called 'an approver'. This was a witness who was himself facing similar charges to the accused and who was turning in evidence to save his own skin. In this instance, the 'approver' was Patrick Mullany, a Dublin tailor who was implicated in the Manchester and Clerkenwell rescue attempts. He told the court that Barrett had been primarily responsible for the explosion. Witnesses were produced who testified that they had seen Barrett in London around the time of the atrocity. But other witnesses – all Irish as it happens – claimed that he had been in Glasgow in December 1867.

Barrett was found guilty and made a speech from the dock proclaiming his innocence. There were numerous appeals for clemency based on the dubious nature of the evidence against him, but these were ignored.

He was hanged on a temporary gallows erected in front of Newgate Prison. The executioner was one William Calcraft who had hanged Frances Kidder a few weeks before. Barrett was one of four hundred and fifty of Calcraft's victims, but the last man he would hang in public. The *Times* reported that the execution was attended by a huge crowd, including women with children in tow. The newspaper celebrated the fact that, as they put it, this would be 'the last such vulgar public display'.

Three days after the execution of Barrett the Capital Punishment (Amendment) Act was passed, and hanging became an indoor sport, still practiced in Britain and Ireland until the 1950s.

Michael Barrett, who may or may not have been involved in the abortive and tragic Clerkenwell bombing, was, nevertheless, the last man hanged in public in Britain, one hundred and forty-nine years ago, on this day.

Broadcast 26 May 2017

6 May, 1882

The Phoenix Park murders

Had it not been for an uncomfortable new pair of boots, nineteenth-century Irish history might have been very different. The boots belonged to Superintendent John Mallon, head of detectives at Dublin Castle. He was on his way to meet an informant near the Viceregal Lodge in Phoenix Park on the afternoon of 6 May 1882. It was warm, and his feet were sore. When he was met near the eastern entrance to the park by one of his officers, who told him not to walk through the park as he had spotted some well-known Fenians in the area, Mallon succumbed to the offending footwear, and the warning, and headed home instead.

Had he strolled on into the park, however uncomfortably, his presence might have prevented one of the most vicious and notorious murders in Irish history. A short while after Mallon did his about-turn, the new Chief Secretary for Ireland, Lord Frederick Cavendish, a nephew by marriage of Prime Minister William Gladstone, decided, on his first day in Dublin, to walk from his office in Dublin Castle to his new lodgings in the Phoenix Park – today it's the US Embassy. While en route he was passed by the carriage of his Under Secretary, Galway native Thomas H. Burke, effectively the head of the Irish Civil Service. Burke was a figure unbeloved in his own country at a time of repressive measures during the Land War, a war that had bedevilled the nation for the past three years.

134

When Burke recognized the lone walker as the new Chief Secretary, he stopped his carriage and offered Cavendish a lift. The Chief Secretary declined, and Burke sealed both of their fates by offering to walk with him instead. As the two men approached the Viceregal Lodge, they were accosted by a group of four men who produced surgical knives and proceeded to attack Burke. When Cavendish intervened to defend his Under Secretary he, in turn, was attacked and murdered. Burke's killers had no idea of the identity or the importance of the man who had tried to defend their intended target.

The intervention of the new Chief Secretary and his brutal murder undoubtedly elevated the status of the crime and increased the intensity of the subsequent investigation. Later that night notes were posted through the letterboxes of the main Dublin newspapers. These claimed that the assassinations were the work of a shadowy new organisation, the Irish National Invincibles. This was a small, ruthless and covert group that emerged from the ranks of the Irish Republican Brotherhood, but which maintained no specific ties with that organization.

The timing of the atrocity could not have been worse. It came a couple of days after an agreement between the British Government and the Irish Party to end the Land War, and almost sabotaged the secret diplomacy that promised to terminate that rancorous conflict.

It took almost a year to apprehend and punish the killers of Cavendish and Burke. Six men were hanged for the crime, including two of the ringleaders, Joe Brady and Daniel Curley. One of the other masterminds behind the assassination, James Carey, escaped with his life by informing on his colleagues. Carey was one of a number of informers produced by the Crown in the case against his fellow Invincibles, but his evidence was crucial. Superintendent Mallon had essentially hoodwinked Carey into confessing and turning in evidence. While Brady, Curley and their associates were either hanged or jailed for lengthy terms, Carey was freed and given a new identity.

Carey's freedom, however, was short-lived. He was smuggled out of Ireland, destined for South Africa, a few weeks after the six Invincible hangings. Recognised on board the ship taking him and his family to their new lives, he was shot dead by one Patrick O'Donnell when they reached dry land. O'Donnell, was, in turn, hanged for his own crime.

The Phoenix Park murders took place, one hundred and thirty-four years ago, on this day.

Broadcast 6 May 2016

5 May 1916

William Evelyn Wylie and the court-martial of William Corrigan

There were many unsung heroes of the 1916 Rising. The courageous Elizabeth O'Farrell, for example, who risked her life to carry Pearse's flag of truce along Moore Street, and then took his surrender note under heavy fire to the remaining Volunteer garrisons. Or Sean McLoughlin, the 'boy commandant' promoted to that rank by James Connolly, who was twenty years old when he played a pivotal role in the evacuation of the GPO.

William Evelyn Wylie may be 'unsung', 'deeply flawed' or just an anti-hero, depending on your point of view. He was a successful barrister who, when the Rising began, helped to seal off Trinity College and deny that strategic position to the rebels.

After Pearse's surrender, Wylie was ordered to participate in the court martial process as lead attorney. He prosecuted 'Prisoner No. 1', Pearse himself, and was hugely impressed by his conduct at the brief trial. At the court martial of one of the most tragic figures of the rebellion, Thomas MacDonagh, Wylie pulled up the presiding judge, whose name was – I kid you not – General Charles Blackader. Blackader sought to use the 1916 Proclamation as conclusive evidence against MacDonagh. Wylie, who actually had a copy of the document in his possession, pointed out that it was inadmissible.

Although MacDonagh's name was appended to the printed version, the court would require the presentation of the original signed copy in order to convict him.

As the courts martial proceeded, Wylie, a unionist and a strong opponent of the principles underlying the rebellion, became concerned at the overriding of due process, in particular the lack of an assigned counsel to speak on behalf of the defendants. He wrote a memoir of that week, which was left to his daughter after his death. In this he described how he took matters into his own hands. Although no defence attorney had been appointed in any of the one hundred and sixty abbreviated trials – an illegal procedure in itself – Wylie took it upon himself to act as both prosecution and defence. While the three presiding military judges were considering their verdict in a case, Wylie would step outside to see who was coming next. He would then advise the accused of their rights and inquire whether they wanted any witnesses to be present. Pearse, MacDonagh and Thomas Clarke had not been made aware that such a facility was available.

It was while engaged in this Janus-like activity on the fourth day of the court martial that Wylie realised, to his intense surprise, that the next prisoner was a Dublin solicitor, William Corrigan, who had briefed him on many occasions in the past. Corrigan had been taken prisoner at the South Dublin Union. When the court martial began, with Blackader presiding, Wylie took the unusual step of arguing the case for and against the prisoner. When Blackader asked why Wylie had adopted this unorthodox approach, the barrister revealed the nature of Corrigan's profession. He then added that he had an uncashed cheque from the accused Volunteer in his pocket that might be void were he to be executed.

Corrigan was one of more than ninety prisoners to be sentenced to death, but in his case the court martial recommended clemency, and Wylie's brief fee was thus secured.

Later, according to his own account, Wylie was consulted by the commander of Crown forces in Ireland, General Sir John Maxwell, about the need to carry out the death sentence passed down on one Éamon de Valera, Third Battalion commandant. Wylie told Maxwell that he didn't see any need to execute de Valera, as he was unlikely to cause trouble in the future. 'I don't think he's very important,' said the clearly misinformed barrister.

Wylie, a keen cyclist, who is mentioned in this context in James Joyce's *Ulysses* (1922), went on to defend Sinn Féin prisoners during the War of Independence, despite his strong unionist sympathies. He was appointed to the High Court by the first Free State Government, and served there until 1936.

William Evelyn Wylie prosecuted and defended Lieutenant William Corrigan of the Irish Volunteers, before a court martial in Richmond Barracks, one hundred and one years ago, on this day.

Broadcast 5 May 2017

12 May 1916

Execution of James Connolly and
Seán Mac Diarmada

Both men came from exceptionally different personal and political backgrounds. One was born in an urban Scottish slum, the other in a small, rural, Irish village. One was a lifelong socialist, committed to proletarian revolution. The other was an equally committed Irish nationalist, and a member of the conservative Catholic organisation, the Ancient Order of Hibernians. But both died on the same day, and for the same cause. James Connolly and Seán Mac Diarmada were signatories to the 1916 Proclamation of the Irish Republic.

Connolly was born to Irish parents in the dismal Cowgate district of Edinburgh in 1868. At age fourteen he lied about his age and joined the British Army. He served in Ireland for seven years. He was to become involved with Keir Hardie in the Independent Labour Party, and James Larkin in the Irish Transport and General Workers Union. He lived in the USA for seven years in the early 1900s, during which time he worked with the famous trade union organisation, the Industrial Workers of the World, better known as the Wobblies. He co-founded the Irish Labour Party in 1912, and the Irish Citizens' Army during the 1913 Lockout. It was this small group of about two hundred men and women – both genders enjoying equal status – that he led into the 1916 Rising, alongside the members of the Irish Volunteers who showed up on Easter Monday after the debacle of Eoin MacNeill's countermanding order.

Connolly, as well as being a man of action, was also a prolific writer and a Marxist intellectual. His most influential work, *Labour in Irish History* (1910), is a clear-headed socialist assessment of Irish history from the late seventeenth century. It contains the following gem: 'The Irish are not philosophers as a rule, they proceed too rapidly from thought to action.'

Sean Mac Diarmada was born in Kiltyclogher in Co. Leitrim in 1883. He moved to Dublin in 1908, where he became involved in a number of cultural and political organisations, including Arthur Griffith's Sinn Féin, and the Gaelic League. He also became a member of the Irish Republican Brotherhood. At an early stage in his revolutionary career he was taken under the wing of the old Fenian Thomas Clarke, and it was these two men, more than any others, who plotted and planned the insurrection in 1916.

The manner of James Connolly's death was the last straw for many Irish people who had initially opposed the Easter Rising. Connolly had been badly wounded in the fighting and was kept in an emergency medical facility in Dublin Castle after the surrender. He was within a few days of death when the British military commander, General Sir John Maxwell, aware that Prime Minister Herbert Asquith was on his way to Dublin to put an end to the executions, ordered that the court martial death sentence be carried out on the last surviving signatories of the Proclamation.

Connolly was brought to Kilmainham Jail in an ambulance, carried to the execution yard on a stretcher, and shot by firing squad while tied to a chair. It was not an astute political move on Maxwell's part, in a week that can generously be described as 'counter-productive'.

Mac Diarmada, owing to the debilitating effects of polio, did not play a large part in the Rising itself. In fact he almost escaped detection and execution. He might not have been identified as a signatory of the Proclamation, and one of the prime movers of the rebellion, had he not been spotted by Dublin Metropolitan Police detective Daniel Hoey. Hoey was later shot dead by members of the assassination squad of Michael Collins.

Other than their Irish nationalism, the two men had little in common. Had they survived a successful Rising – rather a big 'what if' – they might well have found themselves on opposing sides in a subsequent European-style class conflict. But that was not permitted to happen due to the desire of Maxwell to eliminate any future threat from the leaders of radical Irish nationalism and socialism.

James Connolly and Seán Mac Diarmada were executed by firing squad in Kilmainham Jail, one hundred and one years ago, on this day.

Broadcast 12 May 2017

June

"It's actually Copperfaced Jack"
~ *John Scott comes back from the dead* ~

9 June 1739

The birth of the real Copper Face Jack

It is the most famous nightclub in Ireland. By day it's an innocuous basement in Harcourt Street, by night it's frequented by people out to have a good time, or to get drunk, or both. The legend of Copper Face Jack's has not dimmed despite the supposed impoverishment of the entire island of Ireland since 2008. But who exactly *was* Copper Face Jack?

Actually, he was the more grammatically accurate Copper*faced* Jack, and his real name was John Scott, 1st Earl of Clonmel, and was also known as Lord Earlsfort or the Viscount Clonmell at different times.

Scott was born into a landed family in Tipperary in the mid eighteenth century and was educated in Kilkenny College. While there, he came to the defence of a fellow pupil, Hugh Carleton, who was being tormented by another student. Carleton was the son of Francis Carleton, a wealthy merchant from Cork. When he heard of Scott's courage and generosity, Francis Carleton took the young man under his wing and paid for Scott to study at Trinity College, Dublin with his son. Carleton's support, however, turned out to be a mixed blessing – shortly after Scott was called to the Bar in 1765, the Cork merchant prince went bankrupt. It fell to John Scott to support him, to the tune of a hefty three hundred pounds a year until Hugh was in a financial position to do so.

Scott became an Irish barrister at a time when they were anything but a rarity. In late eighteenth-century Ireland, there were over seven hundred barristers; England and Wales had only six hundred between them. The Irish population would have been just over half that of England and Wales combined. Ireland was a litigious nation then, as now, and court cases offered cheap and respectable entertainment for the upper classes of Dublin.

Scott was highly successful at the profession, and used some of the sizeable income he made in the Four Courts to get himself elected to the Irish Parliament as member for Mullingar in 1769. Between 1774 and 1782 he was either Solicitor General or Attorney General for Ireland. In 1784 he became Lord Chief Justice of the King's Bench in Ireland. He was not beloved of those revolutionary nationalists, the United Irishmen, even though he was close to Henry Grattan, and was dismissed from his position as Attorney General for opposing the incursions of English officials on the small measure of Irish sovereignty obtained in 1782. One of the United Irishmen supporters, William Todd Jones, once wrote to Wolfe Tone of his 'contempt and detestation' of Scott.

Were Scott to have read this letter, he might well have challenged William Todd Jones to a duel. He fought four in his lifetime, at least one over his involvement with another man's wife, a Mrs Cuffe, and almost fought a fifth against a political opponent for remarks made in the House of Commons in 1773. Despite his exalted legal position, he even defended duelling in certain instances where there was no recourse to the law. 'In cases of this complexion', he observed, 'the courts will never interfere'.

By the 1790s Scott, by now the Earl of Clonmel, had an income of about twenty thousand pounds per annum from a variety of different sources. He also had at least one thing in common with the venue that is named after him: he enjoyed life to the full. As his income expanded, so did his waistline. His diary suggests that he realized the need to lead a more modest lifestyle, but he never quite got around to it. The increasingly corpulent Clonmel finally succumbed to his own excesses at the early age of fifty-seven. In so doing he missed out on the United Irishmen's rebellion and the Act of Union, either of which might have killed him anyway.

So, what about the famous nickname? Some authorities suggest that this came about because of the incessant consumption of alcoholic beverages, which left him red-faced. Others insist that he had an unusually tanned complexion for his day. Either way, he was stuck with the unflattering moniker 'Copperfaced Jack', which might have been expected to vanish with his passing. Given his elevated status in eighteenth-century Ireland, he would be unlikely to be flattered that his nickname has survived in the way that it has.

The birth of John Scott, aka the Earl of Clonmel, aka Copperfaced Jack, was noted by a breathless nation's newspapers, two hundred and seventy-eight years ago, on this day.

Broadcast 9 June 2017

3 June 1836

Death of Barry Edward O'Meara, surgeon to Napoleon

By 1816 the territory over which he ruled had shrunk to a corner of the small volcanic island of St Helena in the South Atlantic. This was all that Napoleon Bonaparte could call his own after his escape from Elba, the raising of a new French Army, and his final defeat at the hands of Wellington and Blucher at the Battle of Waterloo in 1815.

Sharing Napoleon's exile in St Helena was an Irishman, Barry Edward O'Meara, a British Navy surgeon. O'Meara was born in Newtownpark House in Blackrock, Co. Dublin in 1786. He studied medicine at Trinity College, Dublin, and the Royal College of Surgeons, and joined the army as a medic in 1804. He distinguished himself in fighting in Sicily before being court-martialled for his part in a duel in 1807. He had acted as a second to one of the participants, and was kicked out of the army. What's a young man to do? Well, obviously … join the Navy. This he did almost immediately. He was still a naval surgeon in 1815 when he found himself in the right place at the right time.

Napoleon Bonaparte had been defeated at the Battle of Waterloo and was trying to escape to America, where he would probably have made a fortune on the lecture circuit. Finding his way barred by a naval vessel called the H.M.S. *Bellerophon*, he surrendered to the commander of that ship.

The vessel's surgeon was Dr Barry Edward O'Meara. The unemployed emperor was impressed by the young Irishman's linguistic and medical skills, and invited him to act as his physician in the exciting new opportunity he was being offered by the British Government on St Helena. O'Meara accepted, and over the next three years the two men became good friends.

O'Meara did not enter the arrangement wide-eyed and innocent. During his time with Napoleon he kept a diary with a view to future publication. The two men fared well enough on their new volcanic home under the first two post-war governors of the island. But then, in April 1816, a fellow countryman of O'Meara's, Sir Hudson Lowe from Galway, took over the position, and proved himself to be a Francophobe martinet. He introduced a more spartan regime than that of his predecessors. This became even more restrictive when rumours reached the island of a plot to organise yet another Napoleonic escape. O'Meara's relationship with Lowe deteriorated rapidly, and when he was asked to spy on Bonaparte by the governor, he returned to England.

There in 1822, he wrote *Napoleon in Exile, or A Voice from St Helena*, in which the hero is the late emperor – Napoleon had died the previous year, possibly of stomach cancer, possibly of arsenic poisoning – and the villain is Hudson Lowe. The volume led to his name being removed from the list of naval surgeons, but also attracted much support, including that of Lord Byron.

O'Meara is believed to be the only doctor to have performed a surgical procedure on Napoleon. He extracted one of the emperor's wisdom teeth in 1817. When he died in 1836 the tooth was auctioned, and fetched seven and a half guineas. It was sold again in 2005. This time it cost the buyer thirteen thousand pounds.

After his St Helena experience, O'Meara became a dental surgeon, married a sixty-six-year-old heiress at the age of thirty-seven, and was one of the founders of the Reform Club in London. He died of complications following a chill contracted while attending a fundraising meeting organized on behalf of fellow Reform Club member Daniel O'Connell. Some accounts have him catching his death of cold at one of O'Connell's monster meetings – a much less mundane demise I'm sure you'll agree.

Dr Barry Edward O'Meara, brief and controversial physician to Napoleon Bonaparte, died, one hundred and eighty years ago, on this day.

Broadcast 3 June 2016

24 June 1845

The unveiling of a statue of
Rollo Gillespie, colonial soldier

Few Irishmen are associated with the states of Java, Sumatra or Nepal, but the elegantly named Rollo Gillespie had ties to all three in his short and eventful life. He served in army units in the Far East, hence the link with these exotic locations.

Gillespie was born in Comber in Co. Down, on 21 January 1766. At twenty years of age, in the pattern of the times, he was involved in a duel in which he killed his opponent. He fled to Scotland, but returned to stand trial two years later, where he was acquitted when a verdict of justifiable homicide was returned. In those days dueling was as much a rite of passage as an indictable crime.

In 1792 Gillespie was shipped out with his cavalry unit, the Light Dragoons, to Jamaica. The vessel, however, sank, and when he managed to get to the island of Madeira, he contracted yellow fever. After his recovery, he was made Adjutant General of St Domingo where, one night, eight unfortunate thieves broke into his house in an attempt at burglary. Rollo killed six of them with his sword. The other two barely managed to escape. He also survived at least one escapade in which he risked execution as a spy by indicating to one of his accusers that he was a Freemason.

As well as being a Mason, Rollo was also a loyal unionist, as he amply demonstrated in a visit to the theatre in Cork in the late 1790s. At the conclusion of the night's entertainment, a section of the audience refused to doff their hats and sing 'God Save the King'. Gillespie was seated beside one of these insolent nationalists and decided to remove his offending headgear for him. This led to a brawl; the recalcitrant nationalist was seriously injured, pressed charges, and Rollo was forced to seek refuge from the law by disguising himself as a woman and hiding out on an obliging naval vessel. When the forces of law and order combed the ship, Gillespie augmented his disguise by acquiring a small child and nursing it as the search took place.

In 1804 he transferred with his unit to India. While there, he was accused of fraud but was once again acquitted by a military court. He also almost single-handedly rescued a unit, consisting of sixty men, during the Vellore mutiny of 1806, when Indian troops rebelled against their overlords in the East India Company. After a subsequent stay on the island of Java – not to be confused with the software of the same name – he transferred to the Himalayan state of Nepal in 1814. There he took part in a small war against the formidable Gurkhas, soon to become an elite unit of the British Army. In an attack on a Gurkha hill fort he was heard to shout the words, 'One shot more for the honour of Down' – a cry normally heard on a football field. They were his last words. A Gurkha sharpshooter, attracted by his sentimental urgings, got Rollo in his sights and put a bullet through his head. He died almost instantly. It was of no consolation that he was posthumously knighted in 1815.

Rollo Gillespie reached the rank of Major General in the British Army. A fifty-five-foot-high memorial was erected to him in Comber in 1845. Fifty lodges of his beloved Masonic order attended the dedication, which took place one hundred and seventy-one years ago, on this day.

Broadcast 24 June 2016

17 June 1867

Birth of John Gregg, populariser of shorthand

It is a skill that has become less significant, but is unlikely to ever disappear completely. Variations were used in Ancient Greece and Imperial China. There was a time when a knowledge of shorthand was *de rigeur* for any print journalist. Nowadays you can transcribe from the quotes you pick up on your mobile phone. We've come a long way since 1888 when the Irishman, John Robert Gregg, developed the system named after him.

Born in Co. Monaghan into a strict Presbyterian family, Gregg was a victim of brutality at school at an early age, when his teacher banged the young Gregg's head against that of another pupil as a form of punishment. The result was a lifelong hearing impairment that seriously affected Gregg's education, and led to the assumption that he was slow and dim-witted. As we will see, nothing could have been further from the truth.

John was prompted to teach himself shorthand as a child after the visit of a journalist friend of his father to the Gregg household. His siblings, deemed far more intelligent than young John, had failed, despite their father's enthusiasm for the project, to acquire the skill themselves.

Forced by family circumstances to leave school at the age of thirteen, John Gregg began working in the office of a solicitor. His interest in shorthand continued, and he began to work on a system of his own. A dispute over the extent of his involvement in a system devised by Thomas Stafford Malone prompted him to go it alone and publish his own system in 1888. Bear in mind that he was only twenty-one years old at this stage. In 1888 he published *Light-Line Phonography: The Phonetic Handwriting*, where his template was unveiled. His system is apparently based on an 1845 publication, *The Anti-Absurd or Phrenotypic English Pronouncing & Orthographical Dictionary* by Bartlomiej Beniowski – you can see that one just walking off the shelves.

The most obvious rival to Gregg's system was one devised by Sir Isaac Pitman in 1837. Pitman was obsessed with the reform of spelling in the English language. This was what led to his innovative work. He was also vice president of the Vegetarian Society, and was knighted by Queen Victoria in 1894, three years before his death.

For his part, Gregg moved to the US in 1893, where he published *Gregg Shorthand* the same year. This does exactly what it says on the tin, and became very popular in America. Gregg shorthand is a phonetic writing system based on the sounds made by the speaker rather than the English spelling of the words he or she is using. Over time, Gregg's system made significant inroads on that of Pitman's. When you look at the loops, dashes, lines and diagonals that make up this invented written language, you can only admire the intelligence, tenacity and persistence of those who managed to master it. Journalists, court reporters, secretarial assistants, policemen and so on would, in different times, have been forced to learn this, or another system in order to record for posterity the words of the wise, the unwise, the important and the merely self-important.

Gregg settled in Chicago, wrote numerous books on shorthand and business, and died in 1948. He had the satisfaction of seeing his system become the dominant form of shorthand in North America.

John Robert Gregg, who overcame severe deafness to devise one of the most popular shorthand systems, was born, one hundred and forty-nine years ago, on this day.

Broadcast 17 June 2016

2 June 1891

The penalty kick is born

In order to resolve a stubborn deadlock, trade unionists, employers, diplomats and politicians could do worse than adopt the policy of the football world and go to penalties. This would, of course, greatly benefit Irish politicians involved in trying to end a stalemate, as many were elected to office based on their sporting prowess rather than any obvious political *nous*.

As a punishment for bad behaviour, or a mechanism to end a stalemate, it is fiendishly simple. The ball is placed on a marked spot eleven metres from the goal line and two negotiators, one at a distinct physical disadvantage, face each other. The principal agent in the process, known as the 'penalty taker', is expected to succeed in achieving his goal, which, of course, puts the party of the second part, known as the 'goalkeeper', at a huge *psychological* advantage.

Footballing nerds will be familiar with the fact that in 1986 the astronomically unfancied Steaua Bucharest won the European Cup – now the Champion's League – beating Barcelona in the process. What may have been forgotten is that their victory was largely down to the fact that their goalkeeper, Helmut Duckadam, saved four consecutive penalties in the shootout after extra time. Penalties have a conversion rate of about eighty to eighty-five per cent, but a missed penalty is not always as a result of a goalkeeper's intervention (Roberto Baggio, Neymar da Silva Santos,

Chris Waddle and David Beckham take a bow at this point). So, go figure the odds against a keeper saving four in a row.

But where did it all begin? Well, it actually began in Milford, in Co. Armagh. And who came up with the idea? Surprisingly, an Irish-born goalkeeper.

William McCrum was the son and heir of a linen millionaire who was so bad at organising the family business when his own turn came that he eventually ran it into the ground and was relegated. Of more significance, however, was his sporting life. He played rugby, cricket and soccer. In the case of the latter, he was goalkeeper for Milford Football Club during the 1890/91 season, when Milford played in the Irish Football League. It wasn't a good year for them, and he can't have been much of a goalkeeper, because Milford lost all fourteen of their games and conceded an impressive sixty-two goals. That's close to four goals per match. For the record, they scored ten goals. You can see why they finished last.

And that would have been it for William McCrum, a lousy goalkeeper on a lousy football team, had he not made a suggestion to his friend Jack Reid. Reid was the Irish Football Association's representative on the International Football Association Board. That's the nineteenth-century FIFA, by the way, only not nearly as evil or corrupt. McCrum's idea was to prevent Victorian defenders from chopping down opponents within inches of the goal line, or cynically handling the ball to prevent a score.

Like all great ideas, it was simple and direct. Such transgressions would be punished by allowing the victims a virtually free shot at the goal.

You'd have thought the idea would have been hailed as a stroke of genius and the triumph of fair play, especially as it was the brainchild of a goalie who obviously had no vested interest in the matter. Instead, McCrum's idea was derided. Harrumphing Victorians lost their monocles in outrage at the suggestion that gentlemen would behave so unsportingly. Clearly the hacking of players about to score an open goal was always a tragic accident. The proposal became known as the 'Irishman's motion' – 'Irishman' being a term of abuse in those days.

The legendary C. B. Fry, captain of the great Corinthians Club – membership for gentlemen only – was apoplectic at the notion, observing that it was:

> A standing insult to sportsmen to have to play under a rule which assumes that players intend to trip, hack and push opponents, and to behave like cads of the most unscrupulous kidney.

Then, on 14 February 1891, in an FA Cup quarter final between Stoke and Notts County (anyone remember them?), an indirect free kick given after a deliberate handball was not converted. Fair play had been stood on its head, and McCrum's idea gained currency in England. Shortly thereafter it became football's Rule No. 13 – unlucky for some, mostly goalkeepers like McCrum.

The next time England are, inevitably, defeated in a penalty shootout, it might be an idea to remind any grieving English friends that the penalty is an invention of the devil … an Irishman.

A proposal to introduce the penalty kick into the game of association football was adopted, one hundred and twenty-six years ago, on this day.

Broadcast 2 June 2017

16 June 1904

James Joyce has his first date with Nora Barnacle

Even though Ted Hughes and Sylvia Plath chose to get married on this particular day, their tragic romance was not the most notable to have had its genesis on 16 June. That honour goes to James Joyce and Nora Barnacle, who first 'stepped out' together on the day in question, causing it to be immortalized by Joyce in his greatest work, *Ulysses* (1922).

Now, according to those in the know, James and Nora did quite a bit more than 'step out' that day, but as we are at least two and a half hours before the traditional watershed, we will draw a veil over what exactly happened.

Joyce went on to set the events of his groundbreaking novel on the day of that fateful assignation, 16 June 1904. In his fictionalized version of the auspicious anniversary, Leopold Bloom goes about his business, reflecting on being cuckolded by the charismatic Blazes Boylan. Meanwhile, Joyce's own alter ego, Stephen Dedalus, is in conflict with his flatmate Buck Mulligan, a virtually undisguised Oliver St. John Gogarty – though the 'flat' in question is actually the rather more striking Martello Tower in Sandycove. Ultimately, Bloom and Dedalus meet after parallel odysseys around the city of Dublin, ending in what Joyce called 'Nighttown', but was more familiarly known at the time as 'Monto'. They head for Bloom's house on Eccles Street. The climax of the novel, and I use the word advisedly, is left to Bloom's wife Molly, who, among other things, reflects on cuckolding her husband with the charismatic Blazes Boylan.

At some point in the course of the novel, the ninety-seventh running of the Ascot Gold Cup takes place, and Bloom is presumed to have had money on the nose of a horse called Throwaway who romps home at long odds. You might assume this was a piece of fiction, but, lo and behold, if you check the honour roll of the Ascot Gold Cup, you will find that it was indeed won in 1904 by a horse called Throwaway, ridden, for the record, by Mr Willie Lane, trained by a Mr Herbert Braime, in the colours of Mr Fred Alexander.

Of course it was never on the cards that we, the people of the nation that forced Joyce into exile, would ever be able to leave 16 June 1904 well enough alone. Instead, we created the benign literary monster that has become Bloomsday, so-called, one presumes, because it is considerably more difficult to say 'Dedalus's Day'. Although, in truth, the day more truly belonged to Stephen than it did to Leopold.

The first iteration of Bloomsday took place on its fiftieth anniversary, when a merry bunch of Dublin's literati, which included authors Brian O'Nolan and Anthony Cronin, poet Patrick Kavanagh, critic John Ryan and Joyce's cousin Tom, engaged two horse-drawn cabs, assumed the identities of some of the novel's characters (Cronin played Stephen, for example) and pledged to visit all the more notable sites featuring in the novel. That, however, was the only 'pledge' in evidence on this Bloomsday debut. The merry band of devotees got no further than the Bailey public house, then owned by Ryan, where they were overwhelmed by thirst and were unable to continue the pilgrimage.

Since that inauspicious, if celebrated, inauguration, other aficionados have more than made up for the failure of O'Nolan, Kavanagh *et al* to complete their self-ordained marathon. It appears the only time since that Dubliners have denied themselves the pleasure of commemorating Bloomsday was in 2006 when the festivities would have clashed with the funeral of former taoiseach, Charles J. Haughey. Many of those involved in the festivities would no doubt have benefitted from the artists' tax relief scheme begun in the 1960s by that latter-day charismatic and political Blazes Boylan.

James Joyce went on his first date with Nora Barnacle, and Throwaway won his first and only Ascot Gold Cup, one hundred and thirteen years ago, on this day.

Broadcast 16 June 2017

30 June 1922

The destruction of the Public Record Office

The regulations for readers consulting documents in the Public Record Office in 1922 contained this ironic and poignant gem: 'Regulation Number 6. Smoking or any other dangerous practice is strictly forbidden within the record building.'

It was ironic because on 30 June of that year, the office disappeared in a huge explosion that destroyed records of Irish administrations from the thirteenth to the nineteenth centuries. It wasn't an accident, of course. Nobody had left an unexpired cigarette butt lying around.

In 1922 the Public Record Office was housed in an annexe of the Four Courts building in Dublin. On 14 April this had been occupied by forces under the leadership of Rory O'Connor, forces opposed to the Anglo-Irish Treaty negotiated in December 1921, and narrowly approved by Dáil Éireann in early 1922. By June of that year, the British authorities had grown tired of the failure of the new Free State Government to deal with this direct affront to its legitimacy. British frustration and impatience had turned to anger after the assassination in London of the Irish-born British military officer, Field Marshal Sir Henry Wilson. Assuming – erroneously, no doubt – that the order to kill Wilson had come from the Four Courts, the British Government issued an ultimatum to Michael Collins: dislodge the anti-Treaty rebels, or else. British artillery was supplied for the purpose, and the pro-Treaty attack on the Four Courts garrison began on 28 June 1922.

The effect of the bombardment left much to be desired from a pro-Treaty point of view as it failed to dislodge the rebels. The British Government offered to bomb the Four Courts from the air, which would probably have incurred dozens of civilian casualties, but Collins declined the generous offer. The attack was renewed the following day, and on 30 June, the Four Courts' defenders, by now under the command of Ernie O'Malley, surrendered.

But not before the biggest explosion ever seen in Dublin, to this day.

The 'Irregulars', as the anti-Treaty troops came to be known, had stored their ammunition and explosives in the Public Record Office. There were allegations that the office had also been mined. The Four Courts garrison had been approached on a number of occasions and asked to respect the country's archival heritage and remove their munitions from such a sensitive location. They had failed to do so. Hundreds of years of census returns, wills, land transactions, court reports, military records and parish registers went up in the spectacular blast, for which each side blamed the other.

Ernie O'Malley, who must accept some responsibility for the destruction, as must Collins and the Free State Government, described the aftermath of the explosion thus:

> A thick black cloud floated up about the buildings and drifted away slowly. Fluttering up and down against the black mass were leaves of white paper; they looked like hovering white birds.

A member of the staff of the Public Record Office, S.C. Ratcliff, left this account of the consequences of the blast:

In the vaults were deed boxes on iron racks. The racks were evidently softened by the great heat, and the weight of the boxes has bent them and drawn them forward; the lids of the boxes have fallen in, and the contents have been reduced in every case to a little white ash.

What was lost? The census returns for 1821, 1831, 1841 and 1851. Those for 1861, 1871, 1881 and 1891 had already been pulped during the Great War. Also destroyed were around one thousand parish registers of the Church of Ireland. The only ones that survived were those that had never been sent to Dublin in the first place. The majority of the new nation's wills and testamentary records also went up in smoke. Thankfully, the 1901 and 1911 census records survived, as did the historically vital Griffiths valuation records, which assessed mid nineteenth- century land values across the country.

The Free State Government, despite straitened times and circumstances, had the Public Record Office up and running again by 1928. Would that our current administration was as generous with the modern equivalent, the overstretched National Archives in Bishop Street.

Almost a millennium of official Irish documents disappeared in what was described as 'a mushroom cloud', ninety-five years ago, on this day.

Broadcast 30 June 2017

23 June 1959

Seán Lemass becomes Taoiseach of the Republic of Ireland

It was a long apprenticeship. Not quite on a par with that of the current Prince of Wales as he waits to become King of England, but not far off. Seán Lemass was elected to the Dáil in 1927 as a member of the newly created Fianna Fáil party. The previous year he had resigned from Sinn Féin, along with Eamon de Valera, because of Sinn Féin's insistence on retaining its abstentionist policy. De Valera contemplated leaving politics altogether. Instead, Lemass persuaded him to form a new political party.

Thus began that long apprenticeship. It finally ended thirty-two years later, and within a further four years Lemass had reached the dizzy heights of the cover of *Time* magazine, and an article entitled 'New Spirit in the Ould Sod'. Could it possibly get any better?

Lemass was just sixteen years old when he and his brother Noel took part in the 1916 Rising. Ironically, they had been told by the sons of Eoin MacNeill that the Rising had started and headed straight for the GPO. So theirs was a sort of countermanding order in reverse.

Seán was sent up to the roof of the building and was armed with a shotgun. Because of his youth he was only detained for a month after the Rising ended. He continued in the service of the Irish Volunteers/IRA during the War of Independence. There is still historical controversy about whether Lemass was one of the IRA hitmen who murdered a number of British agents on the morning of what would become known as 'Bloody Sunday', on 21 November 1920. It was not something he ever talked about.

He and his brother – still only in their early twenties – took the anti-Treaty side in the Civil War. Sean Lemass was second-in-command of the force that occupied the Four Courts in defiance of the new Free State Government. But the Civil War ended in defeat and personal tragedy. In 1923 Noel Lemass was kidnapped and murdered; his body was dumped in the Dublin Mountains. The following year Seán Lemass was elected Sinn Féin TD for Dublin South City.

In 1932, three years after Lemass had famously described it as a 'slightly constitutional party', Fianna Fáil entered government for the first time. Lemass was given responsibility for Industry and Commerce and that was, more or less, where he remained for much of the next three decades. Although he has been lauded as the 'architect of modern Ireland' during his tenure in Industry and Commerce, he was responsible for a tariff policy that ultimately did little for Irish industrial development, as it sheltered inefficient Irish industries behind protective tariff walls.

It's hard to say exactly when he became heir apparent. Perhaps he always was, or maybe he didn't get the noble call until 1945, when de Valera made him Tánaiste. He was promoted over the heads of older men after having spent much of the Emergency – our colourful euphemism for World War Two – as Minister for Supplies. In that department he was responsible for the production and distribution of vital goods at a time of huge shortages. So no great pressure there.

While he waited for de Valera to retire, he had the great good sense to become the father in law of one Charles J.

Haughey in 1951. You may have heard of him. Eventually the Long Fellow opted to move to the Phoenix Park in 1959. De Valera became president and the interminable internship of Seán Lemass was at an end. Ireland's greatest civil servant, T. K. Whitaker, beckoned, and the rest is economic history. The two would drag the country into economic modernity as the orthodoxy of de Valera was abandoned. The first and second programmes for economic expansion, launched in 1958 and 1963, kick-started a moribund economy. Ireland, under Lemass, became a more industrialised and urbanised society. In 1965 he took the unprecedented step of travelling across the border for talks with the Prime Minister of Northern Ireland, Terence O'Neill. If this was Russia it would have been called *perestroika*. Under Lemass Ireland was, at last, open to the outside world rather than just populating it.

Seán Lemass became Ireland's fourth taoiseach, in succession to Eamon de Valera, fifty-eight years ago, on this day.

Broadcast 23 June 2017

10 June 1997

Jimmy Kennedy is inducted into the Songwriters' Hall of Fame

It is always interesting to discover the genesis of a popular and memorable poem or piece of music. You assume, for example, that William Wordsworth actually based his poem about daffodils – the one that begins with the immortal line 'I wandered lonely as a cloud' – on a field of the bright yellow blooms. And you wouldn't be too far wrong.

Then there's the sultry pop song from the 1930s, 'South of the Border', which simply has to have been written by someone in the aftermath of a romantic trip to Mexico. But that's where you'd be mistaken. Its inspiration was a postcard from Tijuana. The recipient of the card was Northern Ireland songwriter Jimmy Kennedy. The song may have been voted one of the top one hundred Western songs of all time by the Western Writers of America, but Jimmy Kennedy was closer to Tyrone than Tijuana when he wrote it.

Kennedy was born near Omagh, Co. Tyrone, in 1902, son of a member of the Royal Irish Constabulary. The family later moved to Portstewart in Derry, the seaside town that would inspire another of the writer's classic numbers, 'Red Sails in the Sunset'. He graduated from Trinity College, Dublin, taught for a while in England, and then joined the Colonial Service. But he also moonlighted with a music publisher called Bert Feldman as a pen for hire. By the end of a career that lasted half a century, he had written the lyrics for over two thousand songs, many of which became international hits. For a number of years he was the most successful non-American songwriter in the US, before being supplanted in the 1960s by a pair of scruffy young Liverpool composers named John Lennon and Paul McCartney.

One of his earliest successes was with 'Red Sails in the Sunset'. The song was inspired by the colourful sails of the *Kitty of Coleraine*, a yacht sailing off the Derry coastline that Kennedy would often see from his home. One of the first recordings of the song was by Bing Crosby in 1935. Vera Lynn had a version the same year; Louis Armstrong followed in 1936, and Kennedy was on his way.

In 1907 a composer named John Walter Bratton had written a musical piece that his publishers entitled 'The Teddy Bears' Picnic'. But nobody had thought to add lyrics until Kennedy got hold of it in 1932 and turned it into one of the most popular children's songs of all time.

Kennedy spent the years 1939–1945 in the British Army – serving in the Royal Artillery – where he reached the rank of captain. German defences in 1939 included a chain of fortifications known as the Siegfried Line. Early in the war, Kennedy wrote the comic song 'We're Going to Hang out the Washing on the Siegried Line' as a morale booster. The British didn't actually get near the line until 1945, but the song was hugely popular with the troops and on the 'home front'.

Kennedy won two Ivor Novello awards for his contribution to the music industry, and an OBE in 1983. He died the following year, aged eighty-one.

Jimmy Kennedy, gifted lyricist, was posthumously inducted into the Songwriter's Hall of Fame nineteen years ago, on this day.

Broadcast 10 June 2016

July

"Why don't you join me in a toast, Monsieur Lowe"

28 July 1769

The birth of Sir Hudson Lowe

He is one of the most famous jailers in history, not that anybody actually knows his name. He has been portrayed on film and TV by Orson Welles, Ralph Richardson and Richard E. Grant. Not bad for a military type born in Galway who spent much of his life under a cloud just because he was mean to Napoleon.

Hudson Lowe was born into a military family – his mother was Irish – in 1769. His father was an army surgeon, so if he wanted to be like Dad he could have chosen medicine or the army. Unfortunately for Monsieur N. Bonaparte, he chose the latter.

By the end of the Napoleonic wars he had risen to the rank of major-general, and had also been knighted. But that was as good as it got. In 1815, after the seizure of Napoleon on the H.M.S. *Bellerophon* off Rochefort, Lowe was given the responsibility of looking after the irksome emperor on the island of St Helena. At the time the Secretary of State for War, Lord Bathurst, wrote to the Duke of Wellington in glowing terms of Sir Hudson Lowe, observing that:

> I do not believe we could have found a fitter person of his rank in the army willing to accept a situation of so much confinement, responsibility and exclusion from society.

He makes the job sound so appealing, doesn't he?

But the goodwill didn't last for long. It would probably be an understatement to suggest that Lowe and Napoleon didn't get on. In the six years that they spent together on the same tiny volcanic island off the coast of south-west Africa, they only actually met half a dozen times. But Lowe was determined to ensure that Napoleon, although he may have been the former Emperor of France, was well aware that Sir Hudson Lowe was current Emperor of St Helena. Threats to spring Napoleon from captivity allowed Lowe to impose a particularly harsh regime on the little Corsican general with the big ego. As we have already heard, Napoleon successfully engaged the sympathies of another Irishman, Dr Barry O'Meara, his personal physician, who did little to enhance Lowe's reputation in an 1822 book, *Napoleon in Exile*. Mind you, Lowe did himself few favours with a series of petty regulations and restrictions.

One of Lowe's first mistakes was to insist that Napoleon cover some of the cost of his own incarceration. So, the late emperor rather cleverly, and very publicly, put up some French Imperial silver for sale on the open market. This caused a political storm and Lowe was forced to back down. When he refused to supply enough fuel to last Napoleon over the harsh St Helena winter, the emperor, who was well-used to burning things – like Moscow – set fire to some of his furniture to keep warm. When news of that got out, Lowe was forced to make amends with an increased supply of a more orthodox combustible material.

Lowe must have been greatly relieved when Napoleon, with the immortal catchphrase 'France, army, head of the army, Joséphine' on his lips, died in 1821. But the Galwayman was not yet finished with the diminutive Corsican. There was more to come when Barry O'Meara's book came out in 1822, suggesting that Lowe had contributed, through neglect, to the death of Napoleon. Lowe threatened to sue but never did. Ironically, O'Meara went far easier on Lowe in his book than he had done in a series of letters sent to the Admiralty from St Helena, in which Lowe was described as an 'executioner'.

The Duke of Wellington, who hadn't disagreed with Lord Bathurst, his own Secretary of State for War in 1815 when Bathurst had lauded Lowe's appointment, offered his own verdict on the governor of St Helena:

> A very bad choice; he was a man wanting in education and judgment. He was a stupid man, he knew nothing at all of the world, and like all men who knew nothing of the world, he was suspicious and jealous.

Lowe had some satisfaction in outliving his Napoleonic nemesis by twenty-three years, dying in 1844 at the age of seventy-five.

Sir Hudson Lowe, who was once actually billeted in the Bonaparte family's ancestral home in Corsica in 1799 – so much for returning hospitality – was born, two hundred and forty-eight years ago, on this day.

Broadcast 28 July 2017

14 July 1798

The Sheares brothers are hanged in Dublin

Irish rebellions should probably all come equipped with something we could call an I.Q. That's an Informer Quotient. This is a scientific measure of how many secret agents from among the ranks of the rebels it took to betray the insurrection.

The scale would go all the way from 'Genius' at one hundred and fifty, to 'Witless Imbecile' at zero. Let's take a couple of examples. Obviously the 1798 Rebellion was so riddled with spies and informers that if it had been a boat it would have sunk in a calm and windless cup of tea. So, we'll call that an I.Q. of one hundred and fifty. Then, right at the other end of the scale, there's the 1916 Rising. Here the rebels desperately tried to tip their hand repeatedly, even to the extent of calling the whole thing off in a newspaper advertisement, but the exceptionally dim British authorities had no idea what was going on under their noses. We'll call that an I.Q. of zero.

Totally off the scale of course is the War of Independence, where Michael Collins's own spies and informers were tripping over each other in Dublin Castle. That was a minus I.Q. of about fifty for the rebels.

But the prize for individual revolutionaries most beset by informers has to go to two United Irishmen, the Sheares brothers. It took not one, not two, but three spies to bring them down. Given the going rate for intelligence information in 1798, it must have cost the authorities almost as much as the bribes paid to pass the Act of Union two years later.

The Sheares brothers, John and Henry, were both lawyers from Cork who had witnessed the French revolution and the frequent use of the guillotine. On the boat back home from Calais they met an utterly disillusioned Daniel O'Connell, who was pledged to non-violent political action, based on the bloodthirsty slaughter he had observed in Paris. The Sheares brothers were not so easily put off. When they got back to Dublin in 1793 they joined the United Irishmen. Both began organizing in their native Cork.

Enter spy number one. His name was Conway and he kept the Castle well informed of the activities of the brothers while passing himself off as an enthusiastic supporter. He gets the bronze medal.

While busying themselves in Cork, the brothers were also part of the Dublin Society of the United Irishmen. Enter spy number two. Here their nemesis was Thomas Collins, another apparent republican fanatic but, in reality, a well-embedded British spy. Because he ratted on so many other prominent revolutionaries as well as the brothers, he gets the silver medal.

Enter spy number three, where the gold unquestionably goes to Captain Warnesford Armstrong. You'd think his name would have given him away. How could you be called Warnesford and *not* be a British spy? After the capture of most of the members of the United Irishmen's Directory (note the French influence) in March 1798, John Sheares took over the leadership and ordained the date of 23 May for a nationwide uprising. Armstrong insinuated himself into the confidence of the brothers, to the point where he was a regular visitor to their house on Baggot Street and dandled the children of Henry Sheares on his treacherous knee. He recorded that he did not even have to take an oath in order to become a member of the United Irishman. Not that he would have let something as silly as an oath get in the way. John Sheares himself actually warned Armstrong not to come to the house on one occasion as certain activists believed him to be in the act of betraying the movement and were intent on murdering him!

Two days before the planned rising, John and Henry Sheares were arrested on information supplied by Armstrong, and put on trial. Armstrong himself, clearly pleased at his handiwork, testified against them. Despite being defended by the great advocate John Philpot Curran, it took the jury a mere seventeen minutes to convict them.

John and Henry Sheares, victims of three separate informers, were hanged, drawn and quartered, two hundred and nineteen years ago, on this day.

Broadcast 14 July 2017

29 July 1848

The Young Ireland Rebellion

It doesn't augur well if you can isolate a rebellion to a particular day. Irish rebellions were never all that successful militarily – though most added to the sum of Irish recalcitrance – but the Young Ireland Rebellion in 1848 was probably the least effective of the lot if you look at it purely from a military point of view. But only if you adopt such a blinkered perspective.

Not only was it restricted to a single day, but it can also be said to have occurred in a single place, Ballingarry in Co. Tipperary. Furthermore, it was limited to one location within Ballingarry, a building outside the town belonging to one Margaret McCormack – hence the disdainful description of the rebellion as 'The Battle of the Widow McCormack's Cabbage Patch'.

The plain facts are easily related. The year, 1848, had already seen a number of revolutions across Europe, including the declaration of the Second Republic in France. With Ireland still traumatised by the effects of the Great Famine, it was the best of times and the worst of times to take military action against British rule. The Young Ireland movement, consisting largely of intellectuals and romantic idealists, had become radicalized after its split with Daniel O'Connell and the evidence of British neglect and misrule associated with the Famine. Revolutionary France, where the rule of King Louis Phillipe had been brought to an end, became the inspiration for the republicanism of leaders like John Blake Dillon, Thomas Francis Meagher and William Smith O'Brien. Their hope was to emulate many of the political *coups* in Europe and stage a bloodless rebellion.

Rising tensions persuaded the British Government to take the sort of action it often took in the nineteenth century, when it suspended *habeas corpus* and began to arrest the leadership of the Young Ireland movement. Meagher, O'Brien and Dillon now had little to lose, and began to raise a military force to oppose arrest without trial. On 29 July 1848 they found themselves in Tipperary at the head of a small force. A detachment of the Irish Constabulary (it didn't become the Royal Irish Constabulary until 1867) was sent to arrest the leaders of this attempted *coup*. However, finding itself outnumbered, the forty-six-strong force under Sub-Inspector Trant occupied Margaret McCormack's house and courageously took her five children as hostages.

O'Brien attempted to negotiate the release of the children but was instead fired upon from inside the building by the upholders of law and order. The rebels responded in kind. O'Brien had to be dragged away from the line of fire by James Stephens and Terence Bellew McManus, both of whom were hit in the rescue attempt. The shooting went on for a number of hours before the arrival of police reinforcements caused the withdrawal of the Young Irelanders and the collapse of what can only be described as a rebellion by stretching credibility well beyond snapping point.

The aftermath is far more interesting than the fracas itself. The British, who already had one of the leading Young Irelanders, John Mitchel, under lock and key, introduced new legislation, creating the crime of treason-felony. This enabled them to transport to Australia the leaders of the rebellion rather than hang, draw and quarter them, the vile punishment still on offer for the more serious charge of treason.

The transportees – who were mostly sent to Tasmania – read like a 'Who's Who' of nineteenth-century Irish history and rebellion. Mitchel and Meagher both managed spectacular escapes from captivity in Australia and went on to take opposite sides during the American Civil War. Stephens, John O'Mahony and Michael Doheny escaped to France and became the inspiration or the organizational muscle of the Irish Repubican Brotherhood – ultimately responsible for the 1916 Rising. The funeral of Terence Bellew McManus, who died in poverty in San Francisco, acted as a prelude to the abortive Fenian Rising in 1867, after which the constabulary got its 'Royal' prefix. Another lesser light, Thomas d'Arcy McGee, escaped to the US and became one of the founders of modern Canada before being assassinated by a Fenian sympathizer in 1868. So, when you think about the long-term impact of the Young Ireland movement, it is safe to ignore the skirmish in Ballingarry.

The Widow McCormack got her five children back intact – no thanks to the constabulary – and they all later emigrated to the US. Her cottage is still preserved as a national monument.

The Tussle in Tipperary, which constituted the sum total of the military side of the Young Ireland rebellion, took place, one hundred and sixty-eight years ago, on this day.

Broadcast 29 July 2016

21 July 1860

The birth of Chauncey Olcott

CUE MUSIC: 'When Irish Eyes Are Smiling'.

Go on, admit it. It's so grating it brings you out in lumps, not even one of which is located in your throat. It's the most annoying Irish song ever written, right? Or is it? Maybe you love it passionately and can always be prevailed upon to trot it out when requested to do so at birthday parties, and at Christmas after far too much sherry or single malt has been consumed. Maybe you want to tear someone else's hair out – probably the singer – the moment you hear the first notes of the chorus. But one thing is certain, 'When Irish Eyes Are Smiling' is not Irish. At best, it is one sixth Irish, as the mother of one of the three composers was born in Cork.

That was Chauncey Olcott – a good Irish name, I'm sure you'd agree. Actually, that was only a stage name. 'Twas far from Chauncey Olcott he was reared. He was born John Chancellor Brannigan in 1858, in upstate New York. His mother was Margaret Doyle.

But that's not quite as Irish as it gets. Olcott was a graduate of the nineteenth-century minstrel shows, when singers and dancers – many of them Irish – blacked up and performed. Today it seems bizarre, patronising and racist, but even the BBC carried on the practice into the 1970s with the ghastly *Black and White Minstrel Show*. It wasn't taken off the air until 1978, after running for twenty years.

By 1893 Olcott had been liberated from minstrelsy and was a star on Broadway, specialising in nostalgic comic operas on Irish exile. He realised that there was gold in them there faraway Hibernian Hills and, in addition to performing, he began to write the scripts himself. Between 1897 and 1902 he penned *Sweet Inniscarra* (1897), *Garret O'Magh* (1901), *Old Limerick Town* (1902) and *A Romance of Athlone* (1905). And the Irish-Americans of New York lapped it up.

But he really surpassed himself when he got together with a fellow lyricist, George Graff Junior, and an accomplished composer of catchy melodies, Ernest Ball. Let's be clear about their origins, just in case. Ball was from Cleveland and became famous when he composed the music for lyrics written by the famous Mayor of New York, 'Dapper' Jimmy Walker. The song was called 'Will You Love Me in December as You Do in May?' Clearly it was a question intended for the New York electorate.

George Graff Junior, like Ball, had not a single drop of Irish blood coursing through his veins. But boy, could he fake it!

'When Irish Eyes Are Smiling' first appeared in one of their collaborations, the musical comedy *The Isle O'Dreams*, first produced on Broadway in 1913. The 'O' and the apostrophe are vitally important to the entire enterprise. The three also collaborated on the classic 'Mother Machree' – no, it's not Irish either – which was first heard in the ageless musical *Barry of Ballymore* (1911), which I'm sure you're familiar with. Olcott himself is also solely responsible for the creation of the enduring ditty 'My Wild Irish Rose'. You thought that one was Irish too? Sorry! When it comes to gloriously Irish kitsch, always remember, the Americans got there long before we did.

There was a Hollywood film, *My Wild Irish Rose*, made about Olcott's life in 1947, fifteen years after his death. In

1970 he was inducted into the Songwriters Hall of Fame, bless his wild Irish heart.

Chauncey Olcott, aka John Brannigan from Buffalo, New York, who made a fortune from playing 'Irish', was born, one hundred and fifty-nine years ago, on this day.

Broadcast 21 July 2017

15 July 1865

Lord Northcliffe is born in Chapelizod

Behind every great newspaper there is, of course, a proprietor – great or otherwise. These days, while few could name the editor of the *Sun* or the *Times*, most could hazard a guess at the owner. A clue, he's just married Jerry Hall. If you said Rupert Murdoch, go to the top of the class.

Murdoch is only the latest incarnation of the media mogul – in fact his father was one too. He is successor to a tradition that includes Lord Northcliffe, founder of the *Daily Mail* in 1896. The *Daily Mail* was the first, British, mass-circulation daily newspaper, all the more accessible because it sold for a halfpenny, and its content was simple, short and readable – not something that was always true of its rivals. Its sales grew to over a million a day in 1899.

Northcliffe was born Alfred Charles William Harmsworth – a good surname for a newspaper owner – in the Dublin suburb of Chapelizod in 1865. His younger brother Cecil, later Lord Rothermere, also became a newspaper magnate. Big brother Alfred sold him the *Daily Mirror* in 1913.

Northcliffe went on to acquire the *Observer* in 1905 and the *Times* in 1908, the same year he bought the *Sunday Times*. Within less than a decade he had raised the circulation of the *Times* from forty thousand to two hundred and eighty thousand. His obsession with automobiles led him to ban the reporting of car accidents in the *Mail* – a minor but interesting example of the power he yielded,

While he was a man of influence from the end of the nineteenth century, he came into his own during the Great War. In terms of his political interference, he makes Rupert Murdoch look like an affable country squire with despotic control of the village newspaper.

He was instrumental in bringing down the Liberal Government of Herbert Asquith in 1916, and having Lloyd George installed as prime minister. The two men later fell out when the Welsh Wizard refused to accept a list of cabinet members from Northcliffe for his first post-war government.

He reinforced Lord Kitchener's (Secretary of State for War) loathing of newspapers and journalists with another, not entirely undeserved, press campaign. Having been partly responsible for the appointment of Kitchener in the first place, Northcliffe turned on him over the shortage of shells for the Western Front in 1915. The attacks on the beloved Kitchener were not popular, and the daily circulation of the *Mail* alone briefly dropped from over one million to less than three hundred thousand. After Kitchener obligingly drowned in June 1916, the *Mail* was slowly able to exit the doghouse.

It was the anti-German invective of the *Mail* in the run up to the war that helped create the climate for British entry into the conflict. Later, such was the virulence of Northcliffe's anti-German propaganda that the German Navy did him the signal honour of sending a warship to assassinate him by shelling his home on the Kent coast. They only managed to kill the unfortunate wife of his gardener.

Winston Churchill, though hardly an entirely objective source, wrote of Northcliffe that he 'wielded power without official responsibility … and disturbed the fortunes of national leaders without being willing to bear their burdens'. Lloyd George had offered Northcliffe a cabinet position in 1916, but he declined. The new prime minister had decided it was better to have Northcliffe inside the tent urinating outwards. The proprietor of the *Mail* and the *Times* opted to continue to pee wherever he saw fit.

Northcliffe did, however, choose to bear some of the burden of political responsibility. He accepted the role of director of propaganda in the Ministry of Information in March 1918. He was responsible for dropping four million leaflets behind German lines before the end of the war in November. When he died in 1922, he bequeathed three month's salary to each of his six thousand employees.

Alfred Harmsworth, Lord Northcliffe, newspaper magnate, ruthless power broker, scourge of governments, and a mass of contradictions, was born, one hundred and fifty-one years ago, on this day.

Broadcast 15 July 2016

8 July 1889

The last official bare-knuckle title fight ever held

In 1867 the Marquis of Queensberry – nemesis of Oscar Wilde – formulated a set of rules for the sport of boxing. Well, actually he didn't. The rules were compiled two years earlier by a young Welsh sportsman named John Graham Chambers, but when they were published in 1867 they bore the name of the Ninth Marquis of Queensberry, John Douglas. But that's a whole other story.

One of the fundamental requirements of the new regulations governing boxing was that all fighters, amateur and professional, should wear gloves. Prior to the intervention of Chambers (or Queensberry, if you'd prefer), boxing was a bare-knuckle sport, operated under what were known as the London Prize Ring Rules.

Many of the best bare-knuckle fighters, particularly in the heavier divisions, were Irish or Irish-American. Probably the greatest boxer to have fought under both sets of rules was John Lawrence Sullivan, Boston-born son of Michael Sullivan from Abbeydorney, Co. Kerry and Catherine Kelly from Athlone, Co. Westmeath. John L. Sullivan, born in 1858, won over four hundred and fifty fights, most of them exhibitions in which he challenged all-comers.

No formal boxing titles existed until the 1880s, so the defeat by Sullivan of Paddy Ryan from Co. Tipperary in 1882 in a bare-knuckle contest may or may not have seen Ryan surrender the Heavyweight Championship of the World to his young opponent. The fight was supposed to take place in New Orleans, with both sides putting up two thousand five hundred dollars as stake money. It went ahead despite the best efforts of the municipal authorities to prevent it, but it had to be moved to Mississippi first.

Seven years later Sullivan defended his crown in what is definitely seen as a title fight, and was the last to take place under London Prize Ring bare-knuckle Rules. The champion faced yet another Irish-American challenger, New Yorker Jake Kilrain, in what was actually only Sullivan's third, and last, bare-knuckle fight. Sullivan had also been boxing since 1880 under the Queensberry Rules. The champion trained for the fight in Belfast – Belfast, New York. His regime included a number of alcoholic binges and his trainer, the famous wrestler Billy Muldoon, was frequently required to extract his charge from New York bars.

The prelude to the fight received extensive newspaper coverage, even though no one knew where it was going to take place. New Orleans was, once again, the venue of choice, but the governor of Louisiana was very much against the bout taking place in his state, to the extent that he used militia troops to keep the boxers out. The fight eventually went ahead in Richburg, Mississippi in front of three thousand spectators. The timekeeper for the bout was the celebrated lawman of the American 'Wild West', Bat Masterson.

There were rumours before the fight that Sullivan had let himself go, but when he stripped off there was no evidence of that; he looked to be in superb condition. The fight began at 10:30 p.m. and lasted seventy-five rounds. In round forty-five, Sullivan, after a blow to the stomach, threw up in the ring and looked to be quite vulnerable. But it was Kilrain who finally succumbed in the seventy-fifth round when his second threw in the towel, despite the fighter's protests.

Sullivan only defended his title once – this time wearing gloves – in 1892 against yet another Irish-American, James 'Gentleman Jim' Corbett from San Francisco. He lost. It was his only official professional defeat in forty-four bouts. A convert to prohibition in later life, Sullivan, despite his enormous celebrity, died in poverty in 1918, aged only fifty-nine. Jake Kilrain served as a pall-bearer at his funeral.

John L. Sullivan won the last Heavyweight Championship boxing title fought under bare-knuckle rules, one hundred and twenty-seven years ago, on this day.

Broadcast 8 July 2016

1 July 1916

The 36th Ulster Division on the first day of the Somme offensive

It has been said of the Battle of the Somme that it was won and lost in a matter of seconds. This represented the difference between the time it took for British troops to get across no man's land, through ranks of barbed wire, and onto the German trenches, as against the amount of time it took German machine gunners to get from their deep concrete bunkers to their firing positions. The race began after the end of the five-day British bombardment that was supposed to have destroyed the German front-line trenches and/or filleted their barbed-wire defences. Of course, it did neither. The shells were often of the wrong type, or were duds. Furthermore, the German positions were rather better fortified than the British generals had expected. And the machine gunners had no difficulty in picking out their targets – it was 7:30 in the morning, broad daylight.

None of which mattered all that much to the 36th Ulster Division as they waited for the end of the massive artillery bombardment and the beginning of the greatest offensive in British military history. Many of the men from working-class Belfast, or from the farms of Counties Antrim, Tyrone and Fermanagh, were not actually in their trenches. They were already in no man's land, creeping forward cautiously while watching the shells fall on the formidable Schwaben Redoubt, one of their primary targets.

An inspired order from Major General Sir Oliver Nugent, the commander of the 36th Ulster Division – consisting largely of loyalists who had sworn allegiance to their province by signing the Ulster Covenant in 1912 – meant that his troops were instructed not to wait for the official signal to go 'over the top'. They were to steal a march on the Germans, and on the British divisions on either side of them, and creep into no man's land early. It was both their apotheosis and their undoing.

The Ulsters were one of the few British Army units to achieve their objective that day. They got to the German trenches before the machine guns could open up on their ranks and mow them down, as happened almost everywhere else along the British front lines.

But their success was short-lived. Such were the catastrophic losses incurred by the first British assault forces that the 36th Division was left completely exposed. The divisions on either side were back in their trenches counting their dead while the Ulsters tried to hold on to their gains. German reinforcements and German guns had little else to fire at, so the 36th was the focus of the counter-attack in the Thiepval area.

The newspaper coverage of that day, had it not been tragically inaccurate and utterly dishonest, would almost have been amusing. The doyen of the British press in khaki was William Beach Thomas. His account of the first day of the Somme included this piece of heavenly prose:

> The very attitudes of the dead, fallen eagerly forward, have a look of expectant hope. You would say that they died with the light of victory in their eyes.

The light in their eyes was far more likely to have been the earnest desire to meet in the next life the men who had planned the campaign and ushered them to their violent deaths, while *they* observed proceedings, on paper, from well behind the lines.

The 36th Ulster division won four Victoria Crosses that day. It probably would have been more but for the mortality rate amongst officers whose job it was to document the acts of courage. It was miserable compensation for their losses. Of the twenty-thousand British dead, on the most disastrous day in their army's history, the 36th Ulster Division supplied more than two thousand. Another three thousand Ulstermen were wounded or taken prisoner. Writer Sam McAughtry later described regularly seeing many of these men around his native Tiger's Bay in east Belfast, cripples, shadows, wrecks and wraiths. Southern playwright Frank McGuinness paid tribute to them in his greatest play, *Observe the Sons of Ulster Marching Towards the Somme* (1986).

The 36th Ulster Division were beaten and broken by German bombs and bullets, and by the military incompetence of their own side, one hundred years ago, on this day.

Broadcast 1 July 2016

7 July 1930

The death of Sir Arthur Conan Doyle

He is such a quintessentially English writer that it is still something of a surprise to discover that he was actually born in Scotland to an Irish mother, and with a paternal Irish grandfather. Though he himself was a master of the written word, he came from a long line of cartoonists. He was the nephew of the famous *Punch* magazine illustrator Richard 'Dickie' Doyle, and another uncle, Henry, became director of the National Gallery of Ireland. As a writer, he preferred his own historical novels, but nobody really cares for them that much, and today even fans of his work would find it difficult to name a single one of them.

That's because, in 1886, he created the immortal detective Sherlock Holmes. The first appearance of the master-sleuth and his affable but somewhat dim-witted companion and chronicler, Dr John Watson, netted Arthur Conan Doyle the not terribly princely sum of twenty-five pounds, though it was probably the best twenty-five quid the publishing company Ward Lock & Co. ever spent. *A Study in Scarlet* (1886) united the two heroes of Doyle's most enduring fictions. Subsequent stories, like *The Sign of Four* (1890), *The Hound of the Baskervilles* (1902) and *The Valley of Fear* (1915) made him the best-paid author of his day. By *that* time, Watson's old war wound, incurred in the Afghan war, had migrated from his arm to his leg.

Within five years Doyle was already profoundly sick of his creation. In 1891 he wrote to his mother, 'I think of slaying Holmes … and winding him up for good and all. He takes my mind from better things'. His anguished mother wrote back, 'You won't! You can't! You mustn't!' He didn't! She was, after all, an Irish mammy who must be obeyed in all things.

But two years later he defied even his poor Irish mother by having the cleverest Kerryman ever invented, Professor James Moriarty, toss Holmes over the Reichenbach Falls. 'Good riddance,' said Doyle, 'time to get back to the character who will really establish my reputation, Brigadier Gerard.' Sadly, it wasn't to be, and today few people would even remember the estimable French Brigadier had a rather decent thoroughbred racehorse from the 1970s not been named after him.

After killing off his supersleuth, Doyle had to endure the opprobrium normally reserved for figures like Rasputin, Kaiser Wilhelm and Dr Hawley Crippen, the infamous wife-killer. Reaction to the demise of Holmes was a bit over the top, apparently extending as far as death threats. But ever the stoic, Doyle resisted all temptation for a Holmesian return. However, if the Stone Roses can make a comeback, so could Sherlock, and in 1901 Doyle reintroduced him in a pre-Moriarty novel, the gothic *Hound of the Baskervilles*. This was a prelude to bringing him back to life in a new series of stories in 1903. Mammy Doyle was beside herself.

In addition to his novels and short stories, Doyle was, of course, a medical doctor. He was also a failed politician, a Liberal Unionist – a fancy name for a Tory. Not even the creator of Sherlock Holmes could get elected in the two Scottish constituencies in which he stood in 1900 and 1906. He was also an accomplished sportsman, playing soccer for Portsmouth and cricket for the MCC (Marylebone Cricket Club).

Doyle was also a noted mystic and spiritualist, whose unfortunate gullibility led him to accept the bona fides of one Elsie Wright in 1917 when, as a sixteen-year-old, she took an infamous photograph of her nine-year-old cousin Frances Griffiths with four alleged fairies. In the ensuing controversy surrounding the so-called Cottingley fairies, Doyle came down emphatically on the side of fairy-ness. He chose to believe that Elsie had managed to do what no one else had ever done before: to catch those shy and elusive creatures on camera. He was more than fifty years dead before Elsie admitted in the 1980s that it was all a hoax and that the fairies were cardboard cut-outs.

By the way, 'Conan' was his middle name, not part of a compound surname. His knighthood went to plain 'Arthur Doyle', though the man himself had begun to add the second barrel to his surname at an early age.

There is a commemorative statue in Edinburgh outside the location of the house – long since demolished – in which he was born. It is of Sherlock Holmes. Doyle would have loved that!

Sir Arthur Conan Doyle, creator of the immortal Brigadier Gerard, and the barely remembered Sherlock Holmes, died, eighty-seven years ago, on this day.

Broadcast 7 July 2017

22 July 1935

William Mulholland dies in Los Angeles

He is one of the two Irishmen who made an incalculable contribution to the economic development of modern California by bringing water to one of its largest cities. While Kerryman Michael O'Shaughnessy did not endear himself to environmentalists by flooding a beautiful valley in Yosemite National Park to create a water supply for San Francisco, he was a mere also-ran when his unpopularity was set against that of his compatriot William Mulholland.

If you are a fan of the Roman Polanski film *Chinatown* (1974) then you will already know something about Mulholland. Elements of his story and personality are depicted in the film.

Born in Belfast in 1855 and brought up in Dublin, he left home at the age of fifteen and joined the merchant navy. He then decided to try and earn a living in the US instead of at sea. In 1877 he headed west, and the following year arrived in the city that was to be his home for most of the next six decades, Los Angeles.

At that time it was a relatively small and insignificant town, a far cry from San Francisco in terms of size, importance and future prospects. Mulholland's first job was working ditches for a private water company. But he was ambitious, and began to educate himself. Eight years later he was a qualified engineer, and when the LA city authorities took over the company for which he worked, he suddenly became head of something called the Department of Water and Power.

Today the city is an economic giant, but in the late nineteenth century, Los Angeles did not have much to brag about. And it was going nowhere either, not without a sustainable water supply. Mulholland earned the undying gratitude of Angelenos by bringing water to the city, and the unnerving animosity of the population of the Owens Valley in Northern California by stealing it from them.

The Owens River Valley was populated by farmers and orange growers dependent on an irrigation scheme that never happened. By 1905, thanks to a combination of legal land purchases, bribery and political corruption, Mulholland managed to accumulate enough land in the valley to start diverting water from the Owens River to Los Angeles. This is where fiction catches up with reality and *Chinatown* comes true. Mulholland and his cronies had been buying up the waterless San Fernando Valley in LA County. The plan was to divert much of the Owens River water into the 'valley' and make a lot of the new landowners rich in the process.

Mulholland's great achievement was the building of the Los Angeles aqueduct across two hundred miles of arid desert and high mountain. This allowed LA to shrug off the straitjacket of permanent drought, but left the citizens of the Owens Valley angry and extremely hostile to the project. In 1924 they sabotaged the aqueduct repeatedly in what became known as the Owens Valley War. Mulholland expressed wry regret at the devastation of their orange plantations because, as he put it, 'now there are no longer enough trees to hang all the troublemakers who live there'. But he got the water to LA and had a twenty-one-mile highway named after him.

Mulholland didn't have long to enjoy his success, however. On 12 March 1928 he signed off on the St Francis dam, a storage reservoir for the city. Twelve hours later the structure collapsed, releasing fifteen billion gallons of water into Ventura County and killing more than five hundred people. Mulholland had supervised the building of the dam and was blamed for the disaster by an official inquiry. He had apparently chosen to ignore indications that the dam was leaking. He hung on for just over a year before retiring from his position.

William Mulholland, the man who provoked the California water wars and an un-rehabilitated recluse, died, eighty-one years ago, on this day.

Broadcast 22 July 2016

August

"Don't worry Aoife. It'll be fine"

25 August 1170

Richard de Clare (Strongbow) marries Aoife MacMurrough

Irish-Welsh relations have been generally positive over the years. They are, after all, fellow Celts with their own language – though they've taken better care of theirs than we have of ours. Granted, they have beaten us at rugby on more occasions than is healthy, but they did give us St Patrick. Or rather, we took him as a slave.

However, they also gave us Gerald of Wales, a writer who didn't like us very much, and Richard de Clare, better known as Strongbow, who led the Norman conquest of the country from his Welsh base in Pembrokeshire. (That's where the Fishguard and Pembroke ferries land in case you were hazy on Welsh geography).

Gerald, or to give him his posh Latin name, Giraldus Cambrensis, was writing about Ireland roughly twenty years after the arrival of the Normans. In his *Topographica Hibernica* (1188) (that's us by the way – Hibernica), one of his jobs was to convey the impression that the Normans had done the Irish a great favour by invading and taking much of their lands. And he did an excellent job. This is what he said about us:

This people then, is truly barbarous, being not only barbarous in their dress but suffering their hair and

beards to grow enormously in an uncouth manner ...
they learn nothing and practise nothing but the barbarism in which they are born and bred and which
sticks to them like a second nature. Whatever natural
gifts they possess are excellent, in whatever requires
industry they are worthless.

Clearly we were a people who badly needed a lesson in
civilisation from the Normans, followed by a good shave.
The story of that first Welsh incursion is, like so many Irish
stories over the years, one of rank baseness and supreme
treachery. Where, after all, would we be without rampant
treachery?

In 1167 Diarmaid Mac Murchada – may his name
live in infamy – lost his kingdom of Leinster to the High
King Ruaidri Ua Conchobair. In order to get it back, Mac
Murchada travelled to France – as you would – to seek the aid
of the King of England, Henry II, who was actually French.
The visit was quite convenient for Henry who, in 1155,
had been told by Pope Adrian IV in Rome, who happened
to be an Englishman – stay with me now, all will become
clear – that he was entitled to invade and conquer Ireland
whenever he felt up to it. Pope Adrian had issued a Papal
Bull called *Laudabiliter* with words to that effect. However,
no one has ever been able to find a copy of this gift to the
King of England. I'm sure someone just borrowed it from
the Vatican library and forgot to give it back. It is bound to
turn up, justify seven hundred years of domination and incur
a hefty fine.

When approached, Henry had no time to worry about
Diarmaid's minor difficulties, but he did give permission for
him to negotiate with some of his British subjects with a
view to getting up a mercenary army. Henry did emphasise,

however, that if they won a lot of land they were doing it in the name of the king. If they lost, well that was their problem.

Mac Murchada's main ally, and the leader of the WEF (that stands for Welsh Expeditionary Force – which is something I just made up), was Richard de Clare, Earl of Pembrokeshire, nicknamed Strongbow. Were he to use the name today he would be liable for a lawsuit by a certain alcoholic drinks company for breach of copyright. In return, Mac Murchada – may he burn in hell – promised Strongbow lots of land. At the time, this land belonged to his enemies. Diarmaid also promised the hand of his daughter Aoife in marriage. The nuptials took place in Waterford a year after the successful Norman invasion.

The nineteenth-century Irish painter Daniel Maclise was so enamoured of the subject of the marriage that he painted it twice with slight variations, once in oils, followed by a smaller watercolour version in 1854. It adorns a lot of wall space in the National Gallery.

Strongbow only lived to enjoy his gains until his death in 1176. Aoife, however, was certainly still alive in 1188, the year Gerald of Wales published his diatribe against hairy Irishmen with uncouth beards.

The two politically united lovers married so that Strongbow could inherit the estates of Diarmaid Mac Murchada – may he never rest in peace – eight hundred and forty-seven years ago, on this day.

Broadcast 25 August 2017

18 August 1504

The Battle of Knockdoe

I'll start with a question. What was the biggest battle ever fought in Ireland between two warring Irish sides, as opposed to the many involving British or English forces? And the bi-annual clashes between the Munster and Leinster rugby teams don't count.

It can't be the Battle of the Boyne, fought in 1690, or the Battle of Aughrim, which took place the following year. Although both were huge set-pieces, they involved soldiers from all over Europe, though mostly from Ireland, England or the Netherlands. The same is true of the 1798 Rebellion. There were a number of major battles, but none that didn't involve British or French troops.

It's not that the field is narrow; let's face it, the Irish, like everyone else, had been knocking lumps out of each other for centuries before the Normans arrived and started to do it for us.

The answer is the Battle of Knockdoe, fought in 1504. And I'd never heard of it either. Knockdoe is in the parish of Lackagh. That probably doesn't help very much. Lackagh is about half way between Galway and Tuam. So, that fixes the location. Now, what was it all about? It concerned the bad blood between the Burkes and the Fitzgeralds.

The Burke in question was Ulick Burke, descended from a great Norman family, the de Burgos. He was one of the Burkes of Clanricarde, who owned much of Galway. This branch of the Burkes included some of the worst landlords in a long and often repulsive history of Irish landowning. The Burkes of Clanricarde should be distinguished from their cousins, the Burkes of Mayo, a family who gave us, among others, President Mary Robinson. They could have done with her diplomatic skills back in the sixteenth century.

The Fitzgerald was just that. THE Fitzgerald. Gerald Fitzgerald, Eighth Earl of Kildare, the King's deputy, and the most powerful man in Ireland. An illustration of how far the Francophone Normans had come since 1169 is that Fitzgerald was universally known as Garret Mór (the Great) and Burke was Ulick Fionn (the Fair) – thoroughly Gaelicised, with not much of the original French left.

Ulick was very ambitious. Maybe he was tired of being Ulick Fionn, and he wanted to be Ulick Mór. He cherished dreams to be the sole overlord of Connacht, and made it clear that he expected subservience from his Mayo cousins, who were never going to bow their heads to a Galwayman. To forestall a civil war, Gerald Fitzgerald did what you did in those days to placate a stroppy minor potentate: you either put manners on him in battle, or you gave him a spare daughter in marriage. Gerald, initially, opted for the latter course.

But that didn't do the trick and fighting broke out anyway. The Mayo Burkes threw in their lot with Big Fitz, as did Red Hugh O'Donnell and Art O'Neill. Burke managed to attract vital support from the O'Briens of Munster. So, it was all a bit 'Pro-12'. The sides met at Knockdoe. They were said to have numbered more than ten thousand men, many of them mercenaries or *gall óglaigh* (literally 'foreign volunteers') who were being well paid for their participation. At the end of a busy day of slaughter more than two thousand were dead and Ulick

Burke had been routed. The high fatality rate is thought to be due to the use of firearms, one of the first times they were used on an Irish battlefield.

There is a poem about the battle that begins:

Loud blares the trumpet, the field is set.
Loud blares the trumpet, the foe men are met.
Steep slopes the hill, at Knockdoe in the West.

It is supposed to have been found in the pocket of a dead soldier. If that's true, you have to think that he would have been far better off paying more attention to the fighting. It's not much of a poem, and he might have survived.

The opposing sides assembled for what would become the largest battle fought between rival Irish forces, five hundred and thirteen years ago, on this day.

Broadcast 18 August 2017

4 August 1654

The 'South Sea Bubble'

You might well ask what the insitution of 'The Governor and Company of the merchants of Great Britain, trading to the South Seas and other parts of America, and for the encouragement of fishing' has to do with Ireland. Quite a lot really, as a number of Irish fingers were burned by its activities, and an Irishman was left to clear up the mess. Noël Coward also wrote a play about it but, sensibly, didn't call it, 'The Governor and Company of the merchants of Great Britain, trading to the South Seas and other parts of America, and for the encouragement of fishing', or it might have been even less successful than it actually was. It ran on the West End for two-hundred and seventy-six performances, making Coward the only one to have profited from the enterprise.

The shorter and more familiar title of the institution in question was The South Sea Company, incorporated in 1711, whose activities, founded as they were on fraud, corruption and deceit, led to the infamous 'South Sea Bubble' in 1720. It was an early example of a venture that gets a lot of encouragement from governments today: a public/private partnership. The object was to reduce Britain's national debt, mainly incurred in fighting wars that accrued only to the advantage of the British aristocracy.

It all began at the turn of the eighteenth century when the Tories of the British Government did not want to be beholden to the Bank of England any longer. The 'Old Lady of Threadneedle Street' – the pet name for the bank – was a young maiden at the time. It was a privately run Whiggish financial institution which raised loans so that England could carry on its many foreign wars.

The South Sea Company was established to negotiate and trade in debt, which it would then hand over to the Government. It was also given a monopoly of English commerce with South America. But as the continent was almost entirely run by Spain at the time, that was a bit like being offered an exclusive cartel arrangement to trade with Mars.

Some benefit did accrue to the company when it secured a contract to supply certain goods to Spanish South America for thirty years. The goods in question? Five thousand African slaves per annum at a tenner a slave. But the South Sea Company was unable to make a profit even on this dubious transaction.

The infamous 'bubble' began in 1720 with the kind of hype and Chinese whispers with which we have become overly familiar in our own time. Based on nothing other than rumour, the share price of the company rose from one hundred and twenty-eight pounds in January to just over one thousand by the end of June. During that period the Government passed the 'Bubble Act' – designed to prevent just such unsustainable growth. The South Sea Company actually helped promote the legislation. And then proceeded to burst.

The share price rapidly plummeted right back to where it had started, taking a lot of hapless investors with it. One of them was the great scientist Sir Isaac Newton, who reportedly lost twenty thousand pounds.

Enter the Irishman: Thomas Brodrick, born in Midleton, Co. Cork, was a politician who sat in both the Irish and

British Houses of Commons. In 1720 he was MP for the English constituency of Stockbridge. Brodrick was a notoriously anti-clerical figure of whom Jonathan Swift, himself a celebrated cleric, wrote in 1709, 'you have him now in England, I wish you would keep him there'.

It fell to Brodrick to conduct an investigation into the causes of the share price collapse. What he discovered was unedifying. The corruption went as far as the Chancellor of the Exchequer. Thousands of pounds had been paid out in bribes to politicians. The share price had been manipulated by directors of the company who had used agents to buy at high prices to prevent the collapse. Any of this ring a bell? Probably. But what happened after Brodrick's investigation might sound less familiar.

The directors of the company were forced to hand out thousands of pounds in compensation to the victims of the fraud. Various public officials were impeached. The Chancellor of the Exchequer, John Aislabie, was jailed for corruption and financial irregularities.

Thomas Brodrick, the one-man Public Accounts Committee, was born, three hundred and sixty-three years ago, on this day.

Broadcast 4 August 2017

26 August 1725

Smallpox – the first inoculations are administered

Its effects were feared for centuries before it was finally declared to have been eradicated by the World Health Organisation in 1980. The last recorded case of this dreadful disease was in Somalia in 1977. Good riddance to it, because it plagued this country for generations.

Ireland has more than a nodding acquaintance with smallpox. It originally got its name in the fifteenth century, to distinguish it from 'great pox', aka syphilis. Around one third of the victims of smallpox died. Many survivors were left with the scars of the disease in the form of permanently pockmarked skin. As recently as half a century ago, in 1967, two million people died of smallpox worldwide.

The disease inspired particular dread in Ireland, where smallpox and its ugly sisters, cholera, typhoid and dysentery, made themselves at home for hundreds of years and exploited extreme poverty and ignorance to devastating effect. The symptoms of the disease were blisters, high fever, headache and pain in the back and muscles. Children experienced vomiting and convulsions.

If you didn't die of smallpox in eighteenth- and nineteenth-century Ireland, you probably went blind. The next time you hear the music of the great harpist Turlough O'Carolan, from Nobber in Co. Meath, think of smallpox. It blinded him in

1688 when he was just eighteen, making him virtually useless for any occupation until he developed a talent as a harpist and a facility for musical composition. Many other itinerant harpists had been similarly afflicted.

The disease, which was highly contagious and infectious, is believed to have caused about one fifth of all deaths in the city of Dublin between 1661 and 1746. About a third of all child deaths were thought to be caused by smallpox. Although it mainly afflicted the poor, it was no respecter of rank. The children of the rich could die of the disease just as quickly as those closer to the breadline.

Hope emerged towards the beginning of the eighteenth century when the efficacy of inoculation became apparent. Inoculating people with small doses of the virus had been practiced in China since the tenth century, but didn't really begin to make inroads in Europe for another eight hundred years. In Ireland, the technique was first tried on a number of, presumably unwilling, prisoners in a Cork jail in 1721. Four years later the experiment was extended to five children in Dublin.

As the effectiveness became clear, the wealthy began to use inoculation to protect themselves and their children. During periodic epidemics, in the mid to late eighteenth centuries, the survival rate among the wealthy families who had engaged in the practice encouraged its more widespread use. The South Infirmary in Cork even initiated a programme to inoculate the poor.

Naturally, where there was money to be made, there were charlatans. Travelling inoculators with a very basic grasp, if any, of what they were doing, competed for trade. In Donegal in 1781 all but one child of a group of fifty-two died when one unqualified practitioner purported to inoculate them.

Whatever inroads were being made in Ireland against the disease came to virtually nothing with the onset of the Great Famine of the 1840s, when smallpox returned with a grim vengeance. Even for sufferers who survived, the recovery period of the disease ensured that many were pauperized and died anyway, with breadwinners unable to work.

It was only from the 1880s onwards that the disease began to be rapidly eradicated in Ireland. In the 1870s more than seven and a half thousand people died of smallpox. By the first decade of the twentieth century that figure was down to just sixty-five people. Between 1901 and 1910 almost a million Irish people were vaccinated against the disease.

A global campaign in 1967 by the World Health Organisationwas was successful, and now smallpox can only return via the insanity of chemical warfare.

Five Dublin children received the first voluntary smallpox innoculations in Ireland, two hundred and ninety-one years ago, on this day.

Broadcast 26 August 2016

12 August 1773

Robert King and the murder of Henry Fitzgerald

When the members of the Irish House of Lords tried a fellow peer, they did it in style. Such was the case with Robert King, tried for murder of Colonel Henry FitzGerald in 1798. His proper title was the 2nd Earl of Kingston, and he was tried for the killing of the nephew of his wife. King's son, also called Robert, was tried for the same offence.

King had married well. His wife, Caroline Fitzgerald, was one of the wealthiest heiresses in Ireland. She was married off to King in 1769, who was worth a few shillings in his own right, when they were both fifteen years old. They settled into the family home in Mitchelstown, Co. Cork. The couple was probably more distinguished for their choice of governess rather than for anything they ever accomplished themselves. Hired to educate their children was Mary Wollstonecraft, novelist, historian, eighteenth-century feminist and the mother of the woman who wrote *Frankenstein* (1818), Mary Shelley. Shelley would have found it difficult to devise the narrative that saw her employer and one of her pupils arraigned for murder.

The Kings accepted into their family a nephew of Caroline, one Henry FitzGerald, a child born out of wedlock. There were, indeed, rumours to the effect that Henry was not actually Caroline's nephew, but her illegitimate half-brother, the result of a liaison involving her own father.

Henry Fitzgerald, who went on to become a colonel in the military, rewarded the generosity of the King family by seducing one of Caroline's daughters – who may of course have been his half-niece. When Henry Fitzgerald's body was discovered and the truth of the seduction came to light, Robert King Junior and Senior were both charged with his murder.

King Senior, as a peer of the realm, faced his own peers in May 1798 in the Irish House of Lords, a building still intact today (now the Bank of Ireland on College Green in Dublin). The symbolism of the occasion, to paraphrase W. S. Gilbert, fitted the crime. During the trial an executioner stood beside King with an immense axe, painted black except for two inches of polished steel. This served to remind their Lordships of the fate the Earl of Kingston faced should they find him guilty. His actual fate would have been to be hanged by the neck until dead – only afterwards might his head have been separated from his body. However, it never came to that. No witnesses appeared for the prosecution, and King was acquitted. One can't help suspecting that while the Kings had actually done in, or murdered the bounder Henry, anyone who was anyone figured that he'd got what was coming to him. The aristocracy is another country; they do things differently there.

An interesting footnote: the United Irishmen had debated using the trial as an opportunity to kill key members of the Government. But the vote of one Francis Magan, a leading member of the organisation, caused the scheme to be abandoned. Magan, it later emerged, was a Government agent.

While Robert King Senior was tried in splendour by his peers, Robert King Junior was arraigned before the more mundane Cork Assizes on the same charge. Once again no witnesses came forward, so the future Viscount Lorton of Boyle, Co. Roscommon was duly acquitted. The magnificent Boyle Museum, King House, is named after the family.

The dramatic and colourful trial of Robert King, the 2nd Earl of Kingston took place, two hundred and eighteen years ago, on this day.

Broadcast 12 August 2016

11 August 1796

Kilmainham Gaol in Dublin receives its first prisoners

It is such a huge tourist attraction today that it's quite shocking to realise there were proposals as recently as the 1950s to demolish much of it. But Kilmainham Gaol survived intact to play a huge part in the current decade of centenaries.

It opened in 1796, and even then it was a grim place, housing men, women and children as young as twelve. Some were held there prior to transportation to Australia, others were lodged in the prison before their executions, and some served many years there in dreadful conditions, often sharing a cell with up to four others.

Almost every self-respecting nationalist, including some far removed from revolutionary politics, had a spell at their Majesties' pleasure in Kilmainham. A number did so prior to being hanged or shot. The list of some of the guests constitutes a distinguished club: Henry Joy McCracken, Oliver Bond, Napper Tandy, Robert Emmet, Michael Dwyer, William Smith O'Brien, Thomas Francis Meagher, Jeremiah O'Donovan Rossa, Charles Stewart Parnell and Michael Davitt.

Attached to the Gaol was a magistrates' court where cases would be despatched, or, if a serious crime was involved, the preliminary process leading to indictment would take place. It was here that the alleged killers of the Chief Secretary

Frederick Cavendish and his Under Secretary Thomas Henry Burke in Phoenix Park in 1882 appeared for remand hearings before being committed to Green Street Court for trial. And it was here that they first realised the game was up, when one of their number, James Carey, presented himself as a prosecution witness. He had opted to turn in evidence to save his own skin. His first appearance at Kilmainham Magistrates' Court was greeted with roars of rage from the dock. A reporter observed that one of the accused, Joe Brady:

> … glared at him and stretched forward towards him [had he] been able to reach him, I believe he would have been torn to pieces, for Brady was a powerful young fellow, and for the moment he was for all the world like a tiger on the spring.

The prisoners were returned to their cells and a few weeks later Carey's evidence sent five of them to the hangman, a seasoned veteran named William Marwood. His customary advice to his victims before they met their maker was, 'Now then, hold your head back and you'll die easy'. They were all executed in the Kilmainham prison-yard, and their bodies were interred under the scaffold erected to hang them.

Three decades later it was the turn of the leaders of the 1916 Rising. Fourteen were executed there over a nine-day period in May. The first to die, on 3 May, were Patrick Pearse, Thomas Clarke and Thomas MacDonagh. They faced firing squads of twelve British soldiers, mostly drawn from the Sherwood Foresters who had been badly mauled on Mount Street Bridge the previous week. There was little regard to sensitivities on either side. No Catholic priest was allowed to be present to minister to the prisoners, and the same firing squad – consisting mainly of young recruits – was expected to execute all three men. A number of female prisoners, including Countess Markievicz, were awoken by the volleys from the stone-breakers' yard.

The prison continued to be used during the Civil War. Around six hundred Republican prisoners were incarcerated there, many of them women. One of the last to be released was Eamon de Valera.

The prison was closed by the Free State Government in 1929 and might well have been demolished in the 1930s had it not been deemed too expensive to do so. The work of organisations like the Kilmainham Gaol Restoration Society ensured that it was eventually taken over by the Office of Public Works and became one of the most visited historical sites in Dublin.

It has also been a useful location for a number of films. These include the adaptation of Brendan Behan's prison drama, *The Quare Fellow* (1962), as well as the Michael Caine film *The Italian Job* (2003) and Neil Jordan's *Michael Collins* (1996). Collins himself was fortunate – he never actually served time there.

Kilmainham Gaol was finally completed and prepared to accept its first prisoners, two hundred and twenty-one years ago, on this day.

Broadcast 11 August 2017

19 August 1876

The *Catalpa* arrives back in the USA

Anyone who has ever had the pleasure of seeing Donal O'Kelly's memorable one-man show about the 1876 voyage of the whaling barque, the *Catalpa*, will be unlikely to forget the significance of that event. It was *The Great Escape* (1963) crossed with *Papillon* (1973), to create one of the most unorthodox and daring prison breaks in the history of incarceration.

The backstory begins with the abject failure of the Fenian Rebellion of 1867. In its wake, more than sixty IRB prisoners were transported, after treason-felony and rebellion convictions, to the penal colony in Western Australia. Over the years most of the prisoners were amnestied or released, so that by the mid 1870s only a small handful of Fenians remained in Freemantle Prison on the Australian west coast, not far from the city of Perth.

In 1873 one of the men who remained in jail, James Wilson, managed to get a letter to John Devoy of the Irish revolutionary organisation Clan na Gael, in New York. Wilson asked Devoy to launch an operation to free the remaining prisoners. It was a former Fenian transportee, Thomas McCarthy Fennell, who came up with the unorthodox but highly imaginative plan that was put into operation the following year.

The Clan bought a New Bedford whaling barque, the *Catalpa*, in 1874 for over five thousand dollars. A Captain George Smith Anthony agreed to help them. He recruited twenty-two sailors who were not in on the secret; the ship sailed from Massachusetts in April 1875. In the meantime, two senior members of the Clan, John Breslin and Tom Desmond, had been sent ahead to Australia to prepare for the rescue.

Breslin, posing as an American mining speculator, ingratiated himself with the British governor of the colony while Desmond secured transport for the prisoners and devised a means of cutting telegraph lines to impede communications.

A faulty chronometer meant that Captain Anthony had to use his own navigational skills for the first leg of the *Catalpa's* journey. The vessel also lost much of its crew when it landed in the Azores, but the deserters were replaced and the whaling ship finally arrived at the west coast of Australia in April 1876. There it dropped anchor in international waters and waited.

On 17 April six Fenian inmates, working outside the Freemantle prison walls, absconded from their work party. The group included James Wilson. They met up with Breslin and Desmond and were driven to reconnoitre with Captain Anthony. They were then taken on board a small whaleboat. At this point the alarm was raised by a local man, and the search for the escaped prisoners began in earnest. A storm initially prevented Anthony from transferring the freed Fenians from the small whaleboat to the *Catalpa*. It was hours before the storm abated and they could begin to row towards safety.

As Captain Anthony's whaleboat neared the *Catalpa*, moored more than three miles off shore, he noticed a steamer, the *Georgette*, approach the whaling ship. This had been commandeered by the Western Australian governor. Anthony's first mate refused to allow the *Catalpa* to be boarded as it was anchored in international waters. The *Georgette*, short on fuel, withdrew for the moment, and this allowed Anthony to smuggle the six Fenians on board his ship.

However, the *Georgette* returned the following day and attempted to force the *Catalpa* back into Australian waters. A shot was fired across the bow of the small whaling ship. Anthony then raised the US flag and warned the pursuing steamer that any interference with the *Catalpa* would constitute an act of war. The police on board the *Georgette* had been told by the colonial governor not to create an international incident. They were forced to allow the American vessel to escape into the Indian Ocean.

After its return to the US the *Catalpa* was gifted by the grateful Fenians to its captain and leading crew members. Anthony, who courted arrest if he returned to sea, published an account of the operation in 1897 entitled *The Catalpa Expedition*.

The New Bedford, Massachusetts whaling ship, the *Catalpa*, sailed into New York harbour, to a rapturous Irish-American welcome, one hundred and forty years ago, on this day.

Broadcast 19 August 2016

5 August 1901

Peter O'Connor sets the first World Long Jump record

Long jump records stick around for quite a while. On May 25 1935 Jesse Owens jumped over twenty-six feet, eight inches (8.13 metres) in Ann Arbor, Michigan, creating a new world record. It stood for twenty-five years. For good measure, and within an inspired spell of forty-five minutes, Owens also broke two other world records and equalled a fourth. At the Mexico Olympics in 1968 Bob Beamon leaped a phenomenal twenty-nine feet, two and a half inches to break the previous record. When he was told what he had done, he collapsed in a heap and had to be helped to his feet by fellow competitors. That record stood for almost twenty-three years, before being broken by Mike Powell.

So, a record that lasted a mere two decades isn't a lot to get excited about. Unless you're Irish. And even if you are, you've probably never heard of Peter O'Connor. But he won two Olympic medals in 1906, one of them gold. As far as O'Connor was concerned, he won them for Ireland, but they are down in the record books as UK medals.

O'Connor was from Ashford, Co. Wicklow, though he was born in England to an Irish family. A talented athlete, he joined the GAA as a twenty-four-year-old in 1896, and three years later won All-Ireland medals in the long jump, high jump and triple jump – then called the 'hop, step and jump'. In those days, the GAA catered for far more than what we now call Gaelic Games. Over the next decade O'Connor beat all comers, including the best Britain had to offer. In 1900 he was invited to join the UK Olympic team. He declined the invitation as his wish was to represent Ireland internationally.

His opportunity finally appeared in 1906. In that year the International Olympic Committee organized what were formally called the Intercalated Games in Athens. This was due to the 1900 and 1904 Olympics in Paris and St Louis being overshadowed by the World Fairs. The first Olympic games in Athens in 1896 had been the only truly successful ones in terms of attendance and sporting credibility up to that point. The idea was that the Olympics would return to their spiritual home in Greece every two years, and would then be staged at some other international venue two years later. It never quite worked out, and the experiment was only tried in 1906.

But, initially, it looked as if the Intercalated Games would accept the inclusion of an Irish team. So, the rival GAA and Irish Amateur Athletic Association jointly nominated O'Connor along with two other athletes, Con Leahy and John Daly, to compete under an Irish flag. The flag was a golden harp and shamrock on a green background, bearing the legend 'Erin go Bragh'. However, the International Olympic Committee reneged, and permission for the three men to compete for Ireland was withdrawn. When they travelled to Athens and registered, they were told they would have to represent the United Kingdom. With great reluctance, the three athletes bowed to the inevitable.

O'Connor went to the Games as long-jump world record holder. He had leaped almost twenty-five feet in Dublin in 1901. In the Athens event, however, he was opposed by the previous holder of the world best mark, Myer Prinstein of the US. The only judge at the event just happened to be the American team manager; O'Connor protested this but was ignored. Prinstein won the gold, O'Connor finished second. At the medal ceremony O'Connor saw red … white and blue as the Union Jack was raised to mark his silver medal. Carrying the Irish banner he had brought to Athens, he climbed up the pole and replaced the offending Union flag with the 'Harp and Shamrock'. His compatriots Con Leahy and John Daly stood at the bottom of the pole, just in case anyone might try and stymie the gesture.

Later, O'Connor competed against Leahy in the hop, step and jump, his teammate having taken gold in the high jump. Here O'Connor won a gold medal of his own; Prinstein, champion in 1900 and 1904, was not placed.

O'Connor, by then thirty-four years old, and clearly past his best, did not compete in any further Olympic Games. Undoubtedly his nationalism, which did not permit him to represent the United Kingdom until forced by circumstances to do so, denied him numerous Olympic medals in 1900 and 1904.

He settled in Waterford, working as a solicitor, and became a founder member of the Waterford Athletic Club. He died there in 1957 at the age of eighty-five. His long jump world best set in 1901 stood as an Irish record until 1990, when it was finally broken by Carlos O'Connell. The first British competitor to beat O'Connor's mark was the legendary Welsh athlete and Olympic gold medallist Lynn Davis in 1962.

Peter O'Connor set a new long jump world record of twenty-four feet, eleven and three-quarter inches at the RDS in Dublin, one hundred and fifteen years ago, on this day.

Broadcast 5 August 2016

September

"Quick! William! Here comes the Fuzz"

30 September 1598

Edmund Spenser is appointed
Sheriff of Cork

When someone uses the word 'sheriff', we tend to think of a tall, grizzled man with a wide-brimmed hat and a revolver. Like Gary Cooper in *High Noon* (1952). Now *there* was a sheriff. But closer to home, the word itself originally comes from 'shire', meaning county, and the role has had many different definitions over the years. Think 'Sheriff of Nottingham' – Robin Hood's supposed antagonist – at one end of the spectrum, and the man who sends the bailiffs to take back that couch you can't pay for at the other.

Probably the most unfortunate sheriff in Irish history is a man who had a distinguished literary career in England. In his most celebrated work he spent six books brown-nosing Queen Elizabeth I. This was a very healthy thing for a poet to do. Less healthy was being an English planter in Ireland in the late sixteenth century, living on land confiscated from Irish rebels.

The sheriff in question was the writer Edmund Spenser, whose epic poem *The Faerie Queene* (1590) is still one of the most highly regarded works in the English language.

But Spenser had a whole other side to him, far removed from poetic sensibility. Born in London, probably in 1552, he came to Ireland at the age of twenty-eight in the service of the Lord Deputy, Lord Grey. He fought alongside Walter

Raleigh in 1580 at the siege of Smerwick in Kerry, during the rebellion of James Fitzmaurice Fitzgerald. At the end of the siege Grey had five hundred of the Spanish and Italian defenders of Smerwick Fort butchered. Only the officers were spared. *Noblesse oblige*, don't you know.

Like an enterprising carpetbagger, Spenser benefitted from the subsequent plantation of Munster. He settled on the Kilcolman Estate near Doneraile in Co. Cork. He also acquired land overlooking the Blackwater river, where he is said to have written some of the *Faerie Queen*, under an oak tree. The oak was destroyed by lightning in the 1960s.

Spenser published the first three volumes of his most famous work in 1590, and duly received a pension of fifty pounds a year from the grateful and flattered Faerie Queene herself. If he was hoping to get a job out of sucking up to Her Majesty, he probably shouldn't have antagonized her hatchet man, Lord Burghley, with his next piece of work, *Mother Hubberd's Tale* (1591). Getting into Burghley's bad books meant that it was back to Ireland for Spenser. His first wife died there in 1594, and he married Elizabeth Boyle, a relative of Richard Boyle, the First Earl of Cork.

Just because most of Spenser's income came from his Irish estates rather than his pension or his poetry didn't mean he had to like the native Irish. And he duly obliged by disliking them and almost everything about them. In a pamphlet entitled *A View of the Present State of Ireland* (1596), he adopted the view that the default position of Irish peasants was set to 'rebellious', and the only way to stop them revolting was to destroy their language and customs. He also had a high opinion of a scorched-earth policy in the event of war with the Irish. This would helpfully deprive said revolting peasants of food and sustenance.

So, it was ironic that Spenser himself was the one who was scorched, in the Nine Years War. Shortly after his appointment as Sheriff of Cork in 1598 the forces of Hugh O'Neill burned the poet's castle. He was obliged to return to London. There he fell on hard times, and died at the age of forty-six. He is buried in Poet's Corner in Westminster Abbey.

Although the author of many celebrated works, he is possibly best remembered for a quatrain written when his annual pension was overdue, it goes:

I was promis' d on a time,
To have a reason for my rhyme:
From that time unto this season,
I receiv'd nor rhyme nor reason.

Edmund Spenser was appointed Sheriff of Cork, four hundred and eighteen years ago, on this day.

Broadcast 30 September 2016

29 September 1732

The birth of Sir Henry Cavendish

Given the fact that today's politicians complain bitterly that there is very little reporting of parliamentary proceedings, and that, if people choose to do so, they can catch elements of pretty much any parliamentary debate on radio, TV or the web, it is difficult to believe that it has only been made legal relatively recently to report the proceedings of the British House of Commons in newspapers.

Journalists who attempted to report on the deliberations of the 'Mother of Parliaments' in the early eighteenth century qualified as 'strangers' and could be removed from the House at the instigation of a member. This procedure, which still exists in modified form, was used in 1875 by the Irish MP Joseph Biggar, to have no less a personage than the Prince of Wales thrown out of the House. Biggar simply invoked the cry of 'I spy strangers' and everything came grinding to a halt until the prince was ejected.

In the eighteenth century, while it was actually legal to report the outcome of parliamentary deliberations, newspapers were not permitted to report the content of the debates themselves. Some editors and reporters were jailed for violating this parliamentary privilege. Newspapermen, in order to circumvent this passion for secrecy on the part of their betters, would record debates anyway, and then present them as thinly disguised fictional exchanges.

The same was true for the Irish Houses of Parliament for much of their existence prior to their disappearance in 1800. If you had the temerity to report on the musings of our elected representatives, you could be thrown in jail for contempt. Perhaps if our great leaders of today were to threaten similar sanctions, they would find newspapers tripping over themselves to cover their compelling debates.

Which makes the achievement of Henry Cavendish of Lismore, Co. Waterford all the more startling. He was a member of the aristocratic Irish family from which the Dukes of Devonshire are drawn. So he wasn't in it for the money, because he didn't lack for an estate or two.

Cavendish personally recorded over three million words of debate in the House of Commons in London from 1768–74. Without his furious note-taking the contributions to Parliament of the likes of Edmund Burke and Charles James Fox might have gone unrecorded.

However, Cavendish was not some freelance scribe chancing his arm; he was himself a member of Parliament. The journal he kept was for private consumption only. Had he not filled fifty notebooks, the record of that particular period, including important debates on North America, would have been rather more sketchy. Cavendish had done the same thing when he was an MP in the Irish House of Commons between 1776 and 1789. Using a shorthand system developed by Thomas Gurney, Cavendish filled more than fifteen thousand pages in noting down the speeches of the House of Commons in London.

Cavendish served as a member of the Irish Parliament for Lismore for three terms prior to the Act of Union. He also, somewhat bizarrely, was the member for the far distant Killybegs in Co. Donegal between 1791 and 1797. His period as an English MP was spent as representative for one of the most notoriously rotten boroughs in the British Commons, Lostwithiel in Cornwall. By the time of its abolition in the great Reform Act of 1832, it could only muster twenty-four electors and had long been in the pocket of the Earls of Mount Edgecombe, who could allocate the seat to whomever they wished.

While Cavendish didn't exactly invent shorthand (though he is credited by some with the achievement), he made valuable use of the technique with an astonishing display of energy. The fact that he wasn't expected to do much for his constituents, numbering in the dozens, gave him considerable freedom to indulge his hobby.

Sir Henry Cavendish, the one man Irish Hansard, was born, one hundred and eighty-five years ago, on this day.

Broadcast 29 September 2017

15 September 1803

Abraham Lincoln and the trial
of Robert Emmet

They are two very different orations. One is short, a mere two hundred and sixty-nine words, and lasted barely three minutes. The other is in excess of three thousand words, and must have taken closer to half an hour to deliver. The longer speech was given by a man marked for a judicial death, the shorter by one who would be shot down by an assassin's bullet.

Abraham Lincoln, sixteenth president of the United States of America, was born six years after the execution of the young rebel United Irishman, Robert Emmet, but the coincidental connections between the two men are compelling and inescapable.

Both were Republicans, both are perceived by their acolytes as martyrs. Emmet, a post-Enlightenment Irish Republican, atoned for the hapless nature of his one-day rebellion on 23 July 1803 by making the single most famous, effective, and affecting speech in Irish nationalist history. Lincoln was one of the founder members of the anti-slavery Republican Party, and its first successful presidential candidate in 1860. His election precipitated the debilitating four-year American Civil War. His Gettysburg Address was a model of rhetorical clarity, creativity and brevity.

Emmet's speech, made after his conviction for high treason in Green Street courthouse in Dublin, is famous for its passionate peroration, made as he faced death by hanging the following day.

> Let no man write my epitaph: for as no man who knows my motives dare now vindicate them, let not prejudice and ignorance asperse them. Let them rest in obscurity and peace, my memory be left in oblivion and my tomb remain uninscribed, until other times, and other men, can do justice to my character. When my country takes her place among the nations of the earth, then, and not till then, let my epitaph be written.

Lincoln's Gettysburg Address, made on 19 November 1863 at the dedication of the Soldier's National Cemetery at Gettysburg, Pennsylvania – the scene of a bloody and decisive battle four and half months earlier – is more famous for its iconic opening line:

> Fourscore and seven years ago our fathers brought forth on this continent a new nation, conceived in Liberty, and dedicated to the proposition that all men are created equal.

But did Emmet's speech influence the creation of the most famous short oration in history? Very likely. As a boy in Indiana (where his family had migrated from Kentucky), Lincoln is known to have learnt Emmet's valedictory off by heart. As a gangly teenager he would often deliver it as a party piece for dignitaries visiting Perry County, where he lived.

More than a quarter of a century later, at the first Republican National Convention in New York in 1856, where Lincoln was defeated for the party's vice-presidential nomination, the convention chairman was a New York judge and politician, Robert Emmet, the Dublin-born nephew of his celebrated namesake.

In February 1865 Lincoln was reviewing the death sentence on a young Confederate spy. He was considering an appeal for the boy's life from a Delaware senator, Willard Saulsbury, who had once referred to the president as 'a weak and imbecile man'. So, as you would assume, not much hope there.

Saulsbury, however, was both frank and astute in his appeal to Lincoln. He wrote:

> You know I neither ask or expect any personal favor from you or your Administration ... All I ask of you is to read the defence of this young man ... compare it with the celebrated defence of Emmet, and act as the judgment and the heart of the President of the United States should act.

Saulsbury knew his man. The death sentence was duly commuted.

In 1939 the distinguished playwright Robert Sherwood won a Pulitzer Prize for his play, *Abe Lincoln in Illinois* (1938). The significance of the play is in Sherwood's middle name, Emmet. He was the great-great-grandnephew of the executed patriot. It was as if the Emmet family, having accepted the homage of the young Lincoln, was repaying the compliment.

Emmet would have been proud of the famous peroration of his celebrated acolyte.

> We here highly resolved that these dead shall not have died in vain – that this nation, under God, shall have a new birth of freedom – and that government: of the

people, by the people, for the people, shall not perish from the earth.

Robert Emmet was awaiting trial, and probably writing the signature speech that Abraham Lincoln would later learn by heart, two hundred and fourteen years ago, on this day.

Broadcast 15 September 2017

1 September 1830

The Wild Colonial Boy is shot dead in New South Wales

There was a Wild Colonial Boy,
Jack Duggan was his name.

Let me stop you right there. Yes, there was a 'wild colonial boy', an infamous Australian bushwhacker. But his name was John Donohoe, not Jack Duggan, Jack Doolin or Jack Dowling, depending on which version of the folk song you favour.

He was born and raised in Ireland,
In a place called Castlemaine.

Sorry, have to stop you again! He *was* born and raised in Ireland all right, possibly in 1804, but equally likely in 1806. But he wasn't from Castlemaine in Co. Kerry. He was in fact, to the horror of all right-thinking Kerrymen and women, a Dubliner. Neither did he have anything to do with Castlemaine in the state of Victoria – home of a certain beer with a lot of 'X's in its name. He actually did most of his best work in New South Wales.

John Donohoe was the 'full Irish' in a way that his more notorious successor, Ned Kelly, was not. He was transported from Ireland in 1824 for the heinous crime of doing absolutely nothing. He was charged and convicted with '*intent* to commit a felony'. While he never quite got around to actually committing the intended crime, the authorities put him on board the convict ship *Ann and Amelia* anyway and sent him to Botany Bay. There he began his new life, not far from Bondi Beach, on 2 January 1825.

He didn't much take to life in Australia and was twice given fifty lashes for manifesting this dislike in unrecorded ways. He quickly escaped from captivity and formed a gang that operated around the emerging township of Sydney. They were known as the Strippers, not because of any risqué dance moves on their part, but because of their habit of removing the clothes of their wealthy victims. The Strippers quickly assumed a folk status that placed them somewhere between the mythical Robin Hood and the real, but as yet unborn, Jesse James. Employees of the wealthy farmers of New South Wales enthusiastically offered information on the movements of their bosses to make the job of the Strippers that little bit easier.

Despite all the help they were getting, Donohoe and two gang members, Kilroy and Smith, were captured and given two death sentences each. Kilroy and Smith were actually hanged – just once, by the way, in case you were wondering how they were going to be executed twice – but John Donohoe escaped and continued his life as a bushranger.

Apparently the Dubliner was quite a dapper type who took his couture quite seriously. One witness described his outfit thus:

> He was attired in a velveteen coat and vest, cabbage tree hat, moleskin trousers, and a blue nankeen shirt, with a heart worked on the breast in white cotton.

'Nankeen', by the way, is a variety of cotton. All rather natty for a highwayman, and all adding to his popularity with the *hoi polloi*, mostly former convicts themselves.

Within twelve months of eluding the hangman there was a price of two hundred pounds on Donohoe's head. He was finally betrayed by a fellow bushranger – there truly is no honour among thieves. He was tracked down and shot in the head by a policeman named Muggletson, who sounds rather like a character from *Harry Potter*. It was reported that, like the Wild Colonial Boy of the song, he refused to surrender. Instead, according to a newspaper report, he urged the police to 'come on, using the most insulting and indecent epithets'. Which is a bit of a mouthful, and probably not nearly as Anglo-Saxon as what he actually said.

In that macabre sense of humour of which Australians are justifiably proud, a Sydney tobacconist manufactured a line of pipes with the bowls in the shape of Donohoe's head, including the bullet hole. The British authorities tried to ban the song 'The Wild Colonial Boy' with so much success that it became an instant classic.

Dubliner John Donohoe, worthy precursor of Ned Kelly, was shot dead in Campbelltown, New South Wales, one hundred and eighty-seven years ago, on this day.

Broadcast 1 September 2017

9 September 1831

National Schools established in Ireland

Education in Ireland at primary and secondary level has traditionally been the preserve of the country's main religious denominations, and one in particular. That was not quite the intention of the prime movers back when a formal education system was first established in this country in 1831. That year, thirty thousand pounds was allocated to establish a national system of elementary education in Ireland.

There is a myth that prior to this date Irish children were largely taught in what were known as 'hedge schools'. While such informal and occasionally *al fresco* establishments did exist in the 1700s, education had become rather more professionalized by the nineteenth century. The Society for Promoting Elementary Education Among the Irish Poor, better known in its much shorter form as the Kildare Street Society, was in receipt of Government funds from 1812, and ran almost fifteen hundred schools with over one hundred thousand students by 1825.

Despite the allegations of prosleytism made against the society, the influential Roman Catholic Bishop of Kildare and Leighlin, James Doyle – an ally of Daniel O'Connell – saw nothing fatally objectionable to Catholics in the schools. Doyle, although he was uneasy in some respects, was more concerned with low educational standards elsewhere than he was with any perception that the Kildare Street institutions might be trying to convert Catholics to Protestantism.

Others were not quite so sanguine and deprecated the practice in Kildare Street schools of scripture reading or 'unaided private interpretation of the Sacred volume', which was 'peculiarly obnoxious' to other members of the Catholic hierarchy.

In October 1831 it was to 'banish ... even the suspicion of proselytism' that the Chief Secretary Earl Stanley wrote a letter to the Duke of Leinster outlining a system of education more closely associated with the State than the looser regime that prevailed at the time.

The Chief Secretary informed the Duke that the Government would fund the building of schools (with a small amount of local financial input), and would pay the salaries of teachers. Stanley's letter was meant to convey to the Duke, and to the Kildare Street Society, that the Government was no longer prepared to farm out education to an organization that was, in part, privately funded. It then proceeded to do just that, all over again.

The main object of the new regime was to 'unite in one system children of different creeds'. The Board of National Education was told to look most favourably on applications for assistance from schools jointly managed by Roman Catholics and Protestants. But the policy of introducing a system of non-denominational, religiously integrated education was quickly abandoned as the Commissioners of Education caved into demands from the main churches for rigidly denominational, segregated education. Within twenty years, only four per cent of national schools were unassociated with a single religious denomination. The Dublin Castle administration didn't always buckle to the realities of Irish life, but in this instance, it opted for pragmatism over principle.

The sum of thirty thousand pounds was allocated for the development of a new system of national education, one hundred and eighty-five years ago, on this day.

Broadcast 9 September 2016

8 September 1852

The Irish Tenant League Conference

Today is the story of an Irish political party dedicated to the interests of large, comfortable and respectable farmers – but enough about Fine Gael, coincidentally founded eighty-four years ago today. Instead, the story of an Irish political party dedicated to the interests of large, comfortable and respectable farmers. Turns out we've had quite a few over the years.

The Irish Tenant League was the posh cousin of the Land League of the 1880s. Someone like Michael Davitt would never have been allowed near the Tenant League – he was far too working-class. But the League made the 1850s more interesting in Ireland than the decade might otherwise have been, and regularly rattled the cage of the British Government before sliding into the inevitable abyss of corruption and recrimination.

The League was established in the 1850s in the wake of the Great Famine. Under the terms of the Encumbered Estates Acts, a number of vulture funds were buying up distressed properties. Sorry, that's actually more recent. Let me rephrase. A number of wealthy capitalists were acquiring bankrupt estates at knockdown prices and threatening to change the rules for sitting tenants. That's the great thing about history – if you stick around for long enough it just keeps happening all over again.

The leading lights of the new organisation were Charles Gavan Duffy, the former Young Irelander, and the English-born journalist Frederick Lucas, editor of the progressive Catholic weekly newspaper, *The Tablet*.

It was the Tenant League, not its more illustrious and egalitarian successor, that came up with the three famous demands of the Irish agrarian movement, the '3 F's', dreaded by every student of Irish history. You could easily recall two, but damned if you could ever remember the third. For the record, they were fair rent, free sale and … em … em …yes, fixity of tenure.

The organisation of the League's activities fell to another former Young Irelander, Newry-born John Martin, who would later precede Charles Stewart Parnell as MP for Meath. The League attracted the support of the rump of the late Daniel O'Connell's Repeal Party in the House of Commons, and in 1852 managed to return fifty Tenant Right candidates to Parliament. These included Gavan, Duffy, Lucas, the banker John Sadleir from Tipperary, and the lawyer William Keogh, MP for Athlone. The Tenant League MPs were pledged not to align themselves with any British party that failed to endorse the '3 Fs', and to refuse all political preferment.

Of course, it quickly went pear-shaped. A sectarian element intervened when a cohort of Tenant Leaguers decided that the cause of Catholic religious rights was more important than forcing agrarian reform. They broke off to form the Catholic Defence Association, nicknamed 'The Pope's Brass Band'. In response Frederick Lucas ill-advisedly took on the powerful Roman Catholic Cardinal Archbishop of Dublin, Paul Cullen, and lost. Lucas died in October 1855, and the following month Gavan Duffy emigrated to Australia, where he ultimately became prime minister of the state of Victoria.

But it became even worse than that. Defying the pledge to remain aloof from political office, Sadleir and Keogh accepted positions in Lord Aberdeen's coalition government and joined that great anti-pantheon of Irish traitors whom we cherish to this day. Sadlier didn't last long in office; he was gone by 1854, forced to resign when he was found guilty of attempting the imprisonment of one of his bank's customers. This errant depositor had failed to deliver on a promise to vote for Sadleir. Two years later his Tipperary bank went spectacularly bust and he committed suicide by drinking prussic acid.

Keogh became a judge and handed down savage sentences to the Fenian leadership in 1867. It was left to William Gladstone, through his land legislation of 1870, and Davitt's Land League of the 1880s, to bring into effect the principles of fair rent, free sale and … the other one.

A Dublin conference of the Irish Tenant League adopted an ill-starred policy of independent opposition in Parliament, one hundred and sixty-five years ago, on this day.

Broadcast 8 September 2017

2 September 1865

The birth of William Rowan Hamilton

It was perhaps the most important example of anti-social behaviour in scientific history. What today might merely have merited an ASBO for the scrawling of a piece of incomprehensible graffiti, back in 1843 was the breakthrough that William Rowan Hamilton needed to come up with the concept of the quaternion.

No one could have predicted at his birth that the son of Sarah Hutton and Archibald Hamilton, a Meath solicitor, would emerge as Ireland's most significant mathematician – other than Eamon de Valera – and one of the world's foremost scientific minds. But pretty soon after his birth it was clear to the extended Hamilton family that young William was a bit different.

He was sent at the age of three to live with his uncle James, a teacher and cleric, in Trim, Co. Meath, and there began to learn a variety of languages as a hobby. Before his teens he had already acquired a dozen. In addition to the predictable European tongues, he had also picked up Hindustani, Sanskrit and Malay. Clearly the curriculum in Uncle James's school was an interesting one.

It was a sobering experience at the age of eight that caused young William to wise up and stop messing around with foreign languages. Something of a whizz at mental arithmetic, in 1813 he was pitted against the visiting American mathematical genius, Zerah Colburn, in a head-to-head contest. Half the rakes of Dublin probably had money on the outcome. But it wasn't a happy experience for young Hamilton. In this early Ryder Cup of Hard Sums – or 'math' as the young American would have called it – he lost out to Colburn. Realising he needed to improve his game if he wanted to become a famous mathematician, William Rowan Hamilton abandoned the acquisition of languages in favour of the solving of equations.

He entered Trinity College in 1823 and was appointed Professor of Astronomy in 1827. This was pretty rapid progress, as he had yet to even graduate. That same year he took up residence in Dunsink Observatory, and spent the rest of his life working there.

Which brings us to his famous walk. It took place on 16 October 1843, when he and his wife left Dunsink to go for a stroll along the banks of the Royal Canal. We can only assume that they either walked in silence or that Hamilton, as is sadly the case with many husbands, was paying little or no attention to what his spouse was saying, as they neared Broom Bridge in Cabra. While most men in such circumstances might have been idly poring over in their heads the advisibility of Manchester United, Chelsea, Kerry or Dublin acquiring a new head coach, Hamilton's mind was concentrated on higher things – something called quaternions. These, I am forced to concede, I know nothing whatsoever about, and can't even comprehend sufficiently to offer a passable idiot's guide.

As the couple approached Broom Bridge, Hamilton began to behave in a fashion that must have caused his wife some concern. He took out a knife. But his intentions were peaceable. He carved the following legend into the superstructure of the bridge:

$$i^2 = j^2 = k^2 = ijk = -1$$

And no, I'm very sorry, but I don't understand it either. This, it transpired, was the discovery of the quaternion, which apparently extends the range of complex numbers. One can only agree with the use of the word 'complex'. The knowledge that her husband had discovered quaternions, and was not simply vandalizing the bridge, must have come as a great relief to Mrs Hamilton.

Of course, the true moral of the story is, if you are a budding astronomer or mathematician who wants to make a difference, you should never leave the house without carrying a knife.

William Rowan Hamilton, mathematician and astronomer, died, one hundred and fifty-one years ago, on this day.

Broadcast 2 September 2016

16 September 1870

Birth of John Pius Boland,
Olympic gold medallist

When Sinn Féin swept what later became the Irish Free State in the first post-war general election in 1918, one of the political casualties was this country's first-ever Olympic gold medal-winner. Technically though, John Pius Boland did not win a gold medal for his success in the tennis singles event at the first games of the modern Olympiad in Athens in 1896. He was awarded a diploma, a silver medal and an olive crown, the bulk of whose leaves he willingly shed when requested to do so by admiring Greek fans, mostly female.

Boland was born in Dublin in 1870. He was one of seven children of a baker, Patrick Boland, but was orphaned by the age of twelve. He was fortunate, from an educational point of view, to have then been placed in the care of his maternal uncle, Nicholas Donnelly, auxiliary bishop of Dublin. He received a good secondary schooling in Dublin and Birmingham before being sent to do a degree at London University. From there he went to study law in Christchurch College, Oxford. He was called to the Bar in 1897 but never practiced.

His involvement in the 1896 Olympics was one of those very Victorian stories of happenstance, entitlement and frivolity. He was actually in Greece on holidays from his studies in Oxford, hoping to attend a number of Olympic events as a spectator. He was visiting a friend, Konstantinos Manos, who was on the Athens organizing committee and persuaded him to enter the tennis competition. Boland was not exactly prepared for combat. He hadn't come to Athens to play tennis and so had none of the required paraphernalia. Various stories, some perhaps even true, have grown up around his participation. Everything he used was either bought, borrowed or inappropriate. He is supposed to have played with a racquet purchased at an Athens bazaar, and to have worn his own street shoes. Either way, he still won the inaugural tennis event at both singles and doubles. In the latter category, he partnered a German, Friedrich Traun, whom he had defeated in the first round of the singles tournament. Traun's original partner had withdrawn due to injury.

In reality he was competing on his own behalf. Technically he was representing the United Kingdom. He doesn't appear to have had any major problem with this until he returned to Oxford and discovered that his triumph was being represented as an English victory. Now where have we heard that before? Boland's response was to state that, 'I refuse to foreswear my "Hibernian origin" and the green flag in the field of sport.'

Boland's success was his first and his last in major international competition, though he did meet his wife Eileen at a tournament in France in 1897. The sport of tennis itself disappeared after the 1924 games, and did not make an Olympic comeback, other than as a demonstration event, until 1988.

But that wasn't the end of Boland's life in the public eye. In 1908 he was involved in the creation of the National University of Ireland. In the interim he had also learned Irish and developed a great affection for the language. He was instrumental in having Irish made compulsory for NUI matriculation. He was also elected to Parliament in 1900 for the South Kerry constituency as a member of Redmond's Irish Parliamentary Party. He held the seat until 1918 and, like a lot of fellow Irish Party members, avoided being swept aside by Sinn Féin when he opted not to stand in either of the newly created Kerry East or Kerry West constituencies against Piaras Béaslaí and Austin Stack. Nobody else did either, and both men were elected, unopposed, to what became the First Dáil.

Boland's daughter Honor, under the name Crowley, won back the South Kerry seat for the Boland family, and for Fianna Fáil, in a 1945 by-election after the death of the sitting TD, her husband Frederick. She held it until her own death in 1966. This put the Bolands in a similar category to the Healy-Rae dynasty from the same part of the world.

Boland was also general secretary of the Catholic Truth Society from 1926 to 1947. He died in London on St Patrick's Day 1958.

John Pius Boland, first Olympic tennis champion and nationalist politician, was born, one hundred and forty-six years ago, on this day.

Broadcast 16 September 2016

23 September 1875

Billy the Kid is arrested for the first time

While he has Irish connections of his own, it is the involvement of William Henry McCarty in an Anglo-Irish war that is of most Irish interest. Not THE Anglo-Irish war, also known as the War of Independence, you understand, but AN Anglo-Irish war – of sorts. This one was fought out in New Mexico in the 1880s.

So, who is William Henry McCarty? Well, he also went under the name of William Bonney. And if that doesn't ring any bells, his nickname probably will. He was best known as Billy the Kid. It's hardly unusual in the USA that a violent anti-hero and probable psychopath should be viewed with reverence. But the Kid has had more books written about him, more films made about him, and more porkies told about him – some by himself – than any other Western outlaw.

He was born in New York City, probably in 1859, to an Irishwoman, Catherine McCarty. No other name is listed on his birth certificate, though his father may have been a Patrick McCarty. Billy was brought up in the lower east side of the city in the area known as the Five Points – made famous in recent years by the Martin Scorsese movie, *Gangs of New York* (2002).

By 1873 Catherine McCarty and her new husband, William Antrim, were living in New Mexico. In 1874

Catherine Antrim died. The following year her son became involved in petty crime. In September 1875 he robbed a Chinese laundry in Silver City, New Mexico, was arrested, escaped from jail, and went on the run. He was fifteen years old. He didn't have long left.

The most celebrated and persistent myth about the Kid is that he killed a man for every year of his short life (he was dead by the age of twenty-one). This tall tale may have come from the Kid himself to counteract his youthful appearance and enhance his aura of invincibility, but it is well wide of the mark. He is known to have been personally responsible for the deaths of four men, and was complicit in the killing of four more.

His first victim was a thirty-two-year-old Irishman, Frank Cahill, a native of Galway. The two men met, and fought, in Arizona. Cahill came off worse. The Kid was immediately arrested but, once again, displayed his knack for escaping custody. Facing a murder charge in Arizona, he returned to New Mexico. There he became involved in what is known today as the Lincoln County War. This was a power struggle for economic and political domination of southern New Mexico fought out between a group of dodgy Irish businessmen, fraudsters and rustlers, Lawrence Murphy, John Riley, and Jimmy Dolan on the one side, and an equally dubious young English opportunist, John Henry Tunstall, as well as his Scottish-American partner Alexander McSween on the other. The Kid enlisted on the 'British' side of the conflict when he took a job as one of Tunstall's hired thugs.

His career as a practicing psychopath reached new depths in February 1878 when Tunstall was murdered by members of a posse sent out by the sheriff of Lincoln County, William Brady from Cavan. The Kid claimed his second Irish victim a few days later when he and at least two more of Tunstall's former employees gunned down Sheriff Brady in Lincoln.

The Kid went on the run again, but after numerous brushes with the law and a lot more violence, he was captured by the new Lincoln County sheriff, Pat Garrett. He was tried and found guilty of the murder of Brady in April 1881. He was taken to Lincoln Jail to await hanging, but escaped yet again, this time killing two of Garret's deputies, Bob Ollinger and James Bell, as he made his getaway.

New Mexico governor Lew Wallace, the author of *Ben Hur* (1880), put a five hundred dollar reward on Billy the Kid's head, and Garrett went in pursuit again. He tracked the Kid down in July 1881, and shot him dead in Fort Sumner, New Mexico. Garrett, who had been a friend of McCarty – or Bonney, or Antrim – later capitalized on their association by writing a suitably self-serving biography, *The Authentic Life of Billy the Kid* in 1882. As with Jesse James, Jim Morrison and Elvis Presley, there were many reports of sightings of the Kid after his demise. He would now be more than one hundred and fifty years old, so we can be fairly confident that he is actually dead. But his legend lives on. So far he's been played by Audie Murphy, Roy Rogers, Paul Newman, Kris Kristofferson and Emilio Estevez, among many others.

Billy the Kid was arrested for the first time after robbing a Chinese laundry, one hundred and forty-one years ago, on this day.

Broadcast 23 September 2016

22 September 1884

The gunboat H.M.S. *Wasp* is wrecked off Tory Island

If you were asked what the most northerly Irish island is, you would probably hazard a guess that it was Tory Island, off the coast of Donegal. And you wouldn't be too far wrong. The correct answer is Inishtrahull – or the island of the empty beach – which lies ten kilometres north-east of Malin Head. It also boasts the most northerly lighthouse in Ireland, which was manned until 1987.

But the most significant event in the history of the island took place more than a century earlier, and involved the loss of fifty-two lives.

The H.M.S. *Wasp* was a small British naval vessel, built in 1880 in Barrow, Cumbria. It was one hundred and twenty-five feet long, and its on-board steam engine meant that it was capable of achieving a speed of almost ten knots. It was armed with two four-inch and two six-inch guns, and was rigged with three masts. It also carried two machine guns. The *Wasp* was commissioned by the Royal Navy in 1881. It intersected with the story of Inishtrahull when it became an element of the Irish Land War of the 1880s and was used to transport personnel to offshore islands in order to enforce evictions there.

In September 1884 the H.M.S. *Wasp* was dispatched from Westport to Moville in Donegal, under the command of Lieutenant J. D. Nicholls. It was to collect a party of court officials, Royal Irish Constabulary policemen, and bailiffs in Moville and transport them to Inishtrahull in order to carry out evictions at the behest of the local landlord, Sir Robert Bateson Harvey. The tenants were to be dispossessed for the non-payment of rents to the value of just over seventy-six pounds. Keep that figure in your head when you hear what happened.

On the morning of 22 September 1884, with fifty-eight sailors on board, the *Wasp* was off Tory Island. The commander and most of the crew members were asleep. Just before 4:00 a.m. the gunboat hit a reef, the hull was split, and the craft quickly began to take on water. It sank within fifteen minutes. Only six men were able to escape and make their way to Tory Island, where they were looked after by locals.

Astonishingly, after having endured such an ordeal, all six were later court-martialled by the British Navy but exonerated. The cause ascribed to the disaster was a lack of attention to the navigation of the vessel in dangerous waters.

Given the nature of the *Wasp*'s mission, you might have expected a less than totally sympathetic response from nationalist Ireland. That was not the case. The ultra-nationalist *United Ireland* newspaper did point out, however, that the lost gunboat itself had cost fifty thousand pounds to build, and that the loss of fifty-two lives was of incalculable value, all for the sum of seventy-six pounds and five shillings in unpaid rent. The newspaper's editorial was scathing:

May we therefore assume that Sir Robert Bateson Harvey will not again have a gunboat placed at his bailiff's disposal for the asking, and the Government will not imperil their seamen's lives and taxpayer's property to please a landlord? The Crown have always declined in England to provide the landlords of the Isle of Skye with vessels to overawe the crofters.

Among the many ironies of the tragedy was the fact that the total population of the island of Inishtrahull in 1884 was fewer than fifty souls. The previous year, the *Wasp* had been used to transport much-needed food supplies to the island. Inishtrahull was finally evacuated in 1929 during the first years of the new government of the Irish Free State.

The H.M.S. *Wasp* sank without being able to launch its lifeboats, at a cost of fifty-two lives, one hundred and thirty-seven years ago, on this day.

Broadcast 22 September 2017

October

"As shimmering replicas become distorted through an emergent and diverse practice, the viewer is left with an epitaph for the inaccuracies of existence"

7 October 1582

The Gregorian Calendar

Depending on your point of view, today (7 October 2016) is either 7 October 2016 or 27 September 2016. If you are a big fan of Julius Caesar and swear by his mathematical calculations, then it's the latter. If, however, you go along with Pope Gregory XIII, then it's the former.

Without wishing to cause offence or any unnecessary hurt to Caesarians, most of us tend to go along with Pope Gregory on this one. It all depends on how you calculate time. In 45 BC Julius Caesar, the one who died on the Ides of March – whatever they were – introduced a calendar that had three hundred and sixty-five days, and allowed for a leap year every four years. And what's wrong with that, you might ask?

Nothing, except that Caesar's year was three hundred and sixty-five days and six hours, long. Whereas the length of the year is actually three hundred and sixty-five days, five hours, forty-eight minutes and forty-six seconds. A difference of eleven minutes and fourteen seconds; so about as long as a heavy-metal guitar solo.

Given that Julius Caesar was stabbed to death by Brutus, Cassius, and one or two others, he never realised time got a bit out of whack over the years that followed because of this slight discrepancy. For one thing, Easter, the ultimate movable feast, was getting later every year. At some point it would inevitably coincide with Christmas Day. Action was required, and Pope Gregory XIII got off his Vatican throne and did something about it. Accordingly, across most of Europe, people went to bed on 4 October 1582 and woke up on 15 October 1582.

However, in a rather significant and early manifestation of Brexit, the English decided that they would have nothing to do with a calendar devised by the Antichrist himself. Instead they opted to render unto Caesar the things that were Caesar's – starting with his calendar. As the English Crown had claimed Ireland as a gift from the Pope in 1155, we were stuck with the old calendar too.

Of course things got really confusing when it came to Irish rebellions. As the rebels were invariably Catholic, their wars were fought according to the new calendar, devised under the auspices of Pope Gregory. This, presumably, made it easier to identify an Irish Catholic rebel. You just asked him the date.

So the Battle of Kinsale, for example, was, according to the English side, fought on Christmas Eve 1601. But the clash contested and lost by the forces of Hugh O'Neill and Hugh O'Donnell, as well as their Spanish allies, didn't even take place the same year. The Irish fought their Battle of Kinsale on 3 January 1602.

The English, and by extension the Irish, didn't come into line with the Gregorian Calendar until 1752. Given recent history, don't be too shocked if they suddenly change their minds someday and revert to the Julian Calendar.

Not that the Irish are wedded to ancient history or anything like that, but the calendar switch is often cited as having huge philosophical significance in the context of the first day of the Battle of the Somme. On that occasion, 1 July 1916, the 36th Ulster Division went over the top at Thiepval. More than two thousand of them never came back. The date became part of Ulster Unionist folklore. However, it was pointed out at the time that if you ignored the Pope's calendar – something your average unionist didn't have much of a problem with – 1 July 1916 was actually the anniversary of 12 July 1690, when King William led his Protestant forces to victory against the Catholic army of King James. The battle had actually had been fought on the *1* of July 1690, according to King Billy and his followers.

Because of his decision to toss out the calendar of Julius Caesar, and the consequent loss of ten days, Pope Gregory XIII ensured that absolutely nothing happened, four hundred and thirty-four years ago, on this day.

Broadcast 7 October 2016

21 October 1879

The founding of the Irish National Land League

In times when something called the New Land League moves to prevent an eviction from a mansion in Killiney, it might be a good opportunity to remind ourselves about the Old Land League, an organization whose aim was to protect tenant farmers and ultimately abolish landlordism.

The context for its formation in 1879 was a worldwide economic depression, accompanied by one of those periodic Irish agricultural crises. Things were so bad, especially in the west of Ireland, that many actually feared the return of famine on a scale last seen in the 1840s – the potato crop had failed for three years in a row in the late 1870s.

The usual vicious circle that governed Irish agriculture returned with a vengeance. Tenant farmers were so impoverished they couldn't pay their rents and feed their families at the same time. Landlords reacted by evicting defaulters. Secret societies responded with violence against the property and personnel of the landlords. The Royal Irish Constabulary took appropriate action against known troublemakers, whether they'd actually done anything or not. The Government abolished *habeas corpus*, allowing it to arrest and hold whomever it wanted without charge. We've seen it all before.

But this time it was different. Enter Michael Davitt.

Born in Co. Mayo and brought up among the cotton mills of Lancashire where he had lost an arm in an industrial accident, Davitt had joined the Fenian movement and spent some hard years in Dartmoor Prison, much of it in solitary confinement. After his release, he tired of the ideological purity of the IRB leadership, which opposed socially progressive movements on the basis that they tended to distract and depress revolutionary ardour. Davitt abandoned his former allies and sought a means to improve the appalling situation of tenant farmers in his native Mayo.

The origins of the new agrarian movement can be traced to a public meeting on 20 April 1879 in Irishtown, Co. Mayo. Davitt was one of the organisers of the meeting, but stayed away because he was a 'ticket of leave' prisoner out on probation. In August of that same year Davitt was instrumental in the establishment of the Land League of Mayo. One of the first successes of this new agrarianism was a campaign against a landowning Catholic priest, Father Ulick Burke from Knock, who was threatening evictions against his tenants. A campaign of non-payment of rent forced him to withdraw the threat and to reduce his rents by a quarter.

The founding later that year of the Irish National Land League, and the agreement of an up- and-coming nationalist politician, Charles Stewart Parnell, to lead the organization can be said to mark the beginning of the three-year cycle of political activism and agrarian violence that is known as the Land War.

The most famous victim of the activities of the Land League was the land agent Charles Boycott. Parnell had advocated a policy of civil disobedience in the face of obstinate land owners and suggested that belligerent opponents should be sent to what he called 'moral Coventry'. Boycott was the most spectacularly successful victim of this policy – so much so that this practice of ostracism became known as 'boycotting'. A lot snappier than 'moral Coventry', I'm sure you'll agree.

The Land League was formally suppressed in 1882 and morphed into the Irish National League, a Parnellite organization with rather different priorities. Which meant the copyright on the name had expired so that anyone could use it. Hence its reappearance at the gates of a well-appointed mansion on Gorse Hill in Killiney, Co. Dublin in April 2015. Would Michael Davitt have approved? Well, he didn't have a say in the matter, did he?

The Irish National Land League, an organization created to protect the impoverished and the destitute, was founded, one hundred and thirty-seven years ago, on this day.

Broadcast 21 October 2016

14 October 1882

The birth of Éamon de Valera

One of the most successful Irish movies of 2016 was the adaptation of Colm Toibín's novel *Brooklyn*. But that borough of the city of New York has a much more compelling Irish association. It was the chosen destination of Irish immigrant Catherine Coll from Co. Limerick, and it was from there that she met a young Spanish sculptor, got married, and had a son in 1882. That son, their only child, went on to become the dominant Irish political personality of the twentieth century, Éamon de Valera.

Not that the young de Valera, named Edward by his parents, knew much about his mother Catherine or his father Vivion. The latter was dead by the time he was three, and his mother was forced by economic circumstances to have her son sent to Ireland in 1885 to be brought up by relatives in Bruree, Co. Limerick. There he was known as Eddie Coll. He later became a scholarship boy in Blackrock College, where he was to become a teacher. In the 1911 census he was still Edward de Valera, but his involvement in the Gaelic League sparked an increased interest in Irish. Until the formation of the Irish Volunteers in 1913, his politics were those of Home Rule, but the transformation of his philosophy was what ultimately lead to his command of the Third Battalion of the Volunteers in the Easter Rising.

Despite the execution of men far more junior than he, de Valera survived the violent aftermath of the Rising. There is a myth that his death sentence was commuted because of his American citizenship. In fact, it was more to do with timing and happenstance. In the wake of the controversial execution of James Connolly, when General Sir John Maxwell asked the young Irish prosecutor William Wylie whether de Valera should be shot on the basis that he might cause trouble in the future, Wylie made the memorable but hardly clairvoyant observation, 'I wouldn't think so, sir, I don't think he is important enough. From all I can hear he is not one of the leaders'.

After 1916 his star was in the ascendant. He won the East Clare by-election in 1917, led Sinn Féin to a sweeping victory in the 1918 general election, and escaped from Lincoln Prison in 1919. But his personality often let him down. In Lincoln, he made few friends among his fellow Republican inmates. He famously played handball alone in the exercise yard. When he went to the US after his escape to raise funds and awareness for the Irish nationalist cause, he succeeded in falling out with the political leaders of Irish America, John Devoy and Daniel Cohalan.

Never too far from controversy, his decision in late 1921 not to accompany the Irish delegation to the London treaty talks has been condemned, justifiably or otherwise, as a convenient cop-out, designed to ensure that he remained untarnished by the inevitable fudge of the treaty. His subsequent rejection of the agreement signed by Collins and Griffith, and the counter proposals of his 'Document Number Two', have been criticized as Jesuitical and self-serving.

He was largely sidelined during the Civil War – notwithstanding the contrary evidence advanced by the plot of Neil Jordan's film *Michael Collins* (1996) – and seemed to depart from the principles he had enunciated in January

1922 when, in 1926, he and his followers took their seats in the Dáil, an institution that was, essentially, the governing parliament of a state that fell far short of the Republic, for which he had argued in the divisive debate over the treaty.

1932 saw the perennial poacher turn long-term gamekeeper when Fianna Fáil won the general election. Apart from two brief periods of multi-party coalition, he led the country for the next twenty-seven years, wrote the constitution that still, more or less, governs us today, and can be accused of presiding over an economy only rescued from stagnation by his successor Seán Lemass.

But he also, arguably, had the *nous* and the courage to lead Ireland through an economic war with our nearest neighbor in the 1930s, and to keep the country neutral during World War Two, as well as a number of other significant achievements.

Like or loathe him, you cannot ignore Eamon de Valera – a much more impressive name for a political leader, it has to be said, than Eddie Coll.

Eamon de Valera was born in New York, one hundred and thirty-four years ago, on this day.

Broadcast 14 October 2016

6 October 1891

The death of Charles Stewart Parnell

'Under the Great Comedian's tomb, the crowd.'

Thus does W. B. Yeats begin his 1934 poem 'Parnell's Funeral', with a gibe at Daniel O'Connell, whose towering mausoleum dominates the cemetery in which both men were laid to rest: Glasnevin, on Dublin's north side. Yeats, a Protestant, ignored the irony of a co-religionist, Charles Stewart Parnell, being buried in a graveyard that had been opened in 1832 largely at the behest of the Great Comedian himself to allow Catholic funeral ceremonies to take place in the city of Dublin.

Yeats, like James Joyce before him, was in no doubt about where to ascribe the blame for the death of Parnell, who died in October 1891.

> But popular rage,
> *Hysterica passio* dragged this quarry down.
> None shared our guilt; nor did we play a part
> Upon a painted stage when we devoured his heart.

Unlike O'Connell, who lived to witness his own irrelevance, Parnell had the good fortune, at least from a legacy point of view, to die young. Today that would be classified as a good 'branding' decision.

He was superstitious almost to the point of obsession, and one of his phobias related to October. He considered it to be a blighted month. However, up to that point, the worst thing that had happened to Parnell in October was his arrest and incarceration in Kilmainham Gaol in 1881. That was surpassed a decade later by his death following a bout of pneumonia, at the age of forty-five. One of his other phobias was for the colour green, ironic on numerous levels, not least for the fact that the anniversary of his death is remembered each year as 'Ivy Day'.

He died in Walsingham Terrace in Hove, near Brighton, where he had lived with Katharine O'Shea for some time. He had married his 'common law wife' just a few months before, after a semi-covert relationship that had lasted ten years. Her infamous divorce from her Machiavellian husband, Captain William O'Shea, had provoked the political demise which preceded Parnell's actual death. Despite the fact that she often gets bad press here, Katharine O'Shea did this country a huge service when she permitted her husband – the real one, not the cuckold – to be interred in Ireland, a country she might well have blamed for the death of her beloved partner. She could have chosen to bury him on the English south coast and then joined him when she herself died in 1921. Instead, she agreed to have his body returned to Ireland to be buried by the political supporters who had remained loyal to him after he was abandoned by the bulk of his MPs in the wake of the O'Shea divorce revelations.

His funeral, on 11 October 1891, was one of the biggest ever seen in Dublin, comparable to that of O'Connell himself. More than one hundred thousand people lined the route from Sackville Street to Glasnevin. The Fanagan family, still in business today, were the undertakers. When Parnell's remains arrived in Westland Row station, after the boat journey from Holyhead, the wooden box containing the coffin was set upon by mourners and pieces were broken off and retained as relics.

Pride of place in the cortège, immediately behind the coffin, went to Parnell's favourite horse, Home Rule, with the dead leader's riding boots dangling from the saddle. The first three carriages in the funeral procession were filled with close relatives, but the fourth carriage was occupied by leading members of the IRB with whom Parnell had formed a tentative alliance after his fall from grace. So great was the crush to get near the grave that the Glasnevin authorities decided any comparable events in the future would have to be ticketed. This was what happened in the case of Michael Collins, buried in 1922.

The plot allocated to the final resting place of Parnell is now adorned with a large block of Wicklow granite bearing only his surname. It was not placed there until 1940. In the years immediately following his death the plot was a shrine, usually bedecked with flowers. A photograph in the Lawrence collection, taken in 1914, illustrates the fact that this homage continued at least up to the beginning of the Great War. Right up to the present, Ivy Day is still commemorated by members of the Parnell Society in Glasnevin, on the closest Sunday to 6 October.

Charles Stewart Parnell, broken politically and physically, died in the arms of Katharine O'Shea, one hundred and twenty six years ago, on this day.

Broadcast 6 October 2017

27 October 1905

The birth of Bryan Guinness, Lord Moyne, brewer and writer

1929 was quite an eventful year for twenty-four-year-old Bryan Guinness. He married one of the most controversial Englishwomen of the twentieth century, and he perpetrated one of the liveliest artistic hoaxes ever seen in London.

Guinness was born in 1905 with a silver spoon in his mouth. He was an heir to part of the extended family brewing fortune and was also due, at some point, to inherit Daddy's title and become Lord Moyne. He went to Eton, followed by Oxford, and was called to the Bar in 1931. So far so predictable. Except for 1929.

When everyone around him was having a meltdown as the value of their shares plummeted after the Wall Street Crash, Bryan was settling into wedded bliss with one of the Mitford sisters, the famous social gadflies of the 1920s. Unfortunately, he chose one of the 'bad uns', Diana. He might have chosen Debbie who went on to become a Duchess. Or he could have opted for the obscure Pamela, a great lover of poultry, or Jessica, a campaigning investigative journalist. We won't talk about Unity – that would have been almost as bad. But of course *he* had to get hitched to Diana. Today, he could have married the only male sibling, Tom, but in the 1920s that wasn't really an option.

Now the reason you've probably heard of Diana Mitford is not because she married Bryan Guinness and became

Lady Moyne, because she didn't. She married him all right, but then she took up with the Nigel Farage of the 1930s, Oswald Mosley, leader of the British Union of Fascists. As there were too many people in the marriage, Bryan wisely decided to drop out of the arrangement. He divorced Diana, who then went on to marry Ozzie, befriend Hitler, and make a complete ass of herself on *Desert Island Discs* in 1989 by publicly doubting that her mate Adolf had murdered as many as six million Jews. But that's a whole different story.

Now Bryan and Diana, when they were an item, were on matey terms with the writer Evelyn Waugh. His great comic novel *Vile Bodies* (1930) is dedicated to them. Waugh based the character of Anthony Blanche in *Brideshead Revisited* (1945) on a 1920s dilettante named Brian Howard, an aspiring artist. Howard and Guinness were both part of the London social set of the 1920s known as the 'Bright Young People'. Both thought it would be a great idea to play a trick on some of the other Bright Young People who happened to be art critics, by trying to convince them of the boundless talent of an untutored painter they had discovered with the unlikely name of Bruno Hat. Hat, unlike the useful headgear of the same name, was entirely fictional.

Howard provided the paintings, Guinness came up with the gallery – his own London house. Diana Mitford's brother Tom was dressed up as the heavily accented Bruno. The catalogue notes for the exhibition, entitled 'Approach to Hat', were written by Evelyn Waugh. Waugh, in exuberantly pretentious mode, compared Hat to an unschooled Picasso and wrote that:

He is the first natural, lonely, spontaneous flower of the one considerable movement in painting to-day

… Bruno Hat is the first signal of the coming world movement towards the creation of Pure Form.

At the opening, Bruno was almost exposed when someone addressed him in German, but the fast-thinking Tom Mitford, unlike his siblings Diana and Unity, denounced Germany and insisted on speaking 'Englisch'.

The problem was that the paintings weren't half bad. Only the future Labour MP Tom Driberg, writing for the *Daily Express*, didn't fall for the elaborate hoax. He called it 'an excellent hat-trick'. Boom-boom!

Bryan Guinness, who served as a major in the British Army during World War Two, became Lord Moyne in 1944 in tragic circumstances. His father, who was working in the Middle East in a diplomatic capacity, was assassinated in Cairo. In the 1940s and 50s, as the second Lord Moyne, he was in the vanguard of the struggle to have the paintings of the Hugh Lane Bequest returned to Dublin, and was instrumental in the negotiation of the 1959 compromise, which saw them alternate between Dublin and London.

Bryan Guinness, Baron Moyne, was born, one hundred and twelve years ago, on this day.

Broadcast 27 October 2017

13 October 1928

The Dublin Gate Theatre Company produces its first play

It has been running for almost ninety years, yet it only acquired its third artistic director six months ago. It is indelibly associated with the Rotunda Hospital complex, but actually began its life on the premises of its great rival, the Abbey.

The Gate Theatre has survived for nearly nine decades, mostly, but not always, complementing the work of the National Theatre on Abbey Street. But there were times when it looked highly likely to become an artistic casualty rather than an outstanding success.

The Gate actually opened its doors in 1928 in the Peacock Theatre, little sister to the Abbey, under the guidance of the great theatrical and life partners, Hilton Edwards and Micheál Mac Liammóir. Both, as it happens, were born in London around the beginning of the twentieth century.

Mac Liammóir was actually Alfred Willmore, once a child actor working with Noël Coward. He later toured Ireland with his brother-in-law Anew McMaster's company. He fell in love with the country – and with fellow actor Hilton Edwards, whom he met while performing in the Athenaeum in Enniscorthy, Co. Wexford – and decided to remain. He gaelicised his name and learned to speak Irish better than most natives. He also made an – as yet unsubstantiated

278

– claim to have had a sexual relationship with Ireland's premier fascist, the Blueshirt leader Eoin O'Duffy. It could be true, but then Mac Liammóir also had a mischievous and iconoclastic sense of humour.

Edwards and Mac Liammóir were intent on bringing the best of European theatre to Dublin. The work of major playwrights like Henrik Ibsen and August Strindberg was produced, first on the Peacock stage, beginning with *Peer Gynt* by Ibsen in 1928. After some months in Abbey Street, the company moved to Cavendish Row, north of O'Connell Street, and occupied a building on the Rotunda Hospital campus. There, the architect Michael Scott helped create the Gate's compact and iconic home. The theatre seats just under four hundred people.

One of the most enthusiastic early supporters of the venture was the corpulent old Etonian Edward Pakenham, Sixth Earl of Longford, himself a playwright. He became chairman of the theatre in 1930 and helped to raise the funds that kept it alive. Longford could often be found patrolling from Parnell Square to O'Connell Street with a collection box, actively seeking funds.

Despite the fame of its founders and the fact that James Mason and Michael Gambon began their careers at the theatre, there is little doubt that the most distinguished Gate alumnus was Orson Welles, who conned his way into the 1931 production of *Jew Suss* (based on the 1925 novel by Lion Feuchtwanger) as a precocious sixteen-year-old. He told Edwards he was an established Broadway star, and, sixty years before the internet, it was enough to get him a successful audition. He was forced back to the USA after a year because he couldn't get a work permit to stay. How different the Irish theatre and film history might have been had he been allowed to remain in Dublin.

Welles continued his association with Mac Liammóir and Edwards after his later Hollywood success by working on a number of projects with them and casting Mac Liammóir as Iago in his film production of Shakespeare's *Othello* in 1952.

Mac Liammóir died in 1978. Hilton Edwards survived him by four years, but by then the Gate had lost its way. It was rescued from oblivion by the arrival, as second artistic director, of the supremely self-confident and ebullient – some might even say brash – Michael Colgan in 1983. During Colgan's three decades as the Gate's entrepreneur-in-chief, the theatre has often overshadowed the Abbey, and has forged alliances with major dramatists like Samuel Beckett and Harold Pinter. In April of this year Colgan handed over the reins to artistic director number three, Selina Cartmell.

The Gate Theatre opened its doors for the first time, for a production of Henrik Ibsen's *Peer Gynt*, eighty-nine years ago, on this day.

Broadcast 13 October 2017

28 October 1941

The release of *How Green Was My Valley*

You might ask what a Hollywood movie about a Welsh mining village has to do with Ireland. But if the film in question is *How Green Was My Valley* (1941), based on the novel by Richard Llewellyn, the answer is, quite a lot really.

For a start, the film was directed by John Ford (Sean Feeney), who considered himself to be as Irish as they come, and who even pretended to speak the language. Ford was a taskmaster who could be difficult and irascible, but who generally got what he wanted to the benefit of all. He duly won the Oscar for Best Director the year of the film's release.

Then there's the cast, which, by the way, contained one single Welsh actor, Rhys Williams, among the speaking parts. He plays the relatively minor role of a boxer, Dai Bando. The movie was filmed on a Hollywood backlot, rather than the Welsh valleys. Ford would have preferred to film in Wales, but World War Two dictated otherwise.

Continuing the Irish influence, the female lead of Angharad Morgan, as was the case with a number of Ford's films, was played by Maureen O'Hara, a quintessentially Welsh role for this one-hundred-per-cent-Irish actress from Churchtown in Dublin. This was the first of her five films with the director, known to his usually wary cast and crew as 'Pappy'.

Moving down the cast list we find the great Abbey actress Sara Allgood playing the part of Beth Morgan, mother of the young child star of the movie, Roddy McDowall, and 'wife' of the Best Supporting Actor Oscar-winner, Donald Crisp. Allgood was more than just an actress. In her youth, she had been a political activist, a member of Maud Gonne's Ininighdhe na hÉireann, and might well have taken part in the 1916 Rising had she not been touring Australia and New Zealand that year in one of her biggest successes, the play, *Peg of my Heart*. Allgood won the Oscar for Best Supporting Actress for *Valley*.

Then there were the Shields brothers. Arthur played the part of Mr Parry, the deacon. He, at least, had spent some time in Wales. As it happens he was a guest of the British Government in the internment camp of Frongoch. Another highly politicized Abbey actor, he *had* taken part in the 1916 Rising and had been deported to North Wales along with Michael Collins and hundreds of other Irish Volunteers and members of the Irish Citizens' Army.

The other Shields brother, William, is better known as Barry Fitzgerald. The former Abbey Theatre great had come to Hollywood to work with John Ford on his 1936 film version of Sean O'Casey's *The Plough and the Stars*. Fitzgerald, a former roommate of O'Casey's, played the part of a boxing manager in *How Green Was My Valley*.

But perhaps the most interesting Irish connection of all comes through the presence in the film of an English-born actor who played a fascinating peripheral role in an iconic moment in Irish history. Most of us are familiar with the photograph of the surrender of Patrick Pearse to General William Lowe in Dublin as the 1916 Rising ground to a halt. There are four people in the photograph. Pearse, Cumann na mBan nurse Elizabeth O'Farrell – represented by her feet, and who is often controversially expunged from the image – Lowe himself, and to the General's right, a young British officer. This, it turns out, was Lowe's teenage son John, who in some versions of the famous photograph appears to be casually smoking. This is, however, an optical illusion.

After the Rising and the Great War – during which he became a German prisoner – John Lowe went on to become a Hollywood actor under the stage name John Loder. He starred in one of the first talking pictures, married five times – once to Hedy Lamarr – and died in 1988 at the age of ninety. In *How Green Was My Valley* he played one of Roddy McDowall's brothers, Ianto.

Which means that featuring in the same cast of a celebrated Hollywood movie were two men who had fought on opposite sides of the 1916 Rising, Irish Volunteer Arthur Shields, and British Army Lieutenant John Lowe.

By the way, for those with a bent for cinema history, the film won the 1942 Academy Award for Best Picture. Among the other nominees that year was the movie considered by many critics to be the greatest ever made, *Citizen Kane*. But not by the Academy voters.

How Green Was My Valley, a film that lived up to its title as far as the Irish influence was concerned, was released seventy-five years ago, on this day.

Broadcast 28 October 2016

November

Brood, mope, frown, glower, sulk

24 November 1713

The birth of Lawrence Sterne

In this autobiographical novel – in an incident which typifies its lewd humour – the protagonist is accidentally circumcised when a sash falls as he is urinating out a window. The book is full of digressions, to the extent that the author doesn't get around to describing his own birth until volume three. One page is entirely black. A post-modern classic of some kind? Actually, *The Life and Opinions of Tristram Shandy, Gentleman*, was published between 1759 and 1767.

It is the master work of perhaps the greatest and most eccentric novelist of the eighteenth century, Laurence Sterne. He is one of the most accomplished English writers of that golden era. Except, of course, like many other literary giants of the period, Richard Brinsley Sheridan and Oliver Goldsmith, for example, he's not English, but Irish.

Sterne was born in Clonmel, Co. Tipperary in 1713, the son of a British Army officer with Irish family connections. The Sterne family moved around the country a lot – at different times Sterne lived in Clonmel, Wicklow, Dublin, Drogheda, Castlepollard and Carrickfergus. That's an awful lot of blue plaques for one man. During these peregrinations Sterne lost four siblings in an era of horrendous child mortality.

Sterne eventually moved to England at the age of ten where, in the year 1738, he was ordained as a clergyman. In 1759 he intervened in a row among clerics in Yorkshire by publishing a satirical work on the subject entitled *A Political Romance*. This turned out to be both a wise and unwise move. On the positive side, it revealed Sterne's comic and literary talents. However, the novel aroused so much animosity amongst his clerical peers that it ensured he would never become a bishop. Furthermore, at the behest of some of his scandalised and influential colleagues, copies of the book were burnt. Only a handful survived, and most of those did not emerge until long after his death.

Sterne, who had tried to supplement his clerical income by farming – he was no good at it – now concentrated on writing. Despite suffering from tuberculosis from his mid-forties on, he managed to write at prodigious speed and produced more than a volume a year of the lengthy *Tristram Shandy* until it was completed in 1767. The book brought him international renown. When it was discovered that the often bawdy novel was the work of a parson, Sterne was subjected to opprobrium in equal measure. Even the publication of two books of sermons failed to satisfy his prurient critics. This may have had something to do with the fact that a mischievous Sterne chose to publish them under the title *The Sermons of Mr Yorick* (1766), the name of a priest in *Tristram Shandy*.

For the good of his health, he left England for France in 1762. It can't have been an entirely healthy move, because Britain and France were at war at the time. Nonetheless, Sterne's reputation preceded him, and he was treated as a celebrity rather than a spy wherever he went. Some of his travels were incorporated into the later volumes of *Tristram Shandy*, and into his last novel, *A Sentimental Journey through France and Italy* (1768).

After his death, Sterne became the central character in a macabre gothic tale not of his devising. He died at the height of the era of the grave-robber or 'resurrectionist'. These were men whose business it was to provide corpses to the growing number of medical training establishments. Aspiring surgeons could only legitimately practice their anatomical skills on the bodies of hanged men and women. Because of the popularity of transportation as a humane alternative to capital punishment, legally acquired corpses were in shorter supply.

Sterne died in 1768, at the age of fifty-four, shortly after *A Sentimental Journey* was published, and was buried in the churchyard of St George's in Hanover Square. But he didn't rest in peace for long. His body was stolen by grave-robbers and sold to the University of Cambridge. There it was recognised by a surgeon and quietly re-interred in an unknown plot in the original cemetery. A skull, believed to be that of Sterne, emerged when the churchyard was re-developed in the late 1960s, which is highly ironic for someone who extracted so much humour from the name Yorick.

Laurence Sterne, author of *Tristram Shandy* and probably a century and a half ahead of his time, was born in Clonmel, two hundred and four years ago, on this day.

Broadcast 24 November 2017

25 November 1764

The birth of Henry Sirr

Turncoat, informer, abuser of power, or dedicated public servant – it all depends on your political perspective when it comes to Major Henry Sirr. Let's face it, if you were a member of the United Irishmen you probably wouldn't have liked him very much. He was to that revolutionary organisation what Eliot Ness was to Al Capone.

Henry Sirr was a police chief *extraordinaire*. He dedicated his life to catching bad guys for two decades at the turn of the eighteenth century. Well, a lot of his life anyway. He was also a wine merchant. That would be a bit like Garda Commissioner Noreen O'Sullivan owning a few pubs on the side.

Sirr served in the British Army from 1778–91, where one of his military acquaintances was a certain Lord Edward Fitzgerald. Hold that particular thought for just a few minutes.

In 1796 he became acting town major of the city of Dublin – effectively chief of the city's police force. He became a member of the Orange Order, and was permanently appointed to his new role in 1798 – a significant year I'm sure you'll agree. It was certainly significant for Sirr, and for his relentless pursuit of the revolutionary element of the Society of United Irishmen, who were planning a rebellion for that year. Sirr appears to have been well-informed by a network of spies about the activities of the leading lights of the United Irishmen. So much so that he caught almost the entire committee of the Leinster branch at a covert meeting on 12 March 1798, in the house of the woollen merchant Oliver Bond. The only man he missed was his old army colleague Lord Edward Fitzgerald, but he atoned for that oversight on 19 May when he shot and killed Fitzgerald after the aristocrat had tried to stab him to avoid arrest. A few days later he also caught the radical Sheares brothers in two different houses on the same day; this may have given rise to his reputation for bi-location.

Five years later Sirr added to his lustre – assuming you were a major fan of Dublin Castle – by apprehending the young rebel leader Robert Emmet, a month after his ill-starred Dublin rising. He also burst into the home of the eminent barrister John Philpott Curran in a frustrated attempt to locate correspondence between Emmet and Curran's daughter Sarah.

Raiding Curran's house must have given Sirr considerable pleasure, as the two men had rubbed up against each other before. In 1802 Curran had represented one John Hevey in the case of *Hevey v Sirr*. Hevey had been arrested by Sirr and later sued for assault, battery and false imprisonment. Curran went to town on Sirr in his cross examination, and Hevey duly won damages of one hundred and fifty pounds – more than ten thousand pounds today. Testifying to Sirr's lack of popularity, bonfires were lit all around the city and church bells were rung when the verdict was announced.

Sirr paid a personal price for his pursuit of the United Irishmen; he escaped at least three assassination attempts, and was forced to move his family home on no less than six occasions before being quartered inside Dublin Castle. A noted collector of antiques and curios, he is believed to have obtained and retained copies of every broadside, cartoon or satirical article in which he featured.

Sirr, however, was not a stereotypical villain. He was a deeply religious man who was involved with the wonderfully named Association for Discountenancing Vice. He was also a founder of the Irish Society for Promoting Scriptural Education in the Irish Language. Later in life he became a magistrate, was an admirer of Daniel O'Connell, and supported the 1832 Reform Act, which curtailed aristocratic privilege in the House of Commons.

Despite doing the State much service, he was never knighted or elevated to the peerage. Perhaps the civil authorities and the monarchs of his day felt that he was just a little too prone to the odd abuse of power. Or maybe they felt that someone called Sir Henry Sirr had just too much tautology.

Major Henry Charles Sirr, Dublin Chief of Police in interesting times, was born, two hundred and fifty-two years ago, on this day.

Broadcast 25 November 2016

3 November 1831

The birth of Ignatius Donnelly

Talking about the Aryan race was actively discouraged until recently. Then we discovered the so-called 'alt right'. It could become unpopular all over again if the ideas of Ignatius Donnelly are correct. His theory was that Aryans were from the lost island of Atlantis, and that their red-haired, blue-eyed descendants were Irish. So, eat shamrock Breitbart.com!

Ignatius Loyola Donnelly was born to an Irish father and an Irish-American mother in Philadelphia in 1831. He became a lawyer in his twenties, but devoted most of his life to politics and to what would today be described as 'pseudo-science' but which, in the nineteenth century, had a significant constituency.

Donnelly was something of a utopian socialist. In the 1850s he co-founded a commune in Minnesota which went spectacularly bust after one of the cyclical financial downturns of nineteenth-century America. This was the 'panic of 1857' – grandson of the 'panic of 1819', son of the 'panic of 1837', and father of the 'panic of 1873'. You could almost set your alarm clock by them.

After that, Donnelly, who had acquired something of a reputation for financial impropriety, entered politics, the last refuge of the scoundrel. He was a Congressman for the Minnesota Second District from 1863–69, an advocate of female suffrage, and a radical champion of freed slaves. So, not that much of a scoundrel after all. We'll come back to the politics later.

But he was also celebrated in the late nineteenth century for his writing, especially his explorations of the legend of the lost city of Atlantis in his book *Atlantis: The Antediluvian World* (1882). He had an intense Platonic relationship with his subject, as in, he took as gospel everything the Greek philosopher Plato had written about the place. Atlantis wasn't a fable to Donnelly or Plato, it was real. It was where man first rose from barbarism to civilisation. It was destroyed by a natural disaster that gave rise to the biblical stories of the Flood. There's a lot more besides. It's all very 'New Agey', and led to Donnelly being dubbed by some as 'The Prince of Cranks'. In a subsequent work he speculated that the cataclysmic event that had destroyed Atlantis had been caused by a meteor strike. While his work may have been slightly wacky and alternative, it sold very well.

Donnelly also had a bee in his bonnet about William Shakespeare. He was one of many who tried to debunk the notion that the plays ascribed to Shakespeare had actually been written by the humble thespian from Stratford upon Avon. His theory was that they were actually the work of Francis Bacon, the seventeenth-century English philosopher. He theorised that Bacon had inserted a code in the works of Shakespeare which only clever people like Ignatius Donnelly were capable of deciphering. The 'Bacon as Shakespeare' theory had a lot of enthusiastic adherents at the time. It still does today.

In 1891 Donnelly wrote a dystopian science-fiction novel which predicted the invention of radio, TV, the internet and poison gas. *Caesar's Column* is set in 1988 in an America ruled by a ruthless financial oligarchy. So, well off the mark there! The book is about an insurrection against capitalism.

Politically, Donnelly moved leftwards as he got older, from the anti-slavery Republican party of the Civil War to the People's Party of the 1890s. The latter was a coalition of mid-western agricultural and labour interests which sought an eight-hour working day, the abandonment of the gold standard, and the reining-in of the massively wealthy and predatory railway interests. Donnelly was responsible for much of the formulation of the political platform of this short-lived 'third' party.

In 1900, a few months before his death, he was nominated as the vice-presidential candidate for the People's Party in that year's general election.

Ignatius Loyola Donnelly, who, despite being called after the founder of the Jesuit Order renounced his Irish Catholicism early in his life, was born one hundred and eighty-six years ago, on this day.

Broadcast 3 November 2017

10 November 1861

The funeral of Terence Bellew McManus

Say what you like about the Irish republican movement since the 1860s, but you'd have to concede, they do great funerals. There would have been no ... 'The fools, the fools, they have left us our Fenian dead', from Patrick Pearse in 1915 had the IRB not transported the body of Jeremiah O'Donovan Rossa from New York to have him buried in Glasnevin. That was one of the reasons why the British authorities were quick to dispose of the bodies of the executed 1916 leaders 'in-house'. The last thing they wanted was fourteen Dublin funerals.

But the obsequies of Rossa were merely an expert copy, convincing but unoriginal. The first great Fenian funeral was that of a relatively obscure Young Irelander, Terence Bellew McManus. He was no Thomas Davis, no John Mitchel, not even a Thomas Francis Meagher. But he had occupied a prominent position in the mid-1850s generational conflict between the romantic nationalists of the Young Ireland movement and the waning Daniel O'Connell. And he died, in San Francisco, at just the right time.

McManus was a friend of one of the founders of the *Nation* newspaper, Charles Gavan Duffy. He had made a fortune exporting wool, and then lost most of it in the mid-1840s investing in railroad stock. An enthusiastic British-based Young Irelander, he travelled back to this country in 1848 after the authorities declared martial law in anticipation of a rebellion. He was one of the few members of the movement who actually took up arms. He participated in the only military action of the 1848 rising, the infamous skirmish at the Widow McCormack's cottage in Ballingarry, Co. Tipperary. He eluded capture in Ireland and returned to Britain. There he was declared bankrupt and just managed to get on board a ship bound for the USA before he was arrested.

Unfortunately, the ship on which he was travelling was called back to port, he was hauled off, and tried for treason. His famous statement, that he had acted as he did, 'not because I loved England less, but because I loved Ireland more' cut no ice. He was sentenced, like most of his fellow leaders, to be hanged, drawn and quartered – an appalling penalty that remained on the statute books for the crime of high treason. A petition seeking clemency for the convicted Young Ireland leaders, with one hundred and fifty thousand signatures appended, was presented by the Lord Mayor of Dublin to the Lord Lieutenant. The barbaric capital penalties were reduced to the lesser punishment of transportation. By October 1849 he was settling into life in the penal colony of Tasmania, or Van Diemen's Land.

Like a number of his colleagues, McManus managed to escape from captivity – in his case with Thomas Francis Meagher – and made his way to San Francisco in 1851. After which McManus disappeared from sight, abjured most political activity, and tried to build up a respectable business, though without much success. He suffered a fatal accident in January 1861, died and was buried in San Francisco. And that should have been the last we ever heard of Terence Bellew McManus.

However, a campaign was organised to raise money to put a monument over his grave in Lone Mountain Cemetery.

But the IRB had a better idea. Instead of a monument, McManus got a two-month one-way trip back to Ireland, via Panama, New York and Cobh. This was followed by a huge funeral in Dublin, skillfully organised and exploited by the Irish Republican Brotherhood. The organisation had not existed when McManus was in his pomp, but included some of his former Young Ireland chums like James Stephens.

The Cardinal-Archbishop of Dublin, Paul Cullen, was allergic to Fenians and refused to allow McManus's coffin to lie in the Pro-Cathedral. So, instead, he lay in state in the Mechanic's Institute, from where his remains were taken, in solemn procession, to Glasnevin Cemetery, watched by thousands of Dubliners.

Whether or not this indicated growing support for the nascent Fenian movement, or just confirmed the Irish attachment to a good funeral, it emboldened the IRB and greatly vexed their constitutional nationalist opponents, as well as most of the Roman Catholic hierarchy.

McManus eventually got his monument, but not until well into the twentieth century. Funds had been raised to build the monument by 1895 but the inscription was considered too political, and the Glasnevin Cemetery Committee refused to allow it to be erected until 1933. He now shares his grave with, among others, Patrick W. Nally, after whom the Nally Stand in Croke Park was named.

Terence Bellew McManus emerged from relative obscurity to become the central figure of the biggest funeral in Dublin since Daniel O'Connell's, one hundred and fifty-six years ago, on this day.

Broadcast 10 November 2017

4 November 1908

The Irish Women's Franchise League is established

What's the difference between a suffragist and a suffragette? Apparently, the latter is a more militant version of the former. In which case Ireland boasted plenty of suffragettes.

It is a slight misconception that Irish women didn't get the vote until 1918. In 1898 they were granted the vote in local government elections. But the object of suffragists was to secure the franchise for adult women in parliamentary elections, and the right of women to present themselves as candidates. In the self-governing colony of New Zealand women had been entitled to vote since 1893, and full voting rights had also been secured in Australia in 1902. So the UK, which included Ireland, was well behind the colonies.

In the early 1900s a rather genteel organization with the ungainly name of the Irish Women's Suffrage and Local Government Association was in the vanguard of the struggle for votes for women. But it was not the kind of group that *demanded* universal suffrage. It preferred to ask politely. Male politicians liked politeness, but that didn't mean they listened to gentle persuasion.

In 1908 a rather more muscular combination, the Irish Women's Franchise League, was established by, among others, Hanna Sheehy Skeffington and Margaret Cousins. The latter was a remarkable woman who went on to greater fame in

India, where she composed the music for that country's national anthem. Sheehy Skeffington, a secondary teacher, a socialist and a nationalist, was from a political family. Her father, David Sheehy, was a nationalist MP. In 1903 she married Francis Skeffington and took his name. She insisted, however, that he take hers at the same time. He was one of the co-founders of the IWFL.

The newly formed Irish Women's Franchise League was based on the Pankhurst-led – and Pankhurst-ruled – Women's Political and Social Union; but the homage of imitation did not include any desire for affiliation. The Irish suffrage movement remained resolutely separate from its British counterpart. In part, this distinctiveness was expressed in the use of the orange and green colours in the organisation's insignia.

Their differences were seen most clearly at the outbreak of the Great War, when the bulk of the British suffragists sided with the war effort. The same was, however, not true of the Irish Women's Franchise League, which resolutely opposed the war and the drive for recruits in Ireland.

Irish suffragette leaders were required to address numerous public meetings. Margaret Cousins, to whom public speaking was anathema, described how she would practice in an open field with only a donkey looking on. There were obviously quite a few male donkeys who attended Irish women's suffrage meetings because Sheehy Skeffington recalled in later life that speakers had to be 'capable of keeping their temper under bombardments of rotten eggs, over-ripe tomatoes, bags of flour [and] stinking chemicals'.

Sheehy Skeffington was prominent in the militant actions carried out by members of the Franchise League. She was jailed in 1912 for breaking windows in government buildings. She threw a hatchet at British Prime Minister Herbert Asquith, though it probably did not have the effect of waking him up. She lost her teaching job for throwing stones at Dublin Castle and assaulting a policeman. Bear in mind, in relation to the latter charge, that your average member of the Dublin Metropolitan Police would have been close to six feet in height. Hanna was five foot two.

Like many other early twentieth-century feminists, Sheehy Skeffington went on hunger strike while in jail. She was temporarily released under legislation especially devised for hunger-striking suffragettes. It was officially entitled the Prisoner's Temporary Discharge of Ill Health Act, but became better known under its colloquial name, the Cat and Mouse Act. As the name suggests, this allowed the authorities to release a hunger striker and then re-arrest her when her health recovered.

The Irish Women's Franchise League was founded, one hundred and eight years ago, on this day.

Broadcast 4 November 2016

11 November 1918

Armistice Day

The world had seen nothing like it before. At least nine million men had died in combat, and more than twice that number had been wounded. Untold and often uncounted millions of civilians had perished in the conflict itself, and in its many 'Ugly Sisters', such as the Armenian Massacre, and the Russian Revolution. Sadly, the 'war to end all wars' didn't, and the process was repeated twenty years later with even more tragic results.

But it had to come to an end at some point, and eventually it did. Germany was in no position to fight on. The generals did what they often do – made sure the blame was passed to politicians and then retired or waited to get the whole thing started all over again.

Three days of intense negotiations in a forest near Compiègne in France yielded little more than an abject, unconditional surrender for Germany after one thousand five hundred and sixty-six days of fighting. Hostilities were to cease at 11:00 a.m. on 11 November, entirely coincidentally, but poetically and memorably, the eleventh hour, of the eleventh day, of the eleventh month.

For the British Army, it was a clear case of *déjà vu*. Their war ended where it had begun, outside the Belgian city of Mons. Which is why five of the first and four of the final British fatalities of the war are buried in St Symphorien Cemetery, a few yards, and nine million lives, apart.

The last British soldier to die did so at 9:30 on the morning of the 11 of November. George Ellison from Leeds was serving in the Fifth Royal Irish Lancers when he met his end. He is buried facing the grave of John Parr, the first British fatality of the conflict.

You might expect a spirit of 'live and let live' on the last day of such an obscene war. But actually, it was mostly business as usual. The American general John J. Pershing decided his army had not lost nearly enough men, and ordered vigorous actions to be conducted against the Germans right up to the eleventh hour. More than ten thousand men were killed, wounded or were taken prisoner on the ultimate day. Three thousand of the casualties were American.

Irishmen responded in various ways, some with rapture, others with indifference and apathy. One Dublin Fusilier, the unrepentant southern unionist Captain Noel Drury, wrote in his diary that:

It's like when one heard of the death of a friend – a sort of forlorn feeling. I went along and read the order to the men, but they just stared at me and showed no enthusiasm at all. One or two muttered "We were just getting a bit of our own back". They all had the look of hounds whipped off just as they were about to kill.

Another veteran, Frank Hitchcock of the Leinster Regiment, brother of the Hollywood director Rex Ingram, recalled that:

The Brigadier had galloped up and yelled out: "The War is over! The Kaiser has abdicated!" We were typically Irish, and never cheered except under adverse conditions such as shell-fire and rain. Somewhat crestfallen the Brigadier rode slowly off to communicate his glad tidings to an English battalion, who, no doubt took the news in a different way.

Terence Poulter, another Dublin Fusilier, who survived into old age, was more excited at the end of hostilities:

Approaching eleven o' clock in our sector you could have heard a pin drop. When eleven o'clock came, there were loud cheers. The war was over as far as we were concerned.

Back in London, Big Ben was rung for the first time since August 1914, while in Paris, gas lamps were lit for the first time in four years as the Great War finally came to an end, ninety-eight years ago, on this day.

Broadcast 11 November 2016

18 November 1926

George Bernard Shaw refuses the Nobel Prize for Literature

It is one of those great table quiz questions, the answer to which is likely to spark a bun-fight worthy of any UKIP parliamentary party meeting. 'How many Irish writers have won the Nobel Prize for literature?' You'd probably answer 'Four'. And you'd probably be right. Except that our most recent winner, Seamus Heaney, was technically born in the United Kingdom, so if it's a tie at the end of the night that dweeby nerd on the team that finished in joint-first place might insist that your answer to that question was incorrect. Am I speaking from direct experience? Did the adjudicator rule in his favour? Did we lose? Did I want to wring his obsessive, compulsive, pedantic, self-satisfied neck? We will never know.

But the commonly accepted answer – I hope he's listening – is four, namely W. B. Yeats in 1923, George Bernard Shaw in 1925, Samuel Beckett in 1969 and Seamus Heaney in 1995. Beckett, incidentally, is thus far the only first-class cricketer to have received a Nobel Prize. Which is probably not that important really. What is of more consequence is that Beckett's wife Suzanne considered the award to be a 'catastrophe', and Beckett himself gave all his prize money away.

There have been one hundred and thirteen Nobel Literature Laureates, with France leading the way on sixteen wins and the USA – courtesy of Bob Dylan – just ahead of the UK in second place, on eleven. Unless of course you're so pedantic you absolutely *insist* on Seamus Heaney being described as a UK winner (I'm really *not* bitter, you understand) in which case the UK would be joint second. For the record, Ireland lies in joint-eighth place alongside Poland and Russia.

Yeats was cited for 'his always inspired poetry, which in a highly artistic form gives expression to the spirit of a whole nation'. Shaw was honoured for 'his work which is marked by both idealism and humanity, its stimulating satire often being infused with a singular poetic beauty'. Beckett was awarded the prize 'for his writing, which – in new forms for the novel and drama – in the destitution of modern man acquires its elevation', and Heaney 'for works of lyrical beauty and ethical depth, which exalt everyday miracles and the living past'.

Shaw was nearly seventy years of age when he finally won the award. It was his play about Joan of Arc, *St Joan*, written in 1923, the year of her canonization, that seems to have sealed the deal for the Nobel Committee. They had, after all, managed to overlook the Shaw of *Man and Superman* (1903), *Major Barbara* (1905) and *Pygmalion* (1913) while giving the prize in 1907 to the imperialist zealot Rudyard Kipling, who became the first UK winner. Though as he was actually born in Bombay, certain nit-picking know-alls might claim that he was the first *Indian* winner. But we'll let that one pass.

Shaw was about as enamoured of the award as Beckett would be more than forty years later. He didn't quite reject the prize, but he said some pretty scathing things about it, and refused to take the money. He is reported as having observed that, 'I can forgive Nobel for inventing dynamite, but only a fiend in human form could have invented the Nobel Prize'. As regards the prize-fund he pointed out that 'My readers and my audiences provide me with more than sufficient money for my needs'. Shaw thus turned down seven thousand pounds – the equivalent of over three hundred thousand pounds in 2016 – or about half the value of this year's award.

Until the Nobel Committee gave the 2016 award to Bob Dylan, Shaw had been the only writer to have won both a Nobel Prize and an Oscar – in his case for best-adapted screenplay of his own play, *Pygmalion*. He was even less pleased with his Academy Award than he was with his Nobel gong – describing it as 'an insult'. Though apparently he still placed the slim golden statuette on his mantelpiece. He didn't turn up for either the Academy or Nobel awards bash, but he wasn't able to spurn the Oscar dosh because there wasn't any.

George Bernard Shaw turned down the cash element of his Nobel Prize, though not the award itself, ninety years ago, on this day.

Broadcast 18 November 2016

17 November 1930

The first Irish Hospital Sweepstakes draw takes place

For decades, it offered people the hope, or the illusion, of potential riches. It appeared to be a benevolent charity that was channelling vast sums into an underfunded Irish medical system. Granted it caused ructions around the globe because it was a popular but illegal lottery, but there was something poetic, or ironic at least, in the idea of British and American gamblers funding the Irish health service.

Of course, like so many apparently altruistic Irish institutions, it was mostly a sham, a money-grabbing masquerade designed to enrich a small number of already wealthy individuals. The Irish Hospital Sweepstakes bears out the axiom that if something is too good to be true, it's probably not true.

The first draw in November 1930 was, in retrospect, utterly distasteful, but wonderfully stage-managed by the organisation's own P. T. Barnum, Spencer Freeman. Two young boys from St Joseph's School in Drumcondra, both blind and wearing placards bearing the names 'Willie' and 'Peter', were supervised by Garda Commissioner and future Fascist Eoin O'Duffy in drawing the winning tickets. Later, the blind children would be replaced by smiling nurses. Three delighted Belfast men shared an astronomical and life-changing prize fund of over two hundred thousand pounds. The Sweepstakes was well on its way to becoming the employer of up to four thousand people. The surplus was destined, after the deduction of appropriate administration costs, of course, to heal the sick. Everyone was a winner.

Except that everyone wasn't. Less than ten per cent of the turnover – still a considerable sum of money – found its way to the funding of Irish hospitals. Employees, mostly female, were badly paid, and much of the turnover enriched the stakeholders in the private company that ran the enterprise.

The Irish Hospital Sweepstakes was the brainchild of Dublin bookmaker Richard Duggan, War of Independence veteran Joseph McGrath, and Welsh-born Captain Spencer Freeman, a man with a flair for the theatrical. By 1932, after two years of clever marketing, illegal sales, and excessive point shaving, all three were millionaires.

The Sweepstakes also affected political relationships between Ireland and, in particular, Britain and the USA, where the sale of lottery tickets was illegal but widespread. For their part, the British governments of the 1930s were not best pleased that millions of pounds were leaving the country illegally, bound for Eamon de Valera's Irish Free State in the midst of an economic war between the two countries.

In America, McGrath's erstwhile political ally, the veteran Republican Joe McGarrity, was in charge of operations. He wrote in his memoir that he used much of his own considerable personal profits from the venture to purchase IRA guns. This was at a time when that organization was collaborating with Nazi Germany. Recently opened Secret Service files in London revealed that MI5 had fears that the same thing was happening in Britain.

Among the abuses of which the operators stood accused was a sort of 'past-posting' scam. Exploiting the time difference between Europe and the USA, the operators purchased shares in winning tickets from their unwitting holders and claimed some of the prize money themselves. In 1936 Spencer

Freeman, armed with the results of races, used this system to purchase half-shares in eight successful American tickets. He netted nearly a quarter of a million pounds in winnings from his own lottery. By the 1970s the directors had creamed off more than a hundred million pounds in profits.

And, surprise surprise, some of the proceeds from the Sweepstakes were allegedly used to fund the campaigns of friendly Irish politicians.

One distinctly unfriendly politician was Justice Minister Desmond O'Malley who, in the 1970s, sought information on the allocation of the turnover from the lottery. So powerful was the Sweepstakes that he was pressurized into minding his own business. The Government was reminded that any adverse publicity or punitive action against the directors would lead to the loss of hundreds of jobs. In 1973, when the journalist Joe McAnthony finally exposed some of the dubious activities of the lottery in the *Sunday Independent*, all the Sweepstakes' advertising in the newspaper was pulled.

When An Post was awarded the franchise to run the new National Lottery in 1986, that was the end of the Irish Hospital's Sweepstakes. Its employees – mainly elderly women – were discarded, with virtually no provision being made for them.

The notion that it was all 'great craic' and, from a hospital's point of view, better than a poke in the eye from a sharp stick, has its champions. However, at the very least, it is yet another example of the fledgling Irish State farming out vital services to bodies with an agenda of their own. In this case, that of making large fortunes for themselves.

The first winning tickets were drawn in the Irish Hospital Sweepstakes lottery, eighty-seven years ago, on this day.

Broadcast 17 November 2017

December

30 December 1691

Irish scientist Robert Boyle dies

You would think that someone who published a work with the words 'touching the spring of the air' in the title was probably some class of a poet. But in the case of Robert Boyle you would be wrong. The full title of what was actually a scientific paper was *New experiments physico-mechanical, touching the spring of the air and its effects*.

Boyle was one of the most extraordinary and influential Irish-born scientists. In the paper with the semi-poetic title he was experimenting with a vacuum chamber, and assessing the impact of the withdrawal of air on light, flame and living creatures. Not very healthy in the latter case, would have been one of the conclusions, no doubt.

Boyle was the fourteenth child, and seventh son, of the Great Earl of Cork, Richard Boyle, buccaneer, con-man, adventurer, consummate politician and soldier. Born in the picturesque surroundings of Lismore Castle in Waterford, the young Boyle was dispatched to Eton at the age of eight and, thereafter, spent only a few years in Ireland. While Dad was cheating, lying, bullying and finagling his way to a huge fortune and almost unparalleled political influence, young Robert was playing with his chemistry set. Out of this work came recognition as the first modern chemist, and the formula for which he is best known, and which is named after him, Boyle's Law – of which more *anon*.

Boyle, along with a private tutor, Robert Carew, with whom he could converse in Irish, did the Grand Tour of Europe in his mid-teens, in an era well before the Grand Tour became the norm for aristocratic families. In the course of his extended vacation, he visited Florence in 1641, where he may have met an elderly Galileo Galilei. As an aspiring scientist, he did try to live and work in Ireland, but gave up in 1654, describing the land of his birth as 'a barbarous country where chemical spirits were so misunderstood and chemical instruments so unprocurable that it was hard to have any Hermetic thoughts in it'.

From the early 1650s Boyle devoted himself to science and to a variety of potential inventions – according to his own notes his experiments included research into 'the prolongation of life', 'the art of flying', 'perpetual light', 'a certain way of finding longitudes' and 'potent drugs to alter or exalt imagination' – had he been able to paint he might have been a new Leonardo da Vinci. Had he been born a few hundred years later – given the latter topic – he might have been Timothy Leary.

In 1662 he used an air pump, built by his assistant Robert Hooke, to come up with the axiom that bears his name. It goes thus: 'For a fixed amount of a gas kept at a fixed temperature, pressure and volume are inversely proportional.'

And that's as deeply as we are going to go, because I'm already well outside my comfort zone. In coming up with Boyle's Law he got in fourteen years ahead of the French scientist Edme Mariotte, who came to the same conclusion; otherwise the principle would today be known as Mariotte's Law, and Robert Boyle would be familiar only to chemists as an early innovator.

As if all that wasn't enough, Boyle was also a philosopher and theologian – though his work in those areas did attract a certain amount of opprobrium. His 1665 *Occasional Reflections upon Several Subjects* was lampooned by Jonathan Swift in his own *Meditation Upon a Broomstick* (1710).

But of probably greater significance was the work he produced in 1661, the year before the publication of Boyle's Law, called *The Sceptical Chemist*, in which he hypothesized that matter consisted of atoms and clusters of atoms in motion. Not bad for someone writing more than three and a half centuries ago. The Boyle Medal for Science has been presented in his honour since 1899.

Robert Boyle, the Father of Chemistry, died three hundred and twenty-five years ago, on this day.

Broadcast 30 December 2016

22 December 1740

The birth of Bishop Joseph Stock

The United Irishmen's rebellion of 1798 was over – except that it wasn't. Not quite. There would be a sting in the tail for the British authorities who had already savagely put down the main uprisings in Antrim and Wexford and minor eruptions elsewhere. They had been royally assisted by spies and informers, like Francis Magan and Francis Higgins, in anticipating the rebellion in Dublin. Their luck had held out in the winter of 1796 when a French fleet had been unable to land due to adverse weather conditions at Bantry Bay.

But there was a fairer wind off the coast of Mayo on 22 August 1798 when, two months after the United Irishmen had otherwise been defeated, shot, piked, hanged, drawn and quartered, the French arrived in the form of a force of around one thousand men, led by General Jean Joseph Humbert. A little bit *trop tard* but better than *jamais*. The great Irish-American writer Thomas Flanagan called it *The Year of the French* (1979) in his epic novel. In reality it was much closer to 'The Fortnight of the French', a designation that lacks a bit of punch and drama. The intervention, initially successful, was all over by 8 September.

The French invasion force – dispatched on the basis of that age-old axiom that 'the enemy of my enemy is my friend' – gave rise to the short-lived Republic of Connacht, under the presidency of the Mayo landowner John Moore. But it also spawned a fascinating captivity memoir, written by the incumbent Church of Ireland Bishop of Killala, Joseph Stock.

Stock, a fluent French speaker, was born in Dublin in 1740. The son of a wealthy merchant, he was educated at Trinity College. He became a clergyman and was briefly headmaster of Portora Royal School in Enniskillen before becoming a bishop in January 1798. In 1776 he had published a biography of the great Irish cleric and philosopher Bishop George Berkeley, a few years after his death.

Stock had the misfortune to be in the wrong place at the wrong time when the French force arrived. He was captured, along with the British defenders of Killala. That evening he met Humbert. The encounter was extremely revealing. It was clear that Humbert had been led to believe that there would be considerable Irish aristocratic support for the invasion. He actually asked an establishment figure like the Church of Ireland Bishop of Killala if, as Stock puts it, 'he chose to embrace the fortunate opportunity at once of serving himself and liberating his country'. Stock politely declined the offer and chose to become a prisoner.

The French experienced initial success, notably in overpowering a British force at Castlebar in a skirmish that became known as 'The Races of Castlebar' because of the rapidity of the British retreat. This victory prompted uprisings in Longford and Westmeath. These were quickly put down by British troops and loyal Irish militia units. But, no poetry intended, it all came unstuck at Ballinamuck. There, Humbert's force, augmented by Irish rebels, was soundly defeated. The captured French were later exchanged for British prisoners of war, but many of the Irish were immediately executed. Stock demonstrated his personal loyalties by referring in his narrative to 8 September 1798 as 'a day memorable for the victory at Ballinamuck'.

Humbert was later repatriated in a prisoner exchange, rejoined Napoleon's army, and even fought against the British alongside Andrew Jackson in the American war of 1812. A street in Ballina is called after him; on it stands a monument erected in his honour.

Stock's narrative of the rebellion was remarkably nuanced and even-handed for someone who was a bishop of the established Church and who had been a prisoner of the rebels. He emphasised that there was little retribution of any kind on the part of the Irish rebels allied to the French force. The only killings took place in pitched battles. There was some looting and arson, but Stock points out that the depredations of the British forces were far greater than those of the United Irishmen. Stock chose to publish the memoir anonymously in 1800, which was, in retrospect, a wise move. All references to himself or *Monsieur l'Eveque*, as Humbert called him, are in the third person. But he was quickly identified as its author, and subsequent imprints bore his name. His relative fairness probably did him no favours when it came to his subsequent clerical career.

Bishop Joseph Stock, author of a fascinating memoir of one of the most colourful episodes of the 1798 rebellion, was born, two hundred and seventy-seven years ago, on this day.

Broadcast 22 December 2017

15 December 1760

'Half-hanged' MacNaughton
meets his maker

The expressions 'cad' or 'bounder' – defined as a dishonourable man who mistreats a woman – have fallen into disuse since their heyday in the eighteenth century. Which should not be construed as a suggestion that men no longer mistreat women. We just have different terminology for it these days.

By even the lowest possible standards, John McNaughton was a supreme cad and an outrageous bounder. If you befriended him he was likely to steal your wife or daughter. If you lent him money you were unlikely to get it back – *and* he would then go on to steal your wife or daughter, or both. If you shook hands with him, you needed to count your fingers afterwards.

McNaughton, who was born in 1722, was the son of a wealthy landowner. He attended Trinity College, Dublin but didn't graduate. His affection for gambling might have been a contributory factor. However, he cut a handsome and popular figure at Trinity, and was taken under the wing of Lord Massereene, whose family name was, I kid you not, Clotworthy Skeffington. You have to feel sympathetic towards someone whose parents had named him Clotworthy. Even more so when it emerges how shabbily Massereene was treated by McNaughton, who was also a bit of a popinjay, as well as being a cad and a bounder. A popinjay was a flash cad.

McNaughton married Massereene's sister in law, but not before he was obliged to take an oath to foreswear his gambling activities. He was as good as his word ... for two whole years, a lifetime in the career of a rake. A rake, in this case, is not a gardening implement, but a dissolute popinjay. Still with me?

Having built up huge debts – a word still used extensively in the twenty-first century – an attempt was made to arrest McNaughton. He only managed to stay out of jail because the shock induced his pregnant wife into premature labour, and she died. Lord Massereene, who must either have been a saint or a certifiable idiot, then got McNaughton a job as a tax collector in Coleraine. Now, it might have been predictable that a gambling addiction, as well as access to thousands of pounds of excise money, would be mutually destructive. And, so it proved. As a gesture of gratitude to Lord Massereene, McNaughton embezzled eight hundred pounds of the King's tax revenue, and lost it at the gambling tables.

Step forward Andrew Knox, MP for Donegal. He took pity on our rakish cad and invited him to live in his house. His reward was an affair between McNaughton and his fifteen-year old daughter, Mary Anne Knox. Whether this was based on physical attraction, or the fact that she had a fortune of six thousand pounds of her own, or both, we shall never know. McNaughton asked to marry her, and was peremptorily, and sensibly, refused by her father. So he set about kidnapping her instead and forcing her to marry him.

In November 1761 McNaughton and a group of accomplices intercepted the Knox coach on its way to Dublin. But things didn't go according to plan, something of a pattern with McNaughton's life. The attempted abduction was violently resisted, there was a gunfight, and McNaughton ended up shooting dead his intended bride. The star-crossed lover was himself wounded, but escaped, only to be caught and lodged in Lifford Jail. He was tried along with one of his accomplices, John Dunlap. Both men were sentenced to be hanged in Strabane. The gallows was constructed by the uncle of Mary Anne Knox.

Here's where the story gets really interesting. Hanging in those days was utterly unscientific. There was no special knot to cause the neck to break rapidly and avoid strangulation. There was no lever, or trapdoor. You either jumped off the gallows yourself, or you were pushed. If you jumped vigorously there was a good chance your neck would break immediately and you would not be left swinging and strangling agonizingly.

In this case the bounder bounded. McNaughton leaped enthusiastically from the lovingly constructed gallows. So much so that the rope broke. Some reports suggest that this happened on three occasions before he finally died. All kinds of myths surround the hanging. There was a presumption, untrue as it happens, that if a condemned man survived execution the Crown could not attempt to re-hang him. McNaughton, therefore, was said to have offered himself up to the hangman, so broken-hearted was he at the death of Mary Anne Knox. In this version of events, McNaughton was not in mourning for her money. Therefore, he died a noble and courageous death.

More likely, to this cynic at least, the sheriff just kept going until he got it right. The incident earned the late John McNaughton the nickname, 'Half-hanged'. His accomplice John Dunlap met his maker immediately after his employer was finally dispatched.

John McNaughton, murderer, libertine and chronic debtor, was hanged, two hundred and fifty-six years ago, on this day.

Broadcast 15 December 2017

2 December 1802

Sir Dominic Corrigan, cardiologist, is born in Dublin

Next time you're watching TV and you see someone bend over a prone figure, place their finger on his or her carotid artery and pronounce them dead, you can turn to whoever you're with and tell them suavely, 'No Corrigan's pulse'. If the almost inevitable response is 'How do you know their name is Corrigan?' you can then crank the suavity up to the level of smugness by responding, 'I'm not referring to the corpse, but to the technique employed to establish morbidity'.

All right, I accept that's probably too smug. It's also a gross oversimplification on my part.

The Corrigan in question is Sir Dominic John Corrigan, who was born in Thomas Street in Dublin in 1802, on the site of what is now an Augustinian church. Unusually for that time, he received his university education in St Patrick's College, Maynooth, which already had a section for non-clerical students. He qualified as a doctor in Edinburgh in 1825, where he would just have missed dissecting bodies supplied by the notorious grave-robbers and murderers Burke and Hare to the University's anatomy professor Dr Robert Knox.

After qualifying in Scotland, Corrigan returned to practise medicine in Dublin, rising to the dizzy heights of rooms in Merrion Square by 1837. In addition to his lucrative private practice, he also worked extensively amongst the poor of the city, specializing in heart and lung complaints. He incurred considerable personal risk, as did many members of his profession, during the Famine, working with the victims of potentially fatal communicable diseases. His extensive and badly paid public health work made him unpopular with many of his more mercenary colleagues, and he was initially blackballed when he applied for membership of what would become the Royal College of Physicians of Ireland. He circumvented the veto by cheekily taking an entrance examination along with a group of newly qualified doctors in 1855. Revenge was sweet. He was president of the RCPI four years later, the first Roman Catholic to hold the office. His original naysayers would not be pleased by the fact that there is a statue and a portrait of Corrigan in the RCPI building on Kildare Street in Dublin today, while no one even remembers the physicians who blackballed him.

Corrigan appears to have been a patient-centered doctor. He once scolded a junior colleague for consulting his watch in front of a patient. In addition to his work as a cardiologist, he also developed a cauterising device known as Corrigan's Button. This exquisitely painful looking instrument was heated and placed on the skin several times to treat, among other ailments, sciatica. It was also used as a form of shock treatment for psychiatric patients. So, if you were depressed and suffering from back pain, you probably ran a mile when you saw Corrigan approaching. Corrigan's Button has, happily, gone the way of the rack and the thumbscrew. Though it's invention probably contributed to his becoming a baronet in 1866.

In 1870 Dr Corrigan stepped well outside his comfort zone by standing in a parliamentary by-election as a Liberal. It was the year of William Gladstone's first Irish Land Act, and Corrigan was duly elected. He was an ardent advocate of early release for Fenian prisoners, jailed after the 1867 rebellion. But he then did something unconscionable for any Irish politician. He fell foul of the publicans. Corrigan was a temperance advocate actively seeking the Sunday closure of public houses, and thus lost the confidence of his electorate and, more importantly, their extremely active and vociferous publicans. He didn't stand for re-election in 1874, though this probably had little impact on the return to power of Disraeli and the Tories that year.

Sir Dominic John Corrigan, humanitarian, cardiologist and inventor of one of the nastiest looking medical devices ever devised, was born, two hundred and fourteen years ago, on this day.

Broadcast 2 December 2016

8 December 1831

The death of James Hoban, architect of the White House

It is one of the most celebrated addresses in the world – 1600 Pennsylvania Avenue, North West, Washington DC – a large neo-classical building, bigger now than its original incarnation, and it was designed by an Irish architect. The White House and James Hoban are inextricably linked.

Hoban was born in 1755 in Callan, Co. Kilkenny – his actual date of birth was only definitively established in 2016 with the release of millions of Irish-Catholic baptismal records online. He worked as a wheelwright and a carpenter until he was in his twenties. When he showed promise as a scholar he was offered a place to study drawing and architecture in the Dublin Society's Drawing School on Grafton Street. He worked on James Gandon's Custom House project as an artisan, before emigrating to the USA in 1785. There he quickly established himself as an architect in Philadelphia, and later in South Carolina.

In 1791 the first US president, George Washington, then based in Philadelphia, had been impressed by the Charleston, South Carolina County Courthouse designed by Hoban. He asked to meet the architect. The following year he chose Hoban's design for the new presidential mansion from among nine proposals, one of which had been submitted anonymously by Thomas Jefferson, his own secretary of state.

Hoban's original competition entry, for which he won five hundred dollars, and which does not survive, did not entirely meet with the approval of the man after whom the new federal capital would be named. Washington asked Hoban to remove the third floor he had envisaged and to widen the building from nine to eleven bays. Hoban, in putting together his final drawings, was influenced by the design of the town house of the Dukes of Leinster on Kildare Street in Dublin. Today we know this humble mansion as Leinster House. So the annual delivery of a bowl of shamrock is not the only Irish influence on the White House.

Construction began in October 1792, with much of the manual labour being performed by slaves, at least three of whom belonged to the architect himself. Hoban was employed to supervise the construction, and used mostly immigrant Scottish craftsmen to build the sandstone walls. A layer of whitewash finished the job, giving the house its distinctive, though far from unique, colour. It took eight years to build, at a cost of two hundred and thirty thousand dollars (around three and a half million today), and was ready for occupation, though still incomplete, in November 1800. This meant that John Adams, rather than its putative architect, Thomas Jefferson, became the first US president to work in the building. Washington, although he played a major role in its development, never lived there. Adams managed only four months in possession, and thought the mansion was too big. It wasn't until the presidency of Theodore Roosevelt that the building became officially known as the White House.

The original construction, other than the façade, didn't last long. The Americans fell out with their colonial masters in 1812, and went back to war. In 1814 the British set fire to the White House during their occupation of Washington

DC. It was rebuilt, again under Hoban's supervision, and re-occupied by President James Monroe in 1817, though the reconstruction wasn't finally completed until two years before the architect's death. Hoban wasn't responsible for the West Wing or the iconic Oval office, which were much later additions.

His reputation being well-established in Washington, Hoban saw no reason to leave the city, and he set up a lucrative practice there. He wasn't at all hindered by his establishment of the first masonic lodge in Washington, with one J. Hoban as master. He went on to supervise the construction of the Capitol Building and design the Great Hotel. Despite his stature, more than half a dozen of his signature buildings have been demolished, most in the eighteenth or nineteenth centuries. But despite the British in 1814, and Al Qaeda's plans for United 93 back in 2001, the White House is still intact.

James Hoban, Kilkenny-born architect and designer of the one of the world's most iconic buildings, died, one hundred and eighty-six years ago, on this day.

Broadcast 8 December 2017

29 December 1844

The birth of William Martin Murphy

They were sometimes, for geographical reasons, known as the 'Bantry Band'. But their often belligerent Roman-Catholic pietism also earned them the nickname 'The Pope's Brass Band'. Their leader may have been Timothy Healy, MP, but William Martin Murphy, entrepreneur, builder, railway-man, MP, publisher, strikebreaker and zealot, was one of the most influential forces within this group of Irish nationalist politicians who came from this beautiful part of west Cork.

Although Murphy inherited some wealth and a viable building business from his father, he quickly struck out on his own and transformed a small fortune into a much larger one. He turned up in some unexpected places early in his career. While he was known for having made large sums of money building railway lines in Africa, he was also on hand in Milltown Malbay in January 1885 when Charles Stewart Parnell turned the first sod on the project that became the Ennis and West Clare Railway. Three years after breaking the resolve of the workers of the city of Dublin, he became president of the recently established Rathmines and Rathgar Musical Society. He was succeeded in this office by, in turn, his son and daughter.

His ownership of the Dublin United Tramways Company and his leadership of the Dublin employers in their successful fight against James Larkin and the Irish Transport and General Workers' Union renders Murphy infamous, or celebrated, to this day. By locking out workers who refused to sign a pledge not to join Larkin's union, Murphy, in effect, starved them – and their families – into submission.

But of almost comparable significance was his involvement in the newspaper business. This began long before his ownership of the *Irish Independent* newspaper. In 1891, in the midst of the major political rift caused by the O'Shea divorce, Dublin members of the Parnellite faction took over the offices of the Irish Parliamentary Party newspaper, *United Ireland*. They ejected its acting editor, Matthias McDonnell Bodkin, from the premises, offering him the alternative of walking out unscathed or taking his chances being tossed out the window. The anti-Parnellite faction, which included Murphy, needed a propaganda outlet to match *United Ireland*. Murphy's money funded the shortlived *National Press*, although his name does not appear on the list of those who subscribed to the shareholding that established it.

The *National Press* was little more than a vehicle for the anti-Parnellite rhetoric and vitriol of Parnell's greatest antagonist within his own party, Timothy Healy MP. The newspaper was responsible for a series of controversial editorials. The first of these was entitled 'Stop Thief'. In this Parnell was accused of the embezzlement of National League funds. The party leader, it was claimed, had, for a number of years, 'been stealing the money entrusted to his charge'. Parnell's unwillingness to sue the newspaper for libel was exploited in further editorials as the week went on. Emboldened by the non-appearance of a writ, on 2 June the *Press* reminded its readers that: '"Thief" is an unmistakable word. We called Mr Parnell a thief. We now repeat the epithet'.

By the time of his death in October 1891 Parnell had still not sued. While incarcerated in Galway jail the anti-Parnellite leader John Dillon wrote that:

Loathing is the only word that can express my feeling every time I open the *National Press*. If that spirit is to triumph, national politics will be turned into a privy.

Later Murphy guaranteed his dominance of the Irish newspaper market when he acquired the *Irish Daily Independent* in 1905. He would have enjoyed the further acquisition of the old *Freeman's Journal* newspaper by his company in 1924, but by then he was dead. As he had passed away five years before, he was not around to enjoy the demise of the one-hundred-and-sixty-year-old Irish Parliamentary Party newspaper.

One of Murphy's few reversals was his convincing defeat in the 1892 general election for a Dublin constituency by the pro-Parnellite candidate William Field. Murphy lost by a 4:1 margin. Field, as luck would have it, though he ran one of the largest butcher's businesses in the city, had a background in the labour movement. Though he often expressed his opposition to socialism, Field can arguably be cited as the only representative of labour to have given William Martin Murphy a political hiding.

William Martin Murphy, dubbed William Murder Murphy by Dublin trade unionists in 1913, was born, one hundred and seventy-three years ago, on this day.

Broadcast 29 December 2017

1 December 1848

The *Londonderry* tragedy

The great Irish emigration song 'Paddy's Green Shamrock Shore', popularized by Paul Brady, begins with the lines:

From Derry quay, we sailed away on the twenty-third of May
We were boarded by a pleasant crew bound for Amerikay.

The song tells us that those passengers 'safely reached the other side in three and twenty days'. What follows is a very different story of Derry quay, one that ended in the tragic deaths of seventy-two emigrants.

In the mid nineteenth century, the paddle-steamer *Londonderry*, belonging to the North-West of Ireland Steam Packet Company, and manned by a largely Scottish crew, plied a regular route between Sligo and Liverpool. Most of her passengers were set to sail onwards from Liverpool to North America.

In late November of 1848 the steamer was approaching Derry, on the first leg of its journey to England, with around one hundred and eighty passengers – mostly in steerage – and twenty-six crew. The bulk of the passengers were impoverished Mayo and Sligo farmers and their families fleeing the ravages of the Great Famine.

A sudden storm prompted the captain, Alexander Johnstone, to order his crew to force all the passengers into a small aft cabin, measuring about eighteen feet in length and, at most, twelve feet wide. More than one hundred and seventy men, women and children were crammed into this tiny space. The situation was exacerbated when the only ventilation available was covered with a tarpaulin to ensure that water did not get into the cabin. As a result, many of the passengers began to suffocate. One of them finally managed to escape and tell the first mate that the steerage passengers were dying from want of air. A reporter from the *Belfast Newsletter* described what the crew found when the cabin door was opened:

> There lay, in heaps, the living, the dying, and the dead, one frightful mass of mingled agony and death. Men, women, and children, were huddled together, blackened with suffocation, distorted by convulsions, bruised and bleeding from the desperate struggle for existence which preceded the moment when exhausted nature resigned the strife.

All told, seventy-two passengers, thirty-one women, twenty-three men and eighteen children, had died horribly. Wild rumours began to circulate when the steamer pulled into Derry. It was reported that:

> A large number of passengers had been barbarously butchered by a band of robbers, who took passage with them for the sake of plundering the poor emigrants, and, in short, that one of the most frightful massacres on record had been perpetrated.

The authorities were initially inclined to blame criminality for the tragedy. The official narrative that emerged was of belligerent Irish passengers rioting and killing each other. The full truth came out at the inquest, where survivors accused the Scottish crew of extreme cruelty, and the captain insisted in his defence that he had given orders for the decks to be cleared for the safety of the passengers.

One fortunate survivor, Michael Branan from Sligo, told the inquest that he had been on deck when one of the crew cursed him and forced him down below, where, as he put it:

> The place was so thronged that, while those at the sides were obliged to sit down, there was no sitting room for those in the centre, and they were moved to and fro with every motion of the vessel.

A local doctor giving evidence compared the steerage accommodation to the Black Hole of Calcutta. Other witnesses alleged that cattle being transported from Sligo had been better treated than the steerage passengers.

The Captain and two mates were found guilty of manslaughter by the inquest jury. The jurors also called the attention of proprietors of steamboats to what it called:

> The urgent necessity of introducing some more effective mode of ventilation in steerage and also affording better accommodation to the poorer class of passengers.

However, the call fell on deaf ears, and no remedial legislation followed. In 1996 six coffins were found by workmen on a building site in the Waterside area of Derry, in grounds close to the former workhouse. They were believed to be the remains of some of the poverty-stricken travellers from the ill-fated paddle-steamer.

The *Londonderry* pulled into Derry quay, with seventy-two dead passengers on board, one hundred and sixty-nine years ago, on this day.

Broadcast 1 December 2017

23 December 1864

Death of Chartist James O'Brien

It was Brendan Behan who is supposed to have observed that the first item on the agenda of any Irish radical movement was, 'the split'. But it wasn't just true of the Irish. The great British quasi-revolutionary organisation of the 1840s, the Chartists, also fell victim to vicious factionalism. But Behan wasn't too far wrong, because at the centre of the dissension were two Irish journalists.

James O'Brien was born near Granard, Co. Longford in 1804 or 1805. Feargus O'Connor, born in 1794 or 1796, was from West Cork. Both studied at Trinity College, and both are noted for the radical English newspapers they helped establish. In O'Brien's case, it was the *Poor Man's Guardian* to which he contributed articles under the pseudonym 'Bronterre', before eventually adopting the *nom de plume* as his middle name.

O'Connor was the long-time editor of the much more celebrated *Northern Star*, named in tribute to the famous newspaper of the Ulster United Irishmen, and for its home town of Leeds. Both men became central to the organisation of one of the most important radical movements in nineteenth-century British history.

The Chartists sought six basic demands – universal male suffrage for all *men* of sound mind over the age of twenty-one, the secret ballot, the abolition of property qualifications for MPs, the payment of parliamentarians, constituencies of equal size, and annual elections.

The organisation drew its name from the 1838 People's Charter, the document that encapsulated the six demands. Public meetings and demonstrations were held around the country, but the original petition – with one million, three hundred thousand signatures – was rejected by Parliament in 1839. A second petition, this time with three million signatories, followed in 1842. It too was rejected. An economic depression then led to strikes and violence, both of which became associated with the Chartist movement. In 1848, with a wave of revolutions taking place across Europe, Chartism re-emerged in England and Wales as a vibrant radical force. The previous year Feargus O'Connor had been elected as MP for Nottingham. A new petition was prepared, the Chartists claiming it contained five million signatures. It may, however, only have amounted to around two million, and many of those were proven to be bogus. The movement foundered when repressive legislation was introduced by the Government and many of its leaders were arrested and deported.

Charged with sedition in 1840, James O'Brien served eighteen months in jail, during which time his wife and four children were virtually destitute. Feargus O'Connor was charged with seditious libel via the pages of the *Northern Star* in 1839, and also served eighteen months in prison. The split between the two men came about after their release from incarceration, when O'Connor advocated support for the Tories against the incumbent Whig Government in a general election of 1841. Their differences became intensely personal and were conducted in the columns of their respective newspapers. O'Brien referred to his compatriot as 'The Dictator' – which was actually not a grossly unreasonable assertion – while O'Connor cruelly dubbed O'Brien 'The Starved Viper'.

Neither man came to a good end. O'Brien died in his late fifties, an impoverished alcoholic. O'Connor suffered poor mental health, possibly exacerbated, or caused, by syphilis. When he physically attacked a fellow MP in 1852 he was committed to an asylum. He died three years later, also in his late fifties.

Although Feargus O'Connor's impressive ego was blamed by many contemporary commentators for the collapse of the Chartist movement, few modern historians accept that the personality of one man could have had such a malign influence. By the end of the Great War all six points of the People's Charter of 1838, other than annual elections, had been implemented, with the considerable bonus of female suffrage thrown in for good measure.

James Bronterre O'Brien, radical journalist and Chartist, died one hundred and fifty-two years ago, on this day.

Broadcast 23 December 2016

9 December 1973

The Sunningdale Agreement is signed

In 1998, after the signing of the Good Friday accord in Belfast, which promised a power-sharing executive to include all the elected Northern Ireland parties, Seamus Mallon, deputy leader of the Social Democratic and Labour Party, memorably referred to the deal as 'Sunningdale for slow learners'. Those of a certain age nodded sagely in agreement and chuckled knowledgeably at his phrasemaking abilities, while many more, particularly in the Republic, wondered why Seamus had invoked a posh English golf course in the context of the Belfast Agreement.

But they probably got distracted by the sheer joy of the complexities of the previously unheard of d'Hondt method of ministerial selection and just put it all down to Mr Mallon's legendary fondness for the game of golf.

But the soon-to-be Deputy First Minister didn't actually have a sporting context in mind. He was referring to the December 1973 Sunningdale Agreement which, lo and behold, had established … a power sharing executive, almost a quarter of a century before the Good Friday deal.

The background to Sunningdale was the attempt by the British Government to end direct rule of Northern Ireland from London. The Stormont Parliament, established under the 1920 Government of Ireland Act, had been suspended on 30 March 1972. That institution had been described by Sir James Craig – first Northern Prime Minister – as, in effect, a Protestant parliament for a Protestant people. So, it wasn't greatly missed by Northern nationalists.

In March 1973 elections took place for a new Northern Ireland assembly, and this was followed by negotiations between the SDLP and a divided Ulster Unionist party with a view to forming a power-sharing executive and bring about the ending of direct rule. In November the Ulster Unionist Party leader Brian Faulkner agreed to take his increasingly fractious party into government with the SDLP, under Gerry Fitt, and the Alliance party, led by Oliver Napier.

The next step was the negotiation of a North-South arrangement, with the formation of a Council of Ireland that had actually been envisaged by the 1920 Government of Ireland Act but had never come to pass. Talks were held in the Berkshire town of Sunningdale, which does indeed have a championship golf course. This led to the establishment of a cross-border council which would include a sixty-member North-South Assembly, and would have thirty-two-county responsibility for 'tourism, conservation and animal health'. But the right wing of the Ulster Unionist Party wasn't even prepared to countenance 'Rome rule' over hotels, exhaust fumes and deadly clostridial diseases, and the day after the agreement was signed by British Prime Minister Edward Heath and Taoiseach Liam Cosgrave, all hell broke loose.

In January 1974 Brian Faulkner was forced to resign as UUP leader, but remained in position as Prime Minister at the head of the executive. In May of that year loyalist opponents of the deal formed the Ulster Worker's Council and called a general strike. This was seen at its most effective in the closing down of the main Northern Ireland power station in Ballylumford. A 1974 poll, which helped shepherd the power sharing executive towards oblivion, included the use of an election poster bearing the pithy slogan 'Dublin is just a Sunningdale away – vote Unionist'.

The executive collapsed on 28 May 1974, and Sunningdale returned to being the home of two picturesque eighteen-hole parkland golf courses.

It took almost twenty-five years, and three thousand deaths, for the Good Friday agreement – the grown-up big sister of the infant casualty Sunningdale – to bring an end to the politics of violence in Northern Ireland. Something which, of course, it has yet to achieve completely.

The Sunningdale Agreement – which promised much but delivered little – was signed forty-three years ago, on this day.

Broadcast 9 December 2016

16 December 1987

'Fairytale of New York' is kept out of Number 1

Back in 2001, on the seventy-fifth anniversary of the establishment of 2RN, forerunner of Radio Éireann and RTÉ Radio, this station conducted two separate polls to attempt to find the seventy-five most beloved Irish songs. One was a poll of music professionals conducted through IMRO, the Irish Music Rights Organisation, the other was a reader/listener poll conducted through the RTÉ Guide. The results were varied, but there was absolute unanimity about the number one song.

Written by Shane McGowan and Jem Finer of the Pogues, and sung by McGowan and the extraordinary Kirsty MacColl, 'Fairytale of New York' has become a Christmas anti-classic all over the world. In the UK it is the most-played Christmas song of the twenty-first century. It's also, arguably, the greatest song *not* to have reached number one in the British pop charts.

The song had its origins two years before its release. As with most of the mythology surrounding the 'Fairytale', there is disagreement about how it began. One version suggests that Elvis Costello jokingly challenged the Pogues, the least sentimental group of all time – outside of the Clash – to write a Christmas hit. Another story has it that the Pogues manager, the late Frank Murray, came up with the idea. Either way, the work was started by the group's banjo player Jem Finer in 1985, and finally completed by Finer and McGowan two years later. Sleighbells, powdery snow, peace on earth and 'ho-ho-ho', would make way for the more realistic Christmas fare of alcohol-induced recrimination and blazing family rows.

A couple of things are fairly certain. At the time the song was being recorded, Jem Finer was reading J. P. Donleavy's novel *A Fairy Tale of New York* (1973), and thus the great Irish-American author unwittingly lent his title to an even more celebrated work. In addition, McGowan was destined to write a great Yuletide song as he was born on Christmas Day in 1957. Though when he began to make his contribution to the song, he'd never actually been to New York. But he had watched Sergio Leone's film *Once Upon a Time in America* (1984) repeatedly – and that seems to have done the trick.

The song, of course, is an antagonistic dialogue between a New York couple fallen on hard times, and the first female vocal – with rather different lyrics – was laid down by the Pogue's bass player, Cait O'Riordan. But when the time came to finish the recording, O'Riordan had left the band. Some thought was given to approaching Chrissy Hynde of the Pretenders, or Suzy Quatro, to do the needful. Instead, Pogues producer Steve Lillywhite – a frequent U2 collaborator – asked his then wife Kirsty MacColl to lay down a new guide track. Whether it was actually Lillywhite's intention or not that MacColl should get the gig – and let's assume that it was for the sake of credibility and posterity – the Pogues decided to leave the female vocal stand. McGowan then re-recorded the male part. The two only got together to make the memorable video, whose opening shot features Matt Dillon as one of 'New York's finest', escorting McGowan, none too gently, to the drunk tank.

In the song, the drunken, down-and-out couple share their recriminations on Christmas Eve. 'I could have been someone,' he sneers, clearly blaming anyone but himself for a life of failure. 'Well so could anyone,' she retorts in one of the great musical putdowns. It's all relentlessly embittered, though the ending offers some hope. It is rather more believable than the 'So here it is, Merry Christmas'-style alternative.

Of course, in a world where genius frequently plays second fiddle to utter mediocrity, the song failed to become the UK Christmas number one. It was kept off the top of the charts by the Pet Shop Boys' cover version of a mawkish 1973 Elvis torch-song 'Always on my Mind'. It did make number one in Ireland, however, which greatly pleased Shane McGowan. 'I wouldn't have expected the English to have great taste,' he told the *Guardian* on the song's twenty-fifth anniversary re-release.

'Fairytale of New York' – far more genuinely Christmassy than 'chestnuts roasting on an open fire' – reached its highest position in the UK charts, twenty-nine years ago, on this day.

Broadcast 16 December 2016